Job and the Excess of Evil

JOB AND THE EXCESS OF EVIL

Philippe Nemo

with a postface by Emmanuel Levinas
translated with a postscript by Michael Kigel

Duquesne University Press
Pittsburgh, Pennsylvania

Introduction and main chapters
first published in French as
Job et l'excès du mal
Copyright © by Philippe Nemo
First published in 1978 by Editions Grasset & Fasquelle
"Transcendence and Evil" published in French as "Transcendance
et Mal" in *Le Nouveau Commerce* 41 (1978). © by Estate of
Emmanuel Levinas
"To Pursue the Dialogue with Levinas" © by Philippe Nemo

English Translation Copyright © 1998 by Duquesne University Press
Translator's Postscript Copyright © 1998 by Duquesne University Pres

Published in the United States of America by
Duquesne University Press
600 Forbes Avenue
Pittsburgh, PA 15282

Library of Congress Cataloging in Publication Data

Nemo, Philippe, 1949–
    [Job et l'exces du mal. English]
    Job and the excess of evil / by philippe nemo; translated by
michael kigel; postface by emmanuel levinas.
        p. cm.
    Includes bibliographical references and index.
    ISBN 0-8207-0285-4 (cloth)
    ISBN 0-8207-0286-2 (paper)
    1. Bible. O.T. Job—Criticism, interpretation, etc. I. Title.
    BS1415.2   .N4513   1998
    223'.106—dc21   98-9000
                                                          CIP

This book is dedicated to
Roland Morillot,
ami disparu 'avant le temps.'

Contents

Introduction

IN WRITING ON "the excess of evil," what I have in mind primarily is not the suffering produced by social injustice, the suffering of prisoners in camps, the suffering of whole peoples immolated in modern wars. I have in mind private suffering. Those who have died in collective catastrophes are first of all private souls, each of whom saw death approaching for himself or herself alone.

Those who denounce evil in its political dimension suppose it to be familiar and simple at the level of the individual soul. The remedy for evil is conceptualized on the same scale that evil itself is conceived: the remedy is political. Yet it is quite possible that the favourable light in which political thought is regarded in modernity, under the influence of the social sciences, Marxism and all the other ideologies belonging to this epoch of multitudes and large numbers, is the result of a weakening within thought itself which ends up hindering and intimidating the question of the soul, the question of its perdition and its beatitude.

I agree that this question is relevant for everyone or for no one. But I must decline the varieties of collectivist thinking precisely because of the inauthenticity into which they lead us. Lacking the question of the soul, they no longer know how to

conceive the individual except as a subject—illusions—or as an
I—trivialities. "Man," as he conforms to the "generic essence of
man," an astonishing concept invented by Feuerbach and Marx,
is truly incapable of discerning between good and evil and, consequently, of coming to the aid of victims who are useless for
the survival of the group. The collective is always the Neutral;
no one is responsible for it. This is the paradox embodied by the
varieties of thought that have the political for their final horizon: they demand commitment, but whose? Commitment is born
there where it hurts: in the soul.

It is this individualized origin of commitment that collectivist thinking denies, in order not to see the truth that lies at the
heart of evil. Evil, in the excess that Job acknowledges, indicates a certain commitment on the part of a certain Intention.

In one of the last volleys of materialist thinking, Ernst
Bloch suggested, in his commentary on the Book of Job,[1] that
evil itself recommends "utopia," and not politics, nor any other
technique, as the only appropriate response. But what is this
utopia? If utopia is not the truth that makes a lie of this world,
it is only a part of this same world; if it neither includes the
world nor deconstructs it, it is lost within it.

Then what must it be? This is the question the Book of Job,
from out of the depths of centuries, answers for us. Recounting
the most private of experiences, the experience of anxiety, it unfolds a distinctive vision of the "Other" that is ready to resolve
some of the aporias of utopia for the benefit of humankind.

What this book says is that the excess of evil does indeed
destroy the world, yet not in order to reveal another "world"—
an inverted image of this one caught in a co-eternal, and

---

[1] Ernst Bloch, "Atheismus im Christentum. Zur Religion des Exodus
und des Reiches," *Gesamtausgabe*, vol. 14 (1968). Cited and commented
on by Henry Mottu, "La figure de Job chez Bloch," *Revue de théologie et de
philosophie* 27 (1977): 307–320.

eternally futile, struggle with it—but to reveal what is other *than* the world, that is to say, what is other than worldliness as such, other than the neutral legality of the world.

The Non-Neutral, the Il-legal that is revealed to Job is precisely—the soul. The soul is not the inverted image of the subject or the I, for it is not an image at all. Nor is it in any way a "being" of this world or of another world. The soul is what "is" when a question is asked *of* the soul by another soul, prior to any constitution of a world, immersed in the medium of a unique history which concerns them alone and which, to this day, is still pending.

Utopia implies two histories in conflict; *eschatology*, only one, and one that ends.

With this difficult and apparently untenable thought, the unknown author of the Book of Job is occupied in an incomparable rigour. For his vision of a soul *in waiting* is not the commentary to a vague conviction: it is the interpretation of the very phenomenon of evil, inasmuch as evil is in excess. This perfect simplicity of Joban thought is no doubt hard to perceive on account of its belonging to the discouraging complexity of the Bible.

The Book of Job,[2] we read in certain Christian interpretations, is "disconcerting," if not "repulsive." After such a first statement, one expects these exegetes to throw in the towel and file the text of Job away—and the text must be very strange

---

[2] The first occasion of the present work was a program in four segments produced for France-Culture and broadcast in June and July 1976 under the title "Job the Iconoclast." The program involved discussions with Michel de Certeau, Olivier Clément, Georges Durand and Jean Lévêque. Following this program three articles were published, the essence of which is reproduced here ("Job et le mal radical," I and II, *Tel Quel* 70 and 71–73; "Job et l'excès du mal" in *La Confession de la foi*, a collective work under the direction of Claude Bruaire (Paris: Fayard, 1977).

indeed in the eyes of their doctrines—under the category of radical interrogation. Yet they make nothing of it. With satisfaction, they note that Job's critical arguments and theological audacity did not ward off those who decided to accept the book into the canon. They probably reason that if Job is in the Scriptures, and if not so much as an echo of disagreement has been passed down to us, it is because the book in some way completes the Scriptures, either because it does not contradict them, or because it contradicts them in a manner that is itself theologically permissible. For example, to invoke the most salient aspect of the book without further ado: Job's dereliction recalls, and therefore in retrospect seems to announce, Christ's solitude on the cross. Thus this disconcerting text does not catch the exegetes off-guard. They explain it in line with its position in the plan of a progressive Revelation that must be read, by subtle practices, along the whole of the biblical canon. If it is a matter of understanding the import of the divine response in the "YHWH speeches," what they see in these is a "theophany" ranking in order with other theophanies in the Old Testament; if it is a matter of evaluating Job's "faith," they compare it to the faith of Abraham; if the "wisdom" of chapter 28 is problematic, they refer it to the *hokhmah* of wisdom literature; and so on. In short, they freely play one text off another.

And this procedure certainly proves fruitful by their standards. They even theorize about its fruitfulness: it is the Bible as a whole that "speaks," and through it, the "Spirit." To play one text off another is not to force it or to obscure it, accordingly, but to illumine it in the only way that is theologically valid and valuable. To take the other route and analyze one text by itself without reference to other texts or to the tradition is to succumb to the false prestige of the social sciences and mere "philology."

On the other hand, one may wonder whether it is really necessary to preserve the bulk of contexts and traditional commentaries in which a given text is ensconced in order to save the meaning of this text from linguistic or historic reduction-ism. For it is quite possible that a text which was inserted at one time into a corpus that eventually became consecrated may never have been read for itself, or at least that it yet may be read one day with different presuppositions and then integrated into a different corpus. Thus Job may be read as a tragedy and may take its place in the corpus of tragedies[3]—and who would judge that corpus not to be "sacred"? A Jew or a Christian, in any case, reads the Book of Job always refracted through the prism of biblical commentary. The tradition of commentary, in turn, expresses the interest of a community. No commentary can break with such an interest without sooner or later usher-ing the commentator to the brink of severing himself from the community. There, if the courage to finalize the break fails him, he has no choice but to compromise his commentary.

Thus Claudel, who has a very traditionalist sensibility by our standards, but who is no less inevitably modern when com-pared to the sensibilities of past centuries, has picked up on the clumsy elements in the speeches of Eliphaz, Bildad, and Zophar.[4] He perceives not only what is unbearable and scan-dalous about them, but above all what is laughable about them when they are measured against Job's intelligence. Thus he writes: "The intention is that of Joe Blow." Why then does he go on to add that in their voices it is none other than the "Holy Spirit" that speaks? Does Claudel take the Holy Spirit and Joe Blow to be one and the same person?—But concerning this morality expounded and defended, brilliantly no doubt, by the ones Claudel calls the *trois compères*, Christian doctrine dic-tates that it not be knocked out cold by the formidable pugilism

---

[3] Hence Horace Meyer Kallen, *The Book of Job as a Greek Tragedy Re-stored* (New York: Moffat, 1918) and Robert Lowth, *Lectures on the Sacred Poetry of the Hebrews* (London: Johnson, 1787); the former argues that Job takes its inspiration from Euripides, the latter from Sophocles.—Tr.

[4] Paul Claudel, *Le Livre de Job* (Paris: Plon, 1946).

of Job's arguments. In other words, the doctrine requires that Claudel compromise himself. The learned exegetes and doctors are better informed than this part-time theologian, but, fundamentally, their method is the same.[5]

---

[5] Still, the comprehensive view of a canonic body of Scripture for which spiritual intelligence requires several reading grids—one text for reading another, the New Testament for reading the Old (in the typological sense), Scripture and Tradition to regulate the Doctors, the Doctors to interpret Scripture, and Tradition to carry it—all this is not yet sufficiently clear in our mind to be rejected altogether. We are not unaware of the fact that the special attention we are paying to Job, among all the texts on "radical" evil which we could draw on from the archive of Western or even non-Western culture, is due to its belonging to the Bible; is not the way in which we examine the Bible directly determined by a tradition that had the force to transmit the text to us? Without this tradition, without the institution which is its vehicle or whose vehicle it is—no matter which is the case here—would we have even opened the Book? And even if we preferred to it the commentary of other discourses, as more true, more exact, less limited, less needlessly obscure, would the interest we felt for them owe nothing to the acquaintance with a first sacred text, which initiates us into the very idea of looking in a text for an absolute and sufficient truth, and opens to us the perspective of exegesis? A vast question which we would take care not to answer too quickly. It is perhaps a question too specifically modern, if it is to be judged by the vagueness with which a Catholic theologian encased it several years ago (A. M. Dubarle, "Introduction à l'Ecriture sainte", in *Initiation théologique*, vol. 1 [Paris: Ed. du Cerf], p. 74): "Individuals are introduced to knowledge of the Scriptures by the community of the faithful in which they live. It is because they received from this community a first initiation into faith and into the affirmation that certain books are sacred, that they have the desire and the possibility of finding religious truth in it. . . . It would be, on the contrary, infinitely rare for an unbelieving reader having encountered Scripture by chance to recognize the Word of God in it. It is only thanks to a key given by a communal faith that the sacred book can reveal its true meaning, that the divine message can pass through it without being misunderstood. This is what Saint Paul teaches us when he compares the conditions in which the Jews and the Christians find themselves when reading Moses. The former are like people whose face is covered with a veil: they can see nothing, or at least their perception is very disrupted

None of this is to say that the present work, by contradistinction, can attempt an objective and ingenuous reading of the Book of Job. No reading is altogether free of interest. But we do claim an "innocent" reading at least with respect to the institutional interests of Jewish and Christian exegetes, for whom the book must be read with reference to the whole Bible and—what is another topic—to the only Bible.

Within the Book of Job itself, the concern with respecting the givens of tradition leads to a new type of error. These are no longer just rude simplifications, but on the contrary inextricable difficulties created artificially. The exegetes agree that the book is to be considered a composite. The prose prologue and epilogue, recounting the "plot" between God and Satan against Job and the happy restoration, are the oldest parts, and were either redacted before the others or were picked up by the principal redactor of the fifth century from an old story transmitted by popular tradition. The poetic dialogue between Job and his friends, as well as the principal portion of YHWH's speeches, are composed by one pen. The discourses of Elihu, the fourth friend, and the Wisdom Poem (chap. 28) are both later additions. The sagacity of the exegetes discerns other brief passages interpolated here and there.[6] But one problem arises immediately. It is the book as a whole that has been canonized

---

and indistinct. On the other hand, the faithful who were converted to the Lord Jesus have an unveiled face, can read without obstacle and understand the meaning (2 Cor., 3.14–18)." This being the case, we for our part will follow the deconstructive hypothesis right through: we wish to read the Book of Job *without* the Bible, for itself alone. We will see if and how it endures this test.

[6] The problems of authorship are exhaustively analyzed in the masterful work to which we will refer often, namely Jean Lévêque O.C.D., *Job et son Dieu*, 2 vols., Etudes bibliques (Paris: Gabalda, 1970). See in particular vol. 1, pp. 119–132, 213–229; vol. 2, pp. 537–543, 593–606.

and not just one of the three or four principal authors. Now, as the development of exegesis made it difficult to attribute the greater part of the biblical corpus to a single great prophet whom everyone would agree to call "inspired," it would have to be established within the Catholic Church as a docrine that *all* the authors of one canonical text must be considered equally inspired with no one of them outranking another.[7] If one wishes to establish an orthodox theology of the Book of Job, therefore, it is vital to take the three or four contributions into account: were one of them completely neglected, the canonicity of the whole would be shattered, together with the canonicity of the remaining contributions. Now, each of the—let us say—four parts is in varying degrees and only with difficulty compatible with the other three. The prose frame—prologue and epilogue—presents a man resigned to his trial, who blesses God instead of rebelling against him, and to whom God promptly replies by restoring his health and his fortune. The body of the poem, on the other hand, presents the complaints of Job at length. While Job's three friends attribute his misfortune to a sin committed by him or by his children against the Law, Elihu, the fourth and last speaker, invokes a sin which is more "interior" than a transgression of the Law: the pride that Job displays in claiming his innocence.

The orthodox exegete must unite all these themes. This sets off an avalanche of problems that are either peremptorily

---

[7] It must also have been postulated that the authors were inspired for the canonical works alone, and not as individuals, so that other works which might have issued from their pen would not be considered equally inspired. God "inspires" the community of redactors of the Book. An exposition of the doctrinal evolution of these questions, which were not asked seriously of the Church until the beginning of the Renaissance and concerning which it was still passing rulings at the First Vatican Council (1871), can be found in *Introduction à la Bible*, 2nd ed., under the direction of A. Robert and A. Feuillet (Paris: Desclée & Co., 1959).

resolved from a partial perspective,[8] or treated prudently, but at the cost of minimalist positions.[9]

For this reason what has presented itself to us as the most coherent approach is to adhere to that which constitutes the body of the Book of Job, to the texts without which the name of

---

[8] Thus Father Bigot, in the article "Job" of the *Dictionnaire de théologie catholique* (Paris: Vacant, Mangenot, Amann et coll., 1925), sees in Elihu's discourses on Job's sin of pride the final explanation of the whole affair. Granted, he considers these discourses as primitive and not interpolated.

[9] This is the case with the majority of modern commentators whom we were able to read. Hans Urs von Balthasar (*La Gloire et la Croix*, vol. 3. Théologie, I. Ancienne Alliance [Paris: Aubier, 1974], pp. 241–249) is more subtle. He perceives very well how Job is confronted with God's absolute silence: anxiety, despair, dereliction, in contrast with the traditional image of YHWH contained in the discourses of the three friends. He understands very well how this absolute silence is in a sense a divine Word: "God is present in the form of absence" (p. 243). But instead of scrutinizing this silence that is Word and seeing precisely what it reveals to Job, he reintegrates the texts of Job's dereliction (the dialogues) into two larger collections. First, the whole Book of Job. Job is the one who uttered the full "yes" to God (in the Prologue), and it is in view of this state of perfect communication between God and Job, and not as an absolute starting point, that the ensuing "interior spiritual darkness" must be understood. In the same way, God's silence takes its true meaning in chapter 28 on Wisdom. Finally, Balthasar sees in Job's final confession, "My ears had heard of you but now my eyes have seen you" (42.5), a "beautiful saying" which "veils over more than it reveals of the true situation" (p. 249). This is because he reads it as a retraction of the dialogues, whereas we (cf. p. 156 below) take it as their confirmation and explanation. On another level, the author situates Job within the "agenda" of biblical revelation. This allows him to propose two hypotheses, which we believe serves at least to turn attention away from the specific problem posed by Job, since at that point the problem's solution must come from elsewhere. First, Job not being a Hebrew, it is not surprising that his simple and pagan human thought, which has been "reduced to forming an image of God for itself simply by reflecting on existence" (p. 248) should end in failure and in darkness. He lacks the Hebrew Revelation (one suspects that this is what numerous Jewish orthodox commentators also say). But how can this be? Is there no "revelation," no epiphany of the Other World and no

Job would be cast into the same oblivion occupied by so many ancient sages: namely, the dialogues and the YHWH speeches which bring the dialogues to a conclusion. If we can conceive of sacrificing the remainder, which is the work of other pens, this is because no orthodoxy of canon or inspiration makes it a crime for us to do so. By our expedient method, we rediscover the text of a single author, a text that is psychologically, dramatically, and "philosophically" coherent. We rediscover the theology of one thinker, not of a mosaic of inspired authors who together create a haze wherein any falsely or veritably ingenuous theology can quickly find a home.

The author of the dialogues is of a very different mindset from the one who can be seen in the apologue of God and Satan. His pithy style little resembles the rhetoric of Elihu. He argues without many references to a theology of the Covenant between YHWH and Israel, or to an "oriental" mythology, or even to a wisdom tradition (as he is not the author of chaps. 28, and 32–37).[10] His God is without name,[11] without a precise

---

angelophany other than the Hebraic? We wish to show, on the contrary, in the dialogues themselves, and "simply by reflecting" with Job and as close as possible to his train of thought, a fully original picture of Revelation. Second hypothesis: Job is in fact a book of Hebrew thought, its issue is in fact integrated into the sequence of biblical problems. But it represents a crucial stage in the sequence, where Mosaic revelation, precisely the pre-exilic Covenant represented by the three friends, appears from that point onward as inadequate, obsolete, absurd, and by its very failure opens up a new experience of an "impenetrable beyond." From that point on, this night will not pass until the dawning of the Christ. There again, this supposes that no illumination, no "*fulgur manens*," in the words of the neo-Platonists, interrupts Job's night, or remains behind for our memories and for a potential theology. We wish to show that this is not necessarily true.

[10] Jean Lévêque does point out the uses of the word "wisdom" in the dialogues. But only in chaps. 28 and 32–37 is the word used in an explicitly theological way, as a notion already formed and contemplated. Elsewhere, it reflects more common and spontaneous uses.

[11] He is called Shaddai, the "Mountain-dweller," the "Almighty."

antecedent revelation, and if, as we shall see, he has a plan concerning the creature, this plan is not a Legislation.

Thus the procedure of the dialogue author becomes clearer. Confronted with the edifying story handed down by tradition (cf. Ezek. 14.14; James 5.11) of Job the "constant" or the "patient," he finds it too beautiful and too unrealistic, and above all too brief. As he himself has evidently been acquainted with a Job-like situation, he feels the need to lend his own feelings and reflections to the legendary Job, instead of taking them entirely into his own account, something that would require more space and time. These reflections are corrosive and "revolutionary." They lead to a religious position by comparison with which it is the traditional theology of Israel that seems lukewarm, ambiguous, unconvincing and paradoxically rather "lay" and "atheistic." He develops these reflections in the form of a dialogue, which he concludes with the mysterious response of YHWH. The fact that the first speech of YHWH acts as a springboard for a second speech where, with completely different intentions, Behemoth and Leviathan are described; the fact that a later redactor interpolated the poem on wisdom, certainly very interesting in itself; the fact that yet another ran to the rescue to salvage the moral of retribution and to expound upon wisdom still further by adding Elihu's speeches; the fact that the author of the dialogues himself, out of concern for symmetry and appeasement, supplemented Job's final reply with a happy ending in conformity to the legend; none of these facts suffices to bring Job's original argument back to the straight theological line of the sages of Israel. That argument stands alone, and wholly embodies the incredible interest of the book— just as the theological corrections which were made to Qohelet

Perhaps the fifth century poet wished to un-baptize God from God's too well-known and dogmatically sealed names with this archaism.

with the pious intention of reconciling it to the Hebrew canon[12] luckily do not attain to the dazzling thought of the Ecclesiast.

The reader will be able to verify of the present work how *all* of the verses of Job 3–27, 29–31 (the dialogues between Job and his first three visitors), constituting the whole of the text which we consider to be the work of the same pen, minus the YHWH speeches (chaps. 38–41), are cited explicitly at least once—thus sacrificing a certain redactionary elegance. Does that mean we identify exhaustiveness with scholarship? Are we naïve enough to believe that nothing essential in a text is lost so long as each of its verses is reproduced? But the task of such an exhaustive reading, as insufficient as it may seem, has been carried out less frequently than one might suppose. One may even wonder whether it is not only the translators—by necessity—and some modern exegetes who have carried the task to completion. According to the study of Charles Kannengieser,[13] commentators of the patristic era, so prolix when writing on certain texts from the New Testament or the Pentateuch, are extremely reserved—to say the least—with regard to Job. When they cite it, it is only by a few verses; and the prologue (chaps. 1–2), curiously enough, is cited with a frequency completely disproportionate to its size. After the first two centuries during which Job receives almost no comment (although it was cited in the New Testament, in Matt. 19.26, Mark 10.27, Luke 1.52, 1 Cor. 3.19, Phil. 1.19, 1 Thess. 5.22, 2 Thess. 2.8, James 5.11, Rev. 9.6, but always in a very elliptical manner and without reference to the central issue of the dialogues), allusions are found in Justin of Rome (who cites 1.6, 2.1 and 1.2), Clement of

---

[12] According to the most probable hypotheses presently supported. Cf. Jean Lévêque, *op. cit.*, vol. 2, pp. 660–662.

[13] *Dictionnaire de spiritualité ascétique et mystique*, ed. Marcel Viller (Paris: Ed. Beauchesne, 1932), article "Job" II.

Alexandria (who is only interested in the cosmology of the book, and briefly so), Cyprian of Carthage (who uses verses 1.21–22, 2.9–10, 1.2–5, 14.4–5, 29.12–13, 15–16 to illustrate lessons on humility). Origen, to be sure, is more thorough: approximately 300 citations. But of these, verses 14.4–5 ("Who can extract what is pure from the impure . . .") is cited 14 times, 1.1 and 5.18 are cited seven times, etc. No allusion whatsoever to what we shall call the "trial" of God. Next, traces are found in Evagrius of Pontus, Athanasius of Alexandria, Hilary of Poitiers, Didymus the Blind (whose commentary ends at 16.1), and John Chrysostome. These texts yet have to be studied in detail. But when we discover that in the work of Saint Augustine, who authored a short commentary, 200 of 400 citations are of 1.21, 2.9–10, 28.28 (none of which are texts of the principal author) and of 7.1 ("Is not man's life on earth nothing more than pressed service . . .") and 14.4–5 (cf., *supra*), we begin to appreciate how difficult a time the Job of the trial of God has in making himself heard by the Catholic doctors.

Without anticipating a study yet to be carried out, one can nevertheless state that the thinkers who put together the doctrine of the Church did so without our text, if not in opposition to it and doing everything to erase it. And this in spite of the fact that they all claim to base themselves on the whole of the Bible "inspired" in its entirety. For let us not say that Augustine did not read the verses of Job which he does not cite. Let us say only that if he had read them without reading them, skimmed them without finding anything noteworthy in them, if their meaning had been "repressed" by his interests as a doctor of the Church, or even just "debarred" by a habit of thinking formed by tradition, we would know nothing certain about this as he did not bother to actually comment on them.[14] Limiting

---

[14] Another example of the ostracism suffered by the Book of Job, or rather by its principal part (chaps. 3–27, 29–31) in the Catholic tradition:

ourselves to what is verifiable, we will say in principle that each commentator in reality only comments on the collection of passages he culls from the book, not on "the" book itself. So many commentaries, so many riddles, so many collections of passages effectively commented upon, so many—definitive—different Books of Job, perceived, but in an *imaginary way*, as being the "same" book, by interpreters who mutually transmit to one another the *signifier*—"the Bible"—of their membership in the same social institution.[15] We hope to show in a future work how the successive divisions of one text, during different epochs of religious thought—but no doubt the phenomenon is to be encountered in other contexts as well—exhibit the heterogeneous, discontinuous, fractured evolution of the thought of commentartors, even as they claim to a continuity of "tradition." In other words, if there is continuity, it must be sought outside the sacred corpus; it is rather to be found in the institution that comments on the corpus; but even and especially at this sociological level, other and more radical discontinuities can be found. *Mutatis mutandis*, one can understand the methodological advantage of exhaustiveness which we have opted for in our own reading of the Book of Job.

---

one of latest complete theologies (of Thomist inspiration and design, claiming to present the latest state of doctrine conforming to Tradition) to have appeared in French (*Initiation théologique*, 4 vol. [Paris: Ed. du Cerf, 1953]) only cites Job, in all its 3000 or so pages, 25 times (by comparison with the Psalms which are cited 184 times, and the fourth Gospel, 428 times. Of these 25 citations, only nine are from the dialogues of chapters 3–27 and 29–31. Eight of these nine concern only the doxographies (God in conflict with Rahab at 9.13; with Tamin at 7.12, etc.). And amid all this we find only *one* allusion to the problem of the suffering righteous man according to Job. Now the work contains a "moral theology" of 1200 pages, and a chapter specially devoted to the problem of evil.

[15] See our article, "Les discours et les pratiques: propositions de recherche," *Annales de l'Institut de philosophie de l'Université libre de Bruxelles* (1976).

What is in danger of being masked by an institutionally determined reading of the Book of Job—be it Jewish or Christian—is the manifestly original problematic that is born there: the question of the excess of evil. A thought that is subtle and labile, easy to miss, easy to evict. But a thought without a price-tag as it concerns an encounter with God.

1. The Anxiety of Job

THE BOOK OF JOB IS SUPPOSED TO BE THE BOOK OF SUF-FERING. It certainly has much to say about physical suffer-ing (Job's skin disease) and moral suffering (utter dereliction). But it has much more to say about a very particular kind of suffering, one which is not reducible to any other kind and is the progenitor of them all: anxiety. The Book of Job contains a rigorous phenomenology of anxiety as it appears by itself and transforms the appearance of everything else.

No reader can overlook the proliferation of terms which des-ignate suffering and anxiety.[1] "May that night be dismal . . . since

---

[1] For the text of Job, we shall be quoting the very beautiful translation of Chrysostome Larcher, *Bible de Jérusalem*, new ed. (Paris: Desclée de Brouwer, 1975). This translation does not always satisfy the demands of Biblical scholarship, not in the way that the translation of Édouard Dhorme, *Le livre de Job* (Paris: V. Lecoffre, 1926) does for example. We shall have equal recourse to Dhorme's translation, as well as to the strokes of inspiration in the T.O.B. (Paris: Les Bergers et les Mages & Ed. du Cerf, 1971), and also to André Chouraqui's *Livre de Job* (Paris: Desclée de Brouwer, 1974). [For the purposes of the present English translation of *Job et l'excès du mal*, we shall be quoting, with modifications, from the

it would not shut the doors of the womb on me to hide *suffering* from my eyes" (3.7, 10). "Months of delusion I have assigned to me, nothing for my own but nights of *suffering*" (7.3). "Death, rather than these my *pains*" (7.15). "My *suffering* remains" (16.6). "*Terrors* turn to meet me" (30.15). "There is no arbiter between us [God and Job]... to keep away his daunting *terrors*" (9.33–34). "You *frighten* me with dreams, and *terrify* me with visions" (7.14). "In the *anguish* of my spirit I must speak" (7.11). "No longer make me cower from your *terror*" (13.21). "Will you *frighten* a wind-blown leaf?" (13.25). "That is why I am full of *fear* before him, and the more I think, the greater grows my *dread* of him" (23.15). The preoccupation of the author of the dialogues is evident not only in the speeches he ascribes to Job, but also in those of Job's interlocutors. When he represents the misfortunes that must befall the wicked, he makes Zophar say: "In his full abundance *anxiety* will seize him" (20.22). And Bildad: "Shaddai fills me with *fright*" (23.16b), etc.

This inventory would be necessary for demonstrating the predominance of the theme of anxiety over that of suffering, even if Job's illness, had it been the only problem at hand, should have put his suffering in center-stage thematically. But the vocabulary taken by itself is not sufficient proof. What will allow us to identify anxiety as the predominant sentiment of Job is the scenario in which this sentiment is implicated.

The scenario is that of the long approach of death. First, the whole of humanity is drawn into it, then Job the individual man. It is something that is worth describing in detail, since here again, the commentators, while they have been attentive to the analogy, even the equivalence, between the "pessimistic" passages which we find in this book and those which can be found elsewhere in the Bible, do not sufficiently inquire into

---

Jerusalem Bible (London: Darton, Longman & Todd, 1966), characterized by its editor as the "English equivalent" of *La Bible de Jérusalem.*—Tr.]

the role the context obliges these passages to play. While in the other contexts, these passages might sound only disillusioned and wry, and hence "wise," here they constitute the first degree of "stress" that belongs to anxiety.

Human existence is presented in a markedly classical manner as something that is incapable of enduring and "passes away." However, while in Isaiah 40.6–8, for example, the man whose flesh "withers away" is immediately confronted by the "Word of God" which "abides eternally," here the theme is presented without any cheerful counterpart. We might also note that the "everything passes" of the Bible stands well apart from the "everything passes" of Heraclitus or of the sophists; the latter is a judgment on the cosmos, while the former very specifically stresses the passing away of the flesh.

The human being passes away like a plant. "He blossoms, and he withers, like a flower" (14.2). "His roots grow withered below, and his branches are blasted above" (18.16). "Drooping like a mallow plucked from its bed, and withering like an ear of corn" (24.24). "Does papyrus flourish, except in marshes? Without water, can the rushes grow? Pluck them even at their freshest: fastest of all plants they wither . . . so perishes the hope of the godless man" (8.11–13). This plant, lacking endurance, is blown away by a breath. Flux to the second degree. It is "a leaf chased by the wind" (13.25). "The wind will carry off this blossom" (15.30). "An east wind picks him up and drags him away" (27.21). "A whirlwind sweeps him off" (27.20). A variety of images of fluidity is proposed. What man holds onto, and man himself, is like water: "A flood sweeps his house away" (20.28). "And now the life in me trickles away" (30.16). Like clouds: "As a cloud dissolves and is gone, so he who goes down to Sheol never ascends again" (7.9). Like breath: "Remember that my life is but a breath" (7.7). "My days are but a breath" (7.16). Like shadows: "Fleeting as a shadow, transient" (14.2). "My limbs wear away like a shadow" (17.7). "Our life on earth passes like a shadow" (8.9). "[Man] vanishes, like a phantom, once for all. . . . Like a dream that leaves no trace he takes his flight, like a vision in the night he flies away" (20.7–8). "My life is crumbling like rotten wood, or a moth-eaten garment" (13.28).

Even so, what all these images evoke is a being that does not stay in place and that precisely never stops passing away. Its inheritance is an eternity of movement. And even putting it that way suggests too much permanence for what the author of Job has in mind. For what he wants to say is that the human being not only slips away, but ultimately falls down. "My breath grows weak" (17.1). "I waste away" (7.16). This fluid, not content to flow, stops flowing, and evaporates. Having long renounced a solid state like ice, which passes into water, Job does not even subsist in a liquid state; he becomes a gas. The sinner is said to disappear "as heat and drought dry up the waters" (24.19). "A wind will wither up his tender buds" (15.30).

Indeed, human existence is not even accorded the time to wither like a plant. The human being is "snatched up from his homestead" (27.21). "Like some lush plant in the sunlight, he sprouted his early shoots over the garden; but his roots were twined in a heap of stones, he drew his life among the rocks. Snatch him from his bed, and it denies it ever saw him" (8.16–18). "He never comes home again, and his house knows him no more" (7.10). "What then of those who live in houses of clay, who are founded on the dust? They are crushed as easily as a moth, one day is enough to grind them to powder" (4.19–20). "The womb that shaped him forgets him, and his name is recalled no longer" (24.20). The disappearance of the individual is so thorough that, beyond being yanked up from the spot where he "took root" (5.3), even the person's name is uprooted from human memory, something that might have otherwise given a semblance of endurance. This already points to a certain treason. When Qohelet comments in a similar vein, "No memory remains of earlier times, just as in times to come, next year itself will not be remembered" (Eccles. 1.11), he means to underscore the indefinite repetition through the generations of the same phenomenon of forgetting, and this repetition itself still presupposes a kind of everlastingness within passing away and despite passing away. On the other hand, what the author of Job insists on is the irreversibility of the past and the vanity of ruminating on it: "But man? He dies, and lifeless he remains; man breathes his last, and then where is he? The waters of the seas may disappear, all the rivers may run dry or drain away; but man, once in his resting place, will never rise again. The heavens will wear away before he wakes, before he rises from his sleep. . . . For once a man is dead can he come back to life?" (14.10–14).

All of these impressions of human existence as something that suffers a vegetal evanescence would provide us with little insight, however, if we did not see how they are linked to an acute personal experience, namely the experience of enfeeblement, of aging, of deterioration, of pain in the flesh, the kind of pain that Job knows all too well: "And [the Satan] struck Job down with malignant ulcers from the sole of his foot to the top of his head" (2.7). This skin disease is undoubtedly incurable. In any event, it is not something that someone in Job's time could imagine being cured of by medical means.

This passes into a full thematization of the injury and the decay of the flesh: "On him God looses all his burning wrath, hurling against his flesh a hail of arrows. No use to run away from the iron armory, for the bow of bronze will shoot him through. Out through his back an arrow sticks, from his gall a shinning point" (20.23–25). "With the vigor of youth his bones were filled, now it lies in the dust with him" (20.11). "Now he rots on the roadside" (8.19). "Disease devours his flesh, Death's First-Born gnaws his limbs" (18.13).[2] "At night-time, sickness

---

[2] All of this is said, not of Job, but of the wicked as they are perceived by Zophar and Bildad. But a full interest in the thought of the Joban author requires us to take our investigations to the far corners of the book. His thought is as evident in the language he entrusts to the three

saps my bones, I am gnawed by wounds that never sleep" (30.17).
"My skin has turned black on me, my bones are burnt with
fever" (30.30). "Vermin cover my flesh, and loathsome scabs;
my skin is cracked and oozes pus" (7.5). "You crush [man]"
(14.20). "Beneath my skin, my flesh begins to rot, and my bones
stick out like teeth" (19.20; Dhorme: "In my skin my flesh has
rotted away, and I have gnawed my bone with my teeth"). "To
my wife my breath is unbearable, for my own brothers I am a
thing corrupt" (19.17).

This process of deterioration can only end badly. Death is
inevitable and irreparable: "He strikes me down on every side
and I perish" (19.10; Dhorme). "So he who goes down to Sheol
never ascends again. He never comes home again" (7.9–10). "I
shall be no more" (7.21). "Before I go to the place of no return,
the land of murk and deep shadow" (10.21). "I shall soon take
the road of no return" (16.22), "Grave diggers are gathering for
me" (17.1). "I know it is to death that you are taking me, the
common meeting place of all that lives" (30.23). "My eyes will
never again see joy. The eye that once saw me will look on me
no more" (7.7–8). Similarly, the friends of Job assert about the
wicked man: "he has no hope of fleeing from the darkness"
(15.22). "He knows that his ruin is at hand" (15.23). "Driven
from light into darkness, he is an exile from the earth" (18.18).
"But he who lays mighty hold on tyrants rises up to take away
that life which seemed secure" (24.22). His death is redoubled
in the death of his descendants: "A sword awaits his sons, however many they may be, and their children after them will

---

friends as in the language he entrusts to Job, even if the latter is the
personage with whom he most readily "identifies." If, in other passages, it
appears that the author works very conscientiously to describe the suffering of Job in the same categories which the friends use to describe the
punishment of the wicked, he does so in order to highlight the paradox.
For the "wickedness" of Job is precisely what is in question. *N.B.*: beginning with the next citation (30.17), it is Job who speaks.

go unfed. Plague will bury those he leaves behind him . . ." (27.14–15).

These assertions, which themselves remain basically objective, are quickly accompanied by others which begin to show signs of anxiety. What governs the texts we presently shall cite is the idea of a "never-again-as-before" that throws light—or perhaps a new shadow—on existence. Henceforward, because one knows that the term of life is short, or more precisely, because the process that invisibly guides all living things to their death suddenly becomes visible (in Job's disease; in the condemnation unleashed against the wicked), even if one has the opportunity to live for a long time or for a time of undetermined ·length, this time is perceived as being too short. It is merely a reprieve. Because the end is henceforth *envisaged*, it is already *present*, even if it is far off in the future. What characterizes the subjective situation here is the impossibility of *forgetting* a truth that, although it has always been true, emerges only now from a sleep wherein it abides in normal time. From the moment this truth emerges, "normal" time becomes inaccessible time, time of what was before, irreparable and un-restorable time. The impossibility of forgetting the truth is the first characteristic of anxiety.[3] At one point, mere thought, in its very quest for truth, is explicitly identified as the cause of anxiety: "The more I think, the greater grows my dread of him" (23.15; cf. 21.6).

As Job says: "And now . . . days of grief have gripped me" (30.16; Chouraqui: "My days of misery embrace me"). "Days of suffering have caught up with me" (30.27). It is as if he cried out: "That's it!" It was foreseeable, it was in the order of things, but one behaved as if it would always be deferred, always come later, always lie in the future. In fact, it was neither really foreseeable nor really in the "order" of things, since what the order

---

[3] "The truth of neurotic suffering is having the truth as cause." Jacques Lacan, *Ecrits* (Paris: Editions du Seuil, 1970), p. 870.

of normal time implies is precisely an obliviousness about the end of time. It is this obliviousness, this infinity of time, that lies inside the order. And if anxiety obligates one to the truth, it is to a truth that is a disorder and a disruption of normal life— proof that the living, for the most part, live by an error.

Now it has arrived. The catastrophe is here. "All my fears come true, what I dread befalls me" (3.25). "I hoped for happiness, but sorrow came; I looked for light, but there was darkness" (30.26). "I lived at peace, until he shattered me" (16.12). Job is obliged to settle down in his new situation, to set up quarters there, to consign his entire existence to the task of waiting upon, and waiting for, death: "I have sewn sackcloth over my skin and rubbed my brow in the dust" (16.15; a sign of mourning). "My harp is tuned to funeral wails, my flute to the voice of mourners" (30.31). He is to station himself henceforth in the camp of the mourners. He is of their race. He has crossed over into their province. The transition from speculative aloofness to anguished situatedness is a transition from a simple judgment—life passes, death comes—to a judgment of value: life passes *too quickly*, death comes *too soon*. "They were borne off *before their time*" (22.16). "Swifter than a weaver's shuttle my days have passed" (7.6). "Man . . . has a short life" (14.1). "For the years of my life are numbered" (16.22). "The days of my life are few enough" (10.20). "My life is not unending!" (7.16). This sudden contraction of time is accompanied by the disappearance of all hopes and all projects. The whole business of projects no longer makes sense, since hoping, projecting, must always assume an undetermined amount of time, a fundamental vagueness shrouding the future as the normal modality for receiving time. Conversely, it is within the modality of the project that we live in the future. The being capable of the project dwells in normal time. What marks the entry into the new modality of time, therefore, is the sudden disappearance of the possibility of the project as all projection suddenly becomes absurd: "My days . . . vanish, leaving no hope behind" (7.6). "My days have fled together with my projects" (17.11; Chouraqui: "my initiatives are cut off"). "Where then is my hope? Who can see any happiness for me? Will these come down with me to Sheol, or sink with me into the dust?" (17.15–16). "My confidence is blown away as if by the wind; my hope of safety passes like a cloud" (30.15). "Soon or late the mountain falls, the rock moves from its place, water wears away the stones, the cloudburst erodes the soil; just so do you destroy man's hope" (14.18–19). "As a man uproots a shrub, so he uproots my hope" (19.10). This hope was planted like a tree, in other words, and then slowly and steadily it gave up its fruit and was rejuvenated ("There is always hope for a tree: when felled, it can start its life again; its shoots continue to sprout. Its roots may be decayed in the earth, its stump withering in the soil, but let it scent the water and it buds, and puts out branches like a plant new set" [14.7–9 ff.]). But no biological model can hold its ground before the neurotic mode of thinking that is condemned to think according to the truth. The uprooting of the tree, which is the paragon of security, of balance, of duration and rejuvenation, shows how security itself was already in need of another system of roots. The efflorescence of the tree issued from an internal sap that surged up through the trunk and the roots. But the tree of Job's hope as a whole was in need of another sap. More than the sap that originates in the earth, it needed an undetermined and "open" time extracted from the earth. What has run dry and is now absent reveals, by contrast, the presence on which everything once depended.

To appeal to "life" would be useless. For life is precisely what has ceased to appear under the aspect of its indefinite efflorescence and perpetual rejuvenation, and changes its appearance imperceptibly and decisively; now instead it slips into its essential fluidity. One is no longer free to reach into a treasure chest and withdraw resources from it without depleting it of all those miracles and the happy twists of fate that keep one alive. One stands facing a boundary which cannot be circumvented. "He has built a wall across my path which I cannot pass" (19.8). One's "heart" is made to "sink" and one's "courage" is "broken" (23.16).

This phenomenology of anxiety and panic is applied across several registers. We would not be going too far if we read allusions in certain places in the text to some of the more somatic manifestations of anxiety. Tears: "My face is red with tears" (16.16). Hyperventilation: "My only food is sighs, and my groans pour out like water" (3.24). Heart-palpitations: "My veins find no sleep" (30.17; Dhorme). Sweat, perhaps, or dizziness: "You bear me away on the wind . . . and a storm drenches me with water" (30.22; Dhorme). Even, crudely enough, bowel movements: "My entrails seethe, are never still" (30.27).

There are other passages which cannot be taken literally like the preceding ones, but which are just as concrete and must not be read as empty ciphers left behind by an obsolete world. They are metaphors consigned to the task of surrounding the object to be described "phenomenologically" step by step. If metaphors are necessary in these passages, it is because literal language is inadequate for the description of extraordinary phenomena. "In his tent the light is dimmed, the lamp that shone on him is snuffed" (18.6). It is "the hour of darkness" (15.24), of "weary eyes" (11.20). One is "driven from light into darkness" (18.18). "The man no longer sees his way" (3.23). "A veil of shadow hangs over my eyelids" (16.16). "My eyes grow dim with grief" (17.7). "He has covered my way with darkness" (19.8). "For darkness hides me from him, and the gloom veils his presence from me" (23.17). "Light has turned to darkness and it blinds you" (22.11). How else could one describe the sudden disappearance of projects that one had in view? As sight, in normal time, is always focused on the thing that is kept in view within the horizon of meaning into which this thing has been projected, the project becomes impossible when it is suddenly robbed of the time required for its realization; sight, having nothing in view, falls upon pitch black.

This image is completed by another image still more faithful to the unfolding scenario, that of a breathless motion as difficult to interfere with as it is brutal in its breaking forth. It is the flight of the blind man who stumbles and keeps on running without being able to balance himself. "For me, there is no calm, no peace; my torments hunt down respite" (3.26). He cannot so much as "swallow [his] saliva" (7.19), or "regain [his] breath" (9.18). His life is a "continual torment" (15.20). "It is no more than a piece of straw on the surface of waters" (24.18). "You carry me up to ride the wind, tossing me about in the tempest" (30.22). But perhaps the keenest description of a consciousness which henceforth is sworn to the forward flight and its continual repetition, a flight of escape necessitated by the fact that every object upon which sight would alight and relax for a short instant immediately provokes a new panic, is the following algorithm for terror: "Lying in bed I wonder, 'When will it be day?' Risen I think, 'How slowly evening comes!' (7.4). "Terrors attack him *in broad daylight*, and at *night* a whirlwind sweeps him off" (27.20).

Even as he speaks of a ceaseless motion, the author imagines a motionlessness from which Job cannot tear himself away. This is understandable since the phenomenon cannot be described in terms of motion and rest; and it is no less coherent. Beside the verse, "He has built a wall across my path which I cannot pass" (19.8), cited above, one finds, "And his is the net that closes round me" (19.6), "His troops have . . . laid siege to my tent" (19.12), he "baulks [man] on every side" (3.23), "For into the net his own feet carry him, he walks among the snares" (18.8), "You . . . who have put my feet in the stocks" (13.27), "Take your hand away, which lies so heavy on me" (13.21). Scenography of a nightmare.

Whether he escapes without stopping or remains nailed to the spot, in either situation he finds himself *attacked*. "Misery descends on him in all its force. On him God looses all his burning wrath" (20.22–23). "An arsenal of terrors falls on him" (20.25). "Terrors attack him on every side, and follow behind him step by step" (18.11). "Distress and anguish close in on him, as though some king were mounting an attack" (15.24). "God's terrors stand against me in array" (6.4). "Why do you choose me as your target?" (7.20). "He has made me a target for his archery" (16.12). "And if I make a stand, like a lion you hunt me down, adding to the tale of your triumphs. You attack, and attack me again, with stroke on stroke of your fury, relentlessly your fresh troops assail me" (10.16–17). "Breach after breach he drives through me, bearing down on me like a warrior" (16.14). "They move as though through a wide breach" (30.14). "His troops have come in force, they have mounted their attack against me" (19.12).

The motion that heaves an entire flood toward him will not abate evidently until it buries him: "A flood of water overwhelms you" (22.11). "Rivers drown the foundations [of the wicked]" (22.16). The army mobilized against him launches spears and arrows that cut sharp and deep, filling him with paroxysms of pain: "Pitiless, through the loins he pierces me, and scatters my gall on the ground" (16.13). "Out through his back an arrow sticks, from his gall a shining point" (20.25). "The arrows of Shaddai stick fast in me, my spirit absorbs their poison" (6.4). The terror of the attack, the pain of the wounds are more than the victim can endure. He is strangled: "With immense power he has caught me by the clothes, clutching at the collar of my coat" (30.18). "He takes me by the neck to dash me to pieces" (16.12). "My suffering drives me to distraction" (16.7). In another image, Job is thrown to the ground by an awesome weight: "If only my misery could be weighed, and all my ills be put on the scales. But they outweigh the sands of the seas . . ." (6.2–3). And by the weight of God's hand: "Your hand lies on me, heavy and hostile" (30.21). "He, who for one hair, crushes me" (9.17). "You plunge me in dung" (9.31). "You crush him once for all" (14.20). "He has overpowered me" (30.11). "He has thrown me into the mud where I am no better than dust and ash" (30.19). "I am crushed beneath the rubble" (30.14).

As there is no recourse, the paroxysm redoubles, if that is possible. "Can any power be found within myself, has not all help deserted me?" (6.13). "They find no escape" (11.20). "If I protest against such violence, there is no reply" (19.7). "They have cut me off from all escape, there is no one to check their attack" (30.13). "I cry to you, and you give me no answer" (30.20); but in this "cry" we do not yet recognize a call to God, and it reads more like a formula for impotence.

Now, in the absence of any radical salvation, Job will at least attempt some of the strategies commonly implemented by anxiety; these have not eluded the keen eye of the author. Unfortunately—"If I resolve to stifle my moans, change countenance, and wear a smiling face, fear comes over me at the thought of all I suffer . . ." (9.27). The attempts fail. The will remains impotent before anxiety. One cannot change one's ideas. One cannot find distraction from anxiety. "While I am speaking, my suffering remains; and when I am not, do I suffer any the less?" (16.6). The buzz of conversations cannot drown out the thunder of death's certainty. And the silence of meditation only prefigures the silence of death. On the one hand, to speak is to close one's eyes to the approach of danger, hence to waver in the vigil that keeps a watchful eye on life, hence, to expose oneself to danger yet again. On the other hand, to be silent is to watch in dumb fear how danger approaches. Anxiety has a much denser consistency than any of the light-hearted distractions, be they ordinary or sophisticated, that one might try to wedge between anxiety and oneself. "If I say, 'My bed will comfort me, my couch will soothe my pain', you frighten me with dreams and terrify me with visions" (7.13). The strategy of sleep no longer "works." Without any break in continuity, the nightmare of sleep picks up where the "nightmare" of the evening left off.

Another recourse is communication with others. As the psychoanalyst, Serge Leclaire, once related to us on this subject matter: "There is no example of a crisis of anxiety that does not yield in the face of a word that communicates effectively."[4] Apparently, the same opinion, in essence, already belongs to the author of the Book of Job, who devotes so much space in his text to a report on the fragility of this opinion. To begin with, a rather astonishing image:

> My brothers have been fickle as a torrent,
>   as the course of a seasonal stream.
> Ice is the food of their dark waters,
>   they swell with the thawing if the snow;
> but in the hot season they dry up,
>   with summer's heat they vanish.
> Caravans leave the trail to find them,
>   go deep into desert, and are lost.
> The caravans of Tema look to them,
>   and on them Sheba's convoys build their hopes.
> Their trust proves vain,
>   they reach them only to be thwarted.
> So, at this time, do you behave to me:
>   one sight of me, and then you flee in fright.
>
> (6.15–21)

Why is it so difficult for Job's three friends, Eliphaz, Bildad and Zophar, and, even more significantly, for Job's own kith and kin, to make a gesture of good-will from where they stand, stretching out a hand to comfort him and reclaim him, as one might reach out from a steady boat to pull in someone who has fallen overboard and is drowning? The problem cannot be that Job's relatives and relations lack compassion for his sufferings

---

[4] In a radio program that we dedicated to the question of anxiety (*France-Culture*, March 23, 1976).

or that they cannot imagine how they might help him. It obviously occurred to the three friends to travel a long distance, each from his homeland, to "offer him sympathy and consolation" (2.11). On the other hand, his relatives do "take fright." They see that the abyss of Job's anxiety is too vertiginous, its slope too steep, for them to try to actually pull him out of it, an enterprise which would put them in serious peril of slipping down the same slope and into the same abyss. They do not engage Job therefore. Which is too bad because such engagement might have comforted him, suggesting to him that those who are reaching out must themselves be standing on firm ground. Instead, their selfish hesitations tell Job that his horror is justified and rationally confirmed. Alas, he is not dreaming. This is not a nightmare from which others might wake him and carry him back to the world's stability. We can imagine that Job might even hope, in his heart, to see his lucidity refuted. But how is he to marshal together enough courage to face an evil which, it is painfully clear, makes all his relatives and closest friends recoil in fear?

Yet he once implored them: "Sombre I go, yet no one comforts me" (30.28; cf. 21.2–3: "Listen, only listen my words; this is the consolation you can offer me. Let me have my say . . ."). He once assumed a sombre countenance in the hope of sparking some gesture of compassion from them, like the child who cries, not because he is actually unhappy, but in order to find a safe haven in the arms of his caregiver before a real reason for unhappiness can arise. We might say: Job tries to "regress." This strategy, this technique fails as well. Perhaps he does not try hard enough? Perhaps it is not enough to effect a somber countenance without saying anything, perhaps it is also necessary to cry out in order to be heard? He takes a risk and cries out: "Pity, pity me, you, my friends!" (19.21). To no avail, again silence greets his cry. And the more distressed the cry, the less are those who hear it disposed to address it and pacify it.

Job falls into total dereliction. This dereliction is not the cause of anxiety, but its consequence, or an aspect of it. Anxiety, arriving on the scene from who knows where, is what causes Job's family and friends to step back from him and to step down from the open stage where they used to communicate with him. "For you have shut their hearts to reason, and not a hand is lifted" (17.4). "My brothers stand aloof from me, and my relations take care to avoid me. My kindred and my friends have all gone away, and the guests in my house have forgotten me. The serving maids look on me as a foreigner, a stranger never seen before. My servant does not answer when I call him, I am reduced to entreating him. To my wife my breath is unbearable, for my own brothers I am a putrid thing. Even the children look down on me, ever ready with a jibe when I appear. All my dearest friends recoil from me in horror: those I loved best have turned against me" (19.13–19). They might have tried to overcome their moral repulsion, perhaps, had Job's physical existence remained intact and healthy. However, confronted with his "putrid" body odor and "unbearable" bad breath, even his wife recoils. If she had communicated with Job at one time, was this not, fundamentally speaking, for the sake of a community based on vital and almost animal interests? And did the clause providing for the indefinite renewal of this tacit contract not stipulate the good physiological operation of the body? The dissolution of the body automatically dissolves the convention of communication implicitly instituted between two living individuals.

Satan spoke prophetically when he proposed that Job, patient in the face of financial loss and the death of his children, would capitulate to the first-person perspective of his own illness: "A man will give away all he has to save his life. But stretch out your hand and lay a finger on his bone and flesh; I warrant you, he will curse you to your face" (2.4–5). And the same goes for Job's close relations. They are quite prepared to forgive him the sin they accuse him of, for the simple reason that this sin wrongs God far more than it wrongs them. After all, it is God who has been ridiculed by the sin of a human being, it is his laws that have been transgressed. What they cannot forgive is his *illness*, which projects the image of their own imminent demise into plain view. In their eyes, or rather in the eyes of their unconscious, Job is *guiltier* of an illness for which, obviously, he can bear no real *responsibility*, than of a transgression which, presumably, he committed freely. They are ready to discuss the latter; from the former they recoil in fear. It is in much the same spirit that we congratulate someone for his good luck, for his inborn talents, for his strength or beauty, which he received from the hand of destiny without having deserved the gift, while we accord little more than polite attention to the efforts of a person straining to climb up from the foot of the slope where nature has placed him: "'Add insult to injury,' think the prosperous, 'strike the man now that he is staggering'" (12.5). It is Job himself who sums it up in this admirable formula. This is the morality of those who are made of flesh. It testifies to a universal type of anxiety that occurs when one is confronted with the *inescapable process* par excellence, the corruption of the flesh; and to a universal and common empathy that occurs when we face its victory. To Satan's thesis, "A man will give away all he has to save his life. But stretch out your hand and lay a finger on *his bone and flesh*; I warrant you, he will curse you to your face," Job offers exact corroboration, term for term: "Let his sons achieve honor, he does not know of it, humiliation, he gives it not a thought. He feels no pain for anything but *his own body*, makes no lament save for *his own life*" (14.21–22).

For Job has read this thesis in the attitude of his close relations. They, like all human beings, lament only over their own bodies and their own selves, and that is why they refuse to lament over Job. This is not a defect in their personalities; it is a shortcoming in our nature. If they were to take an interest in

Job's welfare, it would only be by an inadvertence of their vital interest, and then only if they believed, for example, that charity would be reckoned for a virtue in the last judgment as the fee for immortality. For them it is necessary that the poor man who has been entrusted to their protection already and in advance be a protégé of God. They throw themselves upon Job's apparent atheism and Job's revolt as upon a lucky windfall that can serve to excuse their inexcusable retreat. Faced with a man abandoned by the Lord, they hold that one is permitted, more, required to abandon him.[5]

And so dereliction becomes persecution. Job is no longer simply abandoned, he is held in contempt. He is "sated with ignominy" (10.15). "I am the butt of mockers, and all my waking hours I brood on their spitefulness. . . . I have become a byword among the people, and a creature on whose face to spit" (17.2–6). "The lands of his home are under a curse" (24.18). "Pitilessly he is turned into a target, and forced to flee from the hands that menaced him. His downfall is greeted with applause, and hissing meets him of every side" (27.22–23). And the lament which confuses the aggressiveness of men with the aggressiveness of anxiety itself, if the exaggerated tone is to be believed: "And these are the ones that now sing ballands about me, and make me the talk of the town! To them I am loathsome, they stand aloof from me, do not scrupple to spit

---

[5] And they abandon Job even as he is not just a next-door neighbour but is more like their next of kin; he's "family." Which is why Job cites the proverb: "[You treat me like someone who] invites his friends to share with him, while the eyes of his sons languish with want" (17.5; Dhorme). Moreover, they treat Job not only with indifference, but by playing up their indignation at the assumed scandalous guilt that has cost him such punishment: "At this honest men are shocked, and the guiltless man rails against the godless; just men grow more settled in their ways, those whose hands are clean add strength to strength" (17.8–9). A miserable wretch, far from arousing pity in the heart of a "Philistine," fills him with loathing and a hypocritical and redoubled selfishness.

in my face. Because he has unbent my bow and chastened me, they cast the briddle from their mouth. That brood of theirs rises to right of me, stones are their weapons, and they take threatening strides towards me. They have cut me off from all escape, there is no one to check their attack. They move in as though through a wide breach, and I am crushed beneath the rubble" (30.9–14; cf. 16.5, 7b–10; 30.1–8, 29).

Finally, a description of anxiety that summarizes all the others: the transformation of Job's own person. He speaks "drunk with pain" (10.15), "inebriated" with "delirium" (7.4; T.O.B.) or "obsessed" with "mad thoughts" (Larcher); under the weight of pain "heavier than the sands of the seas," his words are "thoughtless" (Larcher, 6.3), "stammered" (Dhorme), "strangled" (T.O.B.). We must not take these terms to be mere metaphors of excess written in a literary style which is marked by superlatives and which paints the portrait of a man suffering in the extreme while still basically remaining who he is. We must take these passages quite literally and see in them an explicit affirmation, perhaps not of what the psychiatrist understand by "psychosis" or "insanity," but of a "psychopathological" crisis in any case. Job is not all together "there." He is "elsewhere," in some "other" place not related to the normal place. Anxiety has caused him to take leave of himself, has fractured his being, has derailed him.

And as changes take place behind the scenes, the same characters and the same plot take on a new meaning. The text describes it in details which are almost clinical:

Does a wild donkey bray when it finds soft grass,
   or an ox ever low when its fodder is in reach?
Can tasteless food be taken without salt,
   Or is there flavour in the white of an egg?

> The very dishes which I cannot stomach,
> These are my diet in my sickness.
>
> (6.5–7)[6]

For the invalid, food loses its taste. But what changes is not the food itself, only its "subjective" flavour changes. That is to say, the "salt" that usually gives food its flavour is not in the food itself but in a physiological "other scene." Without salt, food is no longer food, though it may possess all substance and reality. This is just barely a metaphor. For here the other scene is indeed the body's physiology. But to this physiological change there corresponds a change in signification. Something is modified, broken, in the "body" of linguistic signification as in the human body. "Sense" is extricable from words as "salt" is separable from food.[7] Words, having lost their sense, become aberrant: "They claim that night is day; they say that light is approaching when darkness falls" (17.12). Job's friends look like characters trapped in a silent film: Job cannot understand what they say, and uselessly addresses them with words they do not understand, although they hold fast to the mistaken belief that they can read his lips. A dream faces a dream. One incommunicability speaks, as it were, face to face with another. Mediation is nowhere in sight.

This evaporation of sense indicates again that the dissension between Job and the visitors does not take place *in* the discussions, and therefore that the alterity between the two parties is not "dialectical." One does not pass from one to the other by a "yes" or a "no." The unity of thought, the continuity of consciousness, is altogether ruptured.

---

[6] Dhorme, v. 7: "My soul has refused to touch it, my heart has been sickened by my bread." T.O.B.: "My mouth vomits them, they are unspeakable rations."

[7] Cf. also: "The ear is a judge of speeches, is it not, just as the palate can tell one food from another?" (12.11).

We cannot really say that the two parties "disagree." A lack of agreement *in* a discussion signifies that at least something has been agreed upon, namely the need for discussion. Disagreement can only take place within a discussion after all. The dissension consists, rather, in the fact that Job's interlocutors stand on the same level with their own discourse, that they find salt and sense in it, while Job has slipped out of the discussion, because, to his great horror, he can no longer find any consistency or any "hold" in the words put forward.

He actually tries to communicate this: "I too could talk like you, were you in my place [Dhorme: if your soul were in the place of my soul—*nephesh*], I too could overwhelm you with sermons, I could shake my head over you, and speak words of encouragement until my lips grew tired" (16.4–5). But "his soul" is no longer "in the place" of "(their) soul." And this *dislodging* is decisive. *Nephesh* here designates the whole being. Anxiety has dislodged Job from the place where the others stand, and plunged him into an unknown place.

This is the ultimate reason for his dereliction. Neither the hostility of others nor the anxiety of others, *nothing that comes from others*, can count as the cause of his forsakenness. For a universal hostility would assume at least a continuity of terrain, so that the hostility could be deployed in Job's direction and reach him. All combat presupposes a site where adversaries can confront each other face to face. Therefore all combat is communication; and all solitude which results from rejection is a communication in the same way. However, the solitude of Job is even less than this minimal communication. For there is no common ground. It is the ground itself that has collapsed under him. Conversely, we could say that an agreement within a discussion demonstrates, not so much a logical agreement of ideas, as if two arguments engaged each other inside the same logical system, as it is an agreement of positions, a common situation on one ground, a situation which the agreement of ideas comes only to ratify.

This almost total independence of words from that which imbues the words with sense is underlined by a decisive argument *a contrario*. Eliphaz says to Job: "Many another, once, you schooled, giving strength to feeble hands; your words set right whoever wavered, and strengthened every failing knee. And now your turn has come, and you lose patience too; now it touches you, and you are overwhelmed" (4.3–5). In other words, Job, when faced with the ordeals of "many another" weary-kneed "Job," *was himself* an Eliphaz, a Bildad, a Zophar. He too had once argued with someone who could not hear him, and the cries of that "Job" who once stood before him had been also the cries of a mute person.

What does this discontinuous succession of anxiety and normalcy signify? ("Now your turn has come. . . .") It signifies that the change, which occurs in your personality as a result of something being dislodged within your unconscious, runs deeper than your imagined identity. If you are Eliphaz one day, this does not prevent you from being Job the next day. And if you ever do become Job, you will pronounce the same words that you used to pronounce. But then they will have lost their meaning, and you yourself will no longer understand, and you will view yourself as one views a silent film.

Before attempting an interpretation of the anxiety of Job, we must take pains to underline how we at least have shown, by the foregoing considerations, that it exists. This anxiety does not easily show itself, it seems, to the theologian commentators, even to the modern ones (but we are not speaking of a Kierkegaard!), who speak of the "suffering" of Job without being more specific. Again, they seem to think that Job's suffering is a consequence of his awareness of the injustice which victimizes him. According to this reading, Job sees himself being treated unjustly, and for this reason alone he experiences pain. A strictly "moral" pain, as we can see.

The many citations which we have brought together and jux-
taposed, we believe, show that Job's anxiety does exist, that
anxiety is what Job suffers from, and that it is the madness
proper to this "species" of suffering that he characterizes as
unjust. It is for the purpose of overcoming anxiety, and nothing
else, that Job initiates a trial demanding justice.

What, after all, would be the value of a debate on justice and
injustice considered as such and in abstraction from the penalty of suffering? It would be a speculative enterprise, another
attempt to penetrate the secrets *of the world*. That is not the
problem here. Here the horror of evil causes the world to fly
into splinters; it matters little that the world is thus or otherwise. It is no longer the world that is in question here, but "Job."

It is one thing to take offence at this or that phenomenon of
signification (classifying one as unjust) or, conversely, to be satisfied with this or that word (declaring one, finally, to be innocent); it is another thing to lose all landmarks and all familiar
signs and to fall into the abyss. Words have value, as we have
seen, when the world is there to sustain them and correspond
to them. In the dizzying void, they lose their correspondence,
their sense, their salt. To interpret the Joban quest for justice
as a speculation on the mysteries of the world is to deny evil, to
shut out its truth. It is to be satisfied with "words" instead of
something which, henceforth, is absent. But who can be satisfied with words and with surrendering themselves to this something, who can be content with the surplus, and announce
themselves as indifferent to the presence or absence of the
necessary—other than those who already *have* what is necessary, those who find themselves possessing, by dint of chance,
what others lack, without knowing that this is a provisional
possession the existence of which is not self-evident and which
can be revoked at any moment? This "something" is the world,
in its full presence, in its endless rejuvenation. It is the "self-
evidence" of the world.

You do not know, or you have forgotten, that the world can

disappear, that the amazing thing is that, usually, the world does not disappear; and as a result of this inauthenticity of yours what you say about misfortune is nothing but words, theories, "sentences of ash" (13.12)—this is what Job has to say to his visitors. That is why they speak as they do: "I wish someone would teach you to be quiet—the only wisdom that becomes you" (13.5).

When we consider evil in its authentic sense, a moment must come when the speculative word, the free interrogation of a thing, grows silent. The one who falls into the abyss is not free at all. If such an individual pretends to be free, in order to "suppress his complaint" and "put on a happy face" (9.27), in order to meditate on the world while *in* the world, as the world in its order itself allows a part of it to meditate on it, then this individual does not allow evil to be what it is in its truth. The truth of evil discloses itself precisely in not allowing the individual who is caught in its vertigo to exit the vertigo and rejoin the world in its stability. And if evil should ever release the person from its grasp, so that, with feet replanted on the solid ground of the world, the individual can say, "What happened?—It was nothing!", this is a sign that evil has *already* withdrawn. For who governs evil? Evidently it is autonomous. If it comes or it goes, the initiative rests with it alone. Whenever anyone speaks of evil as being conquered by some human effort, precisely then one does not speak of evil. One speaks of obstacles, difficulties, even suffering; and of efforts, of heroism and patience in the face of these. But—if we think about it for a moment—all that this evokes, ultimately, is the *happiness* of man, and it assumes Job's problem, the problem of evil, to be resolved.

This problem (which underlies the whole of thought more persistently than any other problem) emerges, and grows to enigmatic proportions, only because in special moments—like anxiety—the world seems to deny us, not just its favors or its cooperation, but also the assistance *of its enmity*. It refuses us combat. It does not help us by extending its hardness to us, so that our human hardness might prove itself in heroic struggle against it. As we know about the most desperate struggles, human beings, whether defeated or triumphant, end up victorious, since it is in the struggle that we comprehend our strength, and it is in our strength that we celebrate ourselves. But in order to bring this about, the struggle has to be given. And unfortunately, in Job's anxiety—the extraordinary character of which only reveals the nature of ordinary evil more vividly—it is this guarantee that disappears. The struggle is not a given. The world shies away, and by its withdrawal releases a crisis where every reference and every common resource is absent. The world, disappearing, dispossesses human beings of all their initiatives. It hurls them toward a consideration of the Other, the one from whom the initiative comes.

2. The "Other" Other Scene

B UT HOW SHALL WE UNDERSTAND THIS ANXIETY OF JOB? Shall we follow Eliphaz, Bildad and Zophar and understand it as punishment for a "sin" committed by Job, which Job must now expiate through practices of purification? To our modern frame of mind, the picture of an anxious Job, sketched with as much clinical detail as the diagnosis of an "anxiety attack" or "nervous breakdown," is a tantalizing subject matter for psychoanalytic interpretation. We can be tempted to argue that, if, henceforth, the initiative comes from the "other," if Job has become an "other" himself, if he is no longer in possession of himself, if he "rambles," all this must be symptomatic of a change that has taken place in the "other scene." That is what Freud called the backstage, the *scene behind the scenes*, of the psyche, where the drama of consciousness and of the emotions is both rehearsed and performed. Assuming that such an interpretation were formulated, however, would it actually cut us loose from that way of thinking that belongs to the three friends, the personae who are supposed to represent the way of thinking of the multitude with its perennial "wise men"? Does modernity actually change something here? Do we dare to believe that Job's response to his friends no longer concerns us, we who are modern?

We shall see that on all accounts the answer is negative. Let us note the following paradox to begin with. The view of the friends—Job suffers because he has sinned—is presented by them as a *religious* view. This fact alone invites us to assume, in line with our modern way of thinking, that the technique which we employ in the task of interpreting anxiety has already ruptured all ties with such a religious viewpoint. As Job himself is a sharp critic of it, moreover, we think we recognize an ally in him (if only an inadvertent one) of our modern atheism. We marvel at the fact that Job's caustic critique was accepted into the biblical canon to begin with.

What we shall discover, however, quite to the contrary, is an almost perfect *homology* between the enterprise of the three friends, its religious connotations notwithstanding, and *technique in general* as the universal program designed to remedy human frailty and the ills besetting it. This includes the most modern manifestation of technique, the now 200-year-old ambition of intervening with the "human" itself, with the human spirit and the secret in the human heart, for the sake of mitigating all those evils which, prior to these last two centuries, had found their best refuge in religion. This homology will help us to understand how the critique of religion, which some have dated from modernity, has actually existed since the time of the Bible and was solidly acclimatized to that time. One finds in the Bible—that is to say, throughout our Book of Job—a critique of the Ab-solute, of the Un-bound, of the free and sovereign Game that is God, in exchange for an affirmation of the unity of the world.

Only, this critique is not the one that Job offers. It is the critique offered by his three pious visitors, on the basis of an uncritical faith in the efficacy of a technique which sets the world aside as a domain for the operations of the human will. But, of course, to make this claim is to imply that "technique" denotes a very broad conceptual category as even the "religion" of the friends can be subsumed under it.

The friends pose a series of questions to Job that are just as much severe judgments. "If one should address a word to you, will you endure it? Yet who can keep silent?" (4.2). "Is there no end to these words of yours, to your long-winded blustering?" (8.2). "Is babbling to go on without an answer? Is wordiness in man a proof of rightness? Do you think your talking strikes men dumb, will you jeer with no one to refute you?" (11.2–3). "Does a wise man answer with airy reasonings, or feed himself on an east wind? Does he defend himself with ineffectual words and unprofitable discourses?" (15.2–3). "Will you never learn to check such words?" (18.2). "To this my thoughts are eager to reply," says Zophar, "no wonder if I am possessed by impatience. I found these admonitions little to my taste, but my spirit whispers to me how to answer them" (20.2–3). "Why do you regard us as beasts, look on us as dumb animals?" (18.3). The violent tone of these questions does not express a general anger though; it is narrowly targeted against Job's obstinacy, as the thing that makes him unavailable for dialogue: "Do you scorn the *moderation* we have used in speaking?" (15.11).

These questions, "moderate" though they may be, mark the *distance* that the friends adopt vis-à-vis Job. They wish to discuss nothing further. Words would be "airy," "ineffectual" and "unprofitable." One could multiply them, but they would be vain: "Is wordiness in man a proof of being right?" If the friends continue to converse with Job, it is not in a tone of cordial argumentation. When a person cannot, or will not, listen, it is necessary to administer a certain *procedure*, even one that is likely to make the person uncomfortable. It is necessary to do violence, to do so for the person's own good. The psychoanalyst, when not responding point-for-point to what the patient says, inflicts the same kind of violence on the patient. This is because the doctor perceives what the patient is unable to perceive. The psychoanalyst possesses a diagnosis and a technique. Similarly, the friends are confident in everything they say because they believe themselves to be in possession of a science that Job does not possess. This science, in which they happen to specialize, is the wisdom of the Law, a Law which is both moral and religious.[1]

Before examining what they say, we may take note of what authority they invoke. First of all, let us note what they take *themselves* to be: "There are among us grey-haired men, old men, heavier with years than your father" (15.10). This means, not just that Job is too young, but, more specifically, that in comparison to the friends, he is inferior in knowledge, both "theoretical" and "practical." In a traditional society like Job's where science hardly evolves, old men are the counterparts to the scientists of our societies. They have accumulated great learning and experience, and therefore, not only must they be addressed with esteem and consideration, but their views and their directives must be studied as the most authoritative.[2] The three old men facing Job do not present themselves to him as companions or peers, veritable *friends* who might engage him

----

[1] If the author of the Book of Job is an Israelite, Job, the personage, is not. The legend says he is a man from the "land of Utz" (1.1). This particularity has caught the attention of a whole class of Jewish commentators who ascribe the aporias of the book to its alien origin. If Job says what he says, it is precisely because he does not know the Jewish version of the Law, namely the Torah. His predicament is characteristic of a relationship with God which the Mosaic revelation does not yet shed light upon. For Christian theologians, it goes without saying, Job's "flaw" is then redoubled. He lacks both the Mosaic and the evangelical revelations. It remains with one group or with the other to show how the Torah is not reducible to the altogether profane and even diabolical Law which Job criticizes (admittedly, they have a number of good arguments for this). Our own suggestion is that the Jewish author of Job makes good use of the fact that the Job of the legend is not an Israelite by stigmatizing a religion of Law without having to stigmatize the Torah.

[2] "Wisdom is found in the old, and discernment comes with great age" (12.12): an ironic citation, made by Job, of Eliphaz's argument.

in speculative debates on an equal footing with him. Rather, they hold over him the superiority of being safe from his predicament, and of having borne witness, in the course of their long existences, to "cases" similar to his, the outcomes of which had been duly observed and interpreted by them in accordance with their moral hermeneutic. They have come, not to debate, but to "pity and console" (2.11), to *do* something.

They decline their titles. "I speak from *experience*" (4.8), says Eliphaz. Experience (cf., *supra*) is what Job lacks, or at least what he has forgotten: "*Remember*, which innocent man has perished?" (4.7). Again: "All this we have *observed*: it true" (5.27). "I will instruct you, listen to me, and that which *I have seen* I will recount to you" (15.17).[3] But this knowledge is not a simple empirical and personal experience. It is a body of science compiled by generations of scientists, confirmed and sanctioned by consensus, so that the polemical opinion of a solitary individual is not something that can counterbalance it: "Meditate on the experience *accrued by the fathers*" (8.8). These are fathers who "will teach you, they will tell to you, and these are the words they will speak from the heart" (8.10), provided that Job poses the "questions" (8.8). Before the eyes of this established science, Job stands naked: "Are you the first born of the human race, brought into the world before the hills?" (15.7). To their personal experience as therapists and to their scientific erudition, the friends add a third excellence: their talent. It is not enough to be a technician. One must also have a gift for one's craft. Eliphaz's "gift," for example, consists in his privileged perception of mysteries: "I have had a secret revelation, a whisper has come to my ears" (4.12).[4] With a receptivity that

---

[3] Dhorme. Larcher translates: "I would like . . . for you to share in my *experience*."

[4] Dhorme: "Now, to me a word was spoken in secret." Here are the circumstances of this revelation: "At the hour when dreams master the mind, and slumber lies heavy on man, a shiver of horror ran through me, and

corresponds to his gift, Eliphaz is the very antithesis of Job who has not "listened to God's counsel or established a monopoly on wisdom" (15.8).

In order to magnify the science of which they are the titular heirs, the friends voluntarily walk into the comparatively colossal shadow of their predecessors: "We sons of yesterday know nothing" (8.9). The reliable transmission of the science grants them knowledge even of what happened in the world's beginning: retributive morality is verified "of all time, since man was set on the earth" (20.4). By way of the tradition, one ascends to the "counsel of God." Finally, the established science renders an account, not only of the rule of retributive morality, but also of its exceptions, even as they are incomprehensible. Tradition knows more than reason, provided that it remains pure. "I will tell you . . . of the teaching of the sages, those faithful guardians of the tradition of their fathers, to whom alone the land was given, with never a foreigner to mix with them" (15.18–19). The fathers were faithful to their own fathers, entrusting us not only with the science of their fathers, but also with the basic requirement for its further preservation: namely that it be recurrent, that it always be transmitted, and that it never try to commence again from scratch. The fact that "foreigners" have mixed in with the true proprietors of the land is insinuated to be the basic cause of current spiritual turmoil. Happiness was promised by God[5] on the condition that the Law[6] be maintained in all its purity, maintained on a land which had to be cleared of foreigners and their idolatrous cults. Evil has resulted from the transgression of this sacred clause—which the Sages, for their part, have not in the least forgotten. In short,

---

my bones quaked with fear. A breath slid over my face, the hairs of my body bristled. Someone stood there—I could not see his face, but the form remained before me. Silence—and then I heard a voice . . ." (4.13–16).

[5] YHWH?

[6] The Torah?

the discourse of the friends is that of the heirs and guardians of a science which is in itself infallible, although it has been rendered less than certain by untimely innovations. Job must accede to those who have made this the better established science among sciences through their wealth of years, their labours and their talents. From the height of a knowledge that has an ultimately divine origin, they lord over the very evils that overwhelm Job.

But again, the divine origin of the Law is perceived, not so much by them personally, as by the mediation of the tradition. God had spoken to certain Fathers some time ago, and these Fathers in turn spoke to the generation that followed them, and so on, and for this reason anyone today can inherit the ancient science. Might we then conclude from this that the Law is human? The voices that articulate it, after all, come from this world, from this side of time and history. True, these voices claim that they themselves have heard it from a voice beyond the world. But this alterity is suspect. The tradition of the Ancients is effectively the authority of the Ancients, and the latter is itself confused with the authority of the one who can, at the very most, only claim to be speaking in the name of the Ancients. The past, with its endless regress to what is original, is the simple sign accompanying the authority of the greatest knowledge.

We begin to understand that if Zophar, Bildad and Eliphaz speak in a religious vernacular exploiting the "revelation" for which Eliphaz has been happily chosen, they do so above all as shareholders in a positive knowledge which they rely upon for the supervision of human action. What is the nature of this knowledge? Is it a theology? It would seem so, since God figures in it quite prominently. But *which* God?

In the friends' discourse, God is represented in an entirely classical fashion, as something beyond thought. "His works are great, past all reckoning, marvels, beyond all counting" (5.9; 9.10). "The secrets of Wisdom put all sagacity to shame" (11.6). "(The limit of Shaddai) is higher than the heavens . . . deeper than Sheol . . . Its length is longer than the earth, its breadth is broader than the sea" (11.8–9). "Can anyone number his armies?" (25.3). "All this but skirts the way he treads, a whispered echo is all that we hear of him" (26.14).

But the unthinkable God soon takes on a more definite shape. God's very unknowableness becomes a known attribute. If our thoughts cannot reach God, it is because "wisdom and power reside with him, in him is counsel and discernment" (12.13). "In him is vigor and wisdom" (12.16). God's attributes are human powers pushed to the extreme. God is big, marvelous, all-powerful. "His works are great, past all reckoning, marvels beyond all counting" (5.9; 9.10; cf. 42.3). God is the Creator: "The hand of God has made all this" (12.9). God is master of the elements. *Of water*: "He sends down rain to the earth, pours down water on the fields" (5.10). "He fastens up the waters in the cloud—the mists do not tear apart under their weight. . . . He has traced a ring on the surface of the waters, at the boundary between light and dark. . . . With his power he calmed the Sea, with his wisdom struck Rahab[7] down" (26.8, 10, 12). God "tramples the Sea's tall waves" (9.8). "Is there a drought? He has checked the waters. Do these play havoc with the earth? He has let them loose" (12.15). See also 38.8–11 where YHWH speaks in the first person. *Of earth*: "The pillars of the heavens [i.e. the mountains] tremble, they are struck with wonder when he threatens them" (26.11). "He moves the mountains, though they do not know it; he throws them down when he is angry. He shakes the earth, and moves it from its place, making all its pillars tremble" (9.5–6). And at 38.4–18: "Where were you when I laid the earth's foundations? . . . What supports its

---

[7] Rahab: personification of the raging sea.

pillars at their bases? Who laid its cornerstone when all the stars of the morning were singing with joy, and the Sons of God in chorus were chanting praise? . . . Have you an inkling of the extent of the earth?" *Of the air and sky*: "His breath made the skies luminous" (26.13). "He it was who suspended the North [quarter of the firmament] above the void, and poised the earth on nothingness. . . . He covers the face of the moon at full, his mist he spreads over it" (26.7, 9). "Can anyone . . . boast of having escaped his lightning?" (25.3; Septuagint: "his ambushes"). "The sun, at his command, forbears to rise, and on the stars he sets a seal. He and no other stretched out the skies, and trampled the Sea's tall waves. The Bear, Orion too, are of his making, the Pleiades and the Mansions of the South" (9.7–9). He "keeps the peace in his heights" (25.2). And at 38.12: "Have you ever in your life given order to the morning or sent the dawn to its post?" And 38.19–20: "Which is the way to the home of the light, and where does the darkness live? You could then show them the way to their proper places, or put them on the path to where they live!"

God is also master of the animals, and does not go unnoticed by them: "If you would learn more, ask the cattle, seek information from the birds of the air. The creeping things of the earth will give you lessons, and the fishes of the sea will tell you all. There is not one such creature but will know this state of things is all of God's own making" (12.7–9). This also holds true for mythical animals: "his hand transfixed the Fleeing Serpent" (26.13). The speeches of YHWH are specially dedicated to celebrating this mastery. (Cf. 38, 39, *passim*, and the discourses on Leviathan and Behemoth [40, 41]).

God is the master of human beings—who can neither face God nor exploit their own faculties. "Who among the wisest and the strongest would defy him" (9.4). "Were he to snatch a prize, who could prevent him, or dare to say, 'What are you doing?'" (9.12). "If he passes and imprisons and calls an assembly, who can turn him back?" (11.10).

The power of God, finally, is superior to that of death: "The Shades tremble beneath the earth; the waters and their denizens are afraid. Before his eyes, Sheol is bare, Perdition itself is uncovered" (26.5–6). This is why God is terrifying: "God never goes back on his anger, Rahab's minions still lie at his feet" (9.13). "What sovereignty, what awe, is his!" (25.2). "[The mountains] are struck with wonder when he threatens them" (26.11).

We will have to return, although from Job's viewpoint, which is a wholly different perspective, to some of these classical expressions of divine power. Here let us simply take note of a certain function which they uniformly exhibit and which illuminates the real nature of the "God" of the three friends. If one reads the expressions closely, one can see how each and every one of them reveals a *power* and an *order*. The description of infinite power does not capitalize on its mystery, its beauty, or its force as attributes of intrinsic value. It is described with a view to its instrumentality. If "God" is omnipotent, it is *for the sake* of being the secular arm of an infallible Justice. If God is omniscient, it is *so that* nothing escape God concerning the merits and demerits of human beings.

Thus, one pictures this God, the same God who, just a moment ago, had been put beyond the reach of knowledge, as a judge whose every sentence can be anticipated. If God is frightening, it is only toward the wicked. They cannot dodge God's eye or punishment by hiding somewhere in the earth, or even somewhere in the heavens: "He let [the tyrant] build his hopes on false security, but kept his eyes on every step he took" (24.23). God becomes the principal component, or motor, of a mechanism which can be described with a good degree of precision. This mechanism is the order of the workings of the world, of things and humans. One knows, on the basis of a consensus tried and tested by generations, that when human beings do such-and-such, everything works according to order, and that when they do not do such-and-such, disorder sets in, and with it misfortune. That which needs to be done is recorded in the Law. And the Law foresees the consequences of transgressing its prescriptions. In this complex mechanism, which only specialists can understand adequately, "God," inevitably, is the metaphor for the Law itself.

Indeed, God *is* the Law itself, since God fills in for its role. One could replace "God" by "Law" at any given moment, and this would not change anything in the order or the parts of the mechanism. In the place that either of these two names can fill, we will say that there is a power, a primary motor, that regulates the cosmic order without either surpassing it or transgressing it. "God" is in this sense nothing other than the mechanism itself, the necessity that regulates the world. And "world" is yet another name for the same necessity.

This equivalence of God, Law, and World, already discernible in the doxographical writings on God we have just looked at, becomes still more obvious in what follows. It becomes transparent in the friends' interpretation of the phenomenon of evil.[8]

"Divine" power does in fact have a strange limit, and this necessity which bears three names, curiously enough, is not monolithic. For it is here that "impure" human beings hold their ground before God and Law.

---

[8] As regards the equation, "World = Law," it plays a central role in the thought of Christian Jambet and Guy Lardreau, in *l'Ange* (Paris: Grasset, 1976) and in Jambet's *l'Apologie de Platon* (Paris: Grasset, 1976); cf. particularly the chapter entitled, "The Political Conception of the World," in the latter book. It is because the Law is the world and the world is the Law that no "rebellion"—no rupture with the order of the Law—can take place, short of the world itself being shattered within an angelophany of "another" world. Here and in what follows we are in accord with this thought, which, with one and the same gesture, revokes monist metaphysics, theories of revolution that usurp the alterity of the Other World by making it a simple future of this world and thereby eternalizing it within the Same, and positive religions, all of which are interpreted by

The dream-revelation of Eliphaz instructs us: "Was ever any man found blameless in the presence of God, or faultless in the presence of his Maker? In his own servants God puts no trust, and even with his angels he has fault to find. What then of those who live in houses of clay . . .?" (4.17–19). Eliphaz will recall this dream in chapter 15: "How can any man be clean? Born of woman, can he ever be good? In his own Holy Ones God puts no trust, and the heavens themselves are not, in his eyes, clean. Then how much less this hateful, corrupt thing, mankind, that drinks iniquity like water!" (15.14–16; see also 25.4–6). All this is summarized in the basic proposition: "Grief does not grow out of the earth, nor sorrow spring from the ground. It is man who breeds trouble for himself as surely as eagles fly to the height." (5.6–7).[9] Misfortunes result from transgressions for which the individual alone is culpable. After enumerating the "sins" Job must have committed, Eliphaz concludes: "No wonder, then, if snares are all around you, or sudden terrors make you afraid" (22.10).

The world, the "earth," the "ground," and above all God, who is the embodiment of order itself—all these are innocent of evil. Evil results from the *human being* making a false step, a *faux pas*, on the ancient path traced out for us.

We will have to return to this rather astonishing possibility of rupture within the order of the world, this odd and unstable

---

the two thinkers (who reserve a special place for mysticism and Gnosticism) as doctrines of Law. Indeed, we can see in the passages of Job just quoted to what extent the "monism" of a unique world, the privileged domain of any positivism, can be conveyed in religious language: the two doctrines, positivism and religion, have this in common, that they always put forward a necessity of things, of a Law, whether this be the collected sum of laws discovered by science, or an eternal Law in the Thomistic sense (although the concept of Law for St. Thomas is in fact something quite different: his *lex divina* makes room for human freedom).

[9] T.O.B.: "Man is born to misery, as the spark to fly upward." Dhorme: "As the sons of the lightning soar aloft in their flight."

play in the gears of the world's mechanics, which causes humans to digress and to stray instead of resting eternally within order. The friends are not surprised by it. They accept this bit of madness as a fact, a revealed given.

But let us turn to these errors for which human beings bear responsibility, these "sins," as the friends call them, which their science classifies with great precision. There are four types. The first type of sin is the *will to dominate*. "Since he once destroyed the huts of poor men, and stole other's houses when he should have built his own, since his avarice could never be satisfied . . . since there was nothing that ever escaped his greed . . ." (20.19–21). "He used to be harsh to the barren, childless woman, and show no kindness to the widow" (24.21). "He had taken possession of ruined towns and made his dwelling in deserted houses" (15.28), thirsty for riches, but riches mingled with impiety, since, at the sight of ruins, the pious man must "whistle," remain "appalled" and "shake his head" (I K 9.8; Jer. 18.16). Ruins are the sign of divine disfavor; in restoring the remains, one risks a verdict from the On-High (Deut. 29.23–27).

The second type of sin or *faux pas* is precisely *impiety.* The wicked are punished "because they said to God, 'Go away! What can Shaddai do to us?' Yet he himself had filled their houses with good things, while these wicked men shut him out of their counsels" (22.17–18). "He raised his hand against God, he ventured to defy Shaddai, he charged against him with head lowered behind a broad shield" (15.25–26). "Such is the fate of all who forget God; so perishes the hope of the godless man" (8.13). "For what hope, after all, has the godless when he prays, and raises his soul to God? . . . Did he make Shaddai all his delight, calling on him at every turn?" (27.8–10). Here is the sin: to fail to make God one's "delight," "at every turn." One must invoke God either always or never. When it is a question of buying insurance, one must do so before the accident. Here the technical character of moral legislation makes its mark, and it is not the mark of the unforseen, of the gratuitous, of the Game. A world is given, in all its presence, in all its coherence. It has a name: Law. One finds oneself always already forewarned. The law is explicit. By transgressing, one breaches the order and begets misery. For this misery, one bears responsibility. One has committed an *error*, and it is not up to the Law to change, it is up to man to redress his error.

The third type of sin consists in *speaking evil.* "Evil was sweet to his mouth, he hid it beneath his tongue; unwilling to let it go, he let it linger on his palate" (20.12–13). The "bile" that consequently ripens in his belly (v. 14), the "venom" (v. 16) of the sins, becomes his punishment: "The viper's tongue kills him" (ibid.).

Finally, sin consists in *pride,* a favorite theme of Elihu, although we will not take it up as such here. Sticking to the dialogues:—"God casts down the boastings of the braggart" (22.29). "But he should not trust in his great stature, if he would not trust in vain" (15.31). "Towering to the sky he may have been, with head touching the clouds; but he vanishes, like a phantom, once for all, while those who saw him now ask, 'Where is he?'" (20.6–7). "Gone that glad face at the sight of his gains, those comfortable looks when business was thriving" (20.18). To sin is to have faith in oneself alone and to turn up one's nose at the Law. Such saucy disrespect is what every good technician avoids. After all, would the technician not "stray," not run headlong into failure, failure pure and simple, upon refusing self-effacement before the Law of the world? Every technician knows: one does not master the world except by respecting its Law, which means abjuring all pride.

To transgression responds punishment. Or rather, prior even to that, the pure and simple failure of all criminal enterprise. Crime cannot transform the order of the world and prevent it from being that which it must be. Technical error is immediately sanctioned by the failure of technique. "Wickedness must shut its mouth" (5.16). "And so the idiot grows wise, and thus a young wild donkey grows tame" (11.12). "[God] does not lend his aid to the wicked" (8.20). "Resentment kills the senseless, and anger brings death to the fool" (5.2). By a kind of natural necessity crime carries failure in its own wake. "His own cunning brings him down" (18.7). "God wrecks the plans of the artful, and brings to naught their intrigues. He traps the crafty in the snare of their own shrewdness, turns subtle counselors to idiots. In daylight they come against darkness, and grope their way as if noon were night" (5.12–14). (Job takes up these sapiental themes in order to refute them word for word; cf. 12.17 ff.). "[Dawn] steals the light from wicked men and breaks the arm raised to strike" (38.15; it is YHWH who speaks).

One should think that the wicked, nevertheless, benefit from the long night for striking out, the delay of sunlight being sufficient for them to accomplish their crimes. For even if "the triumph of the wicked has always been brief, and the sinner's gladness has never lasted long" (20.5), crime *exists*. It, therefore, must be punished, so that the situation preceding it may be restored. "Those who plough iniquity and sow the seeds of grief reap a harvest of the same kind. A breath from God will bring them to destruction, a blast of God's anger will wipe them out. The lion's roar, his savage growls, like the fangs on lion cubs are broken off. For lack of prey the lion dies at last, and the whelps of his lioness are scattered" (4.8–11). "They vanish for ever and no one remembers them. Their tent-peg is snatched from them, and they die for lack of wisdom" (4.20–21). "The life of the wicked is unceasing torment, the years allotted to the tyrant are numbered. The danger signal ever echoes in his ear, in the midst of peace the marauder swoops on him" (15.20–21). "As drought and heat carry away the snow waters, so Sheol kidnaps the sinner" (24.19). "Here is the fate that God has in store for the wicked, and the inheritance with which Shaddai endows the man of violence. A sword awaits his sons, however many they may be, and their children after them will go unfed.

Plague will bury those he leaves behind him, and their widows will have no chance to mourn them" (27.13–15).[10]

That is how transgression is punished. And how is the tort suffered by the victims repaired? By the mechanism of *retribution*. True, we find a number of expressions of absolute hope, in the style of the Psalter: "Can your recall a guiltless man that perished, or have you ever seen good men brought to nothing?" (4.7). "God does not spurn a spotless man" (8.20). "He saves the man of downcast eyes. If a man is innocent, he will bring him freedom" (22.29–30). Again, one receives protection only as recompense for one's merit. But everywhere else, what the just have for their recompense consists of what is recaptured from the hands of the unjust. Justice is like a wheel which, with each full revolution, brings everything that was displaced for a while, in the disorder wrought by the misdeed, back to its proper place. This is retributive justice. It is a revolving mechanism that returns the "algebraic" sum of pleasures and pains back to zero.

"If his will is to rescue the downcast, or raise the afflicted to the heights of joy, he wrecks the plans of the artful. . . . He rescues the bankrupt from their jaws, and the poor man from the hands of the violent. *Consequently* the wretched man can hope again . . ." (5.11–16). "He looses his glad demeanor when *refunding* his gains" (20.18). "His sons must *reimburse* his victims, and his children *pay back* his riches" (20.10). "You may dwell in his tent *which is his no longer*" (18.15). "At the *spectacle* of their ruin, good men rejoice, and the innocent deride them: 'See how their greatness is brought to nothing! See how their wealth has perished in the flames!'" (22.19–20). "He may collect silver like dust, and gather fine clothes like clay. Let him gather! *Some good man will wear them, while his silver is shared among the innocent*" (27.16–17). "I myself have seen how such a one took

---

[10] Cf. 8.14–15; 11.20; 15.22–23, 27–35; the whole of chapter 18, where the accent is placed on the anxiety of the sinner; 20.16–17, 26–27; 27.18–19.

root, until a swift curse fell on his house. His sons at a single blow loose their prop and stay, ruined at the gate with no one to defend them; their harvest goes to *feed the hungry*, God *snatches it from their mouths*, and *thirsty men hanker after their goods*" (5.3–5). "Now he must bring up all the wealth that he has swallowed, *God makes him disgorge it*" (20.15).

The justice in question, then, is not one that breaks the cycle of vengeances and retributions by means of some transcendent principle. It is a distributive justice which ensures the regular succession of phases in the struggle of egoisms. In any given situation, this justice always seeks to reestablish the preceding situation, so that the fight, so to speak, can always begin anew from its initial conditions. For this reason, evidently, it also promotes a general state of combat, and is party to the camp of egoism. It is a justice that eternalizes *the world as it is*, instead of announcing a world where injustice would no longer exist. In its aims, it is similar to a human justice, not to a religious one. And there again, "God," who is the guarantor and the arm of this justice, bears such a strong resemblance to the Law that it is difficult to tell them apart. The world, in so far as it is governed by a Law, can promise nothing to technique other than what strictly conforms to its order. Similarly, divine justice as it is conceived by the technical "religion" of the three friends does protect the human being from an excessive wickedness on God's part, but by the same token, it also dispossesses God of his ability to forgive. "Divine" justice and the order of the Law have this in common, that they enclose human beings within the oneness of a world without an outside, or a flip-side, without origin or end, a world that is eternally self-same.

The machine is so expertly built that it metes out punishment in exact proportion to each iniquity. With each revolution, old guilt finds itself perfectly white again, primed and ready for the perpetration of new sins. And after these new sins cause new stains, a new payment is made and the guilt is once again prepared for washing and bleaching. And so on. This is the scenario that the friends have in mind when they say that God is "correcting" Job (22.4; translation uncertain) when he places him on the rack. "Happy indeed the man whom God corrects! . . . For he who wounds is he who soothes the sore, and the hand that hurts is the hand that heals. Six times will he deliver you from sorrow, and the seventh, evil shall not touch you" (5.17–19). "Thus a blank mind acquires judgment, thus a wild donkey becomes a trusty onager (domestic donkey)" (11.12; T.O.B.). The torture is supposed to break the craving for what is "bigger and better" and what exceeds a person's exact due, whether the person seeks this excess in crime, or perhaps in too much hope. One needs to be hardened through trials and tribulations, protected by a shell of indifference. One must adapt to the machine of the world and acquire a good working-knowledge of all its cogs and wheels. Psalm 94 says this too: "Happy the man whom you instruct, YHWH, the man whom you teach through your law . . ." (v. 12).

With this mechanism of sins and retributions set up to operate as the explanation for evil, nothing remains for the friends to do but to switch it on and process the particular case of Job's suffering. It remains for them to show him that he has indeed committed sins. After that, they can turn to the penal code, the code for the procedures of repair. And lastly, Job will learn about what he is permitted to hope, on condition of yielding to prescriptions. The speeches of the friends fulfill this program scrupulously.

Job, they say, is undoubtedly guilty of the four types of sin which deserve punishment. This was true of his sons: they sinned (cf. 1.4–5), now they are dead (1.19). Bildad: "If your sons sinned against [God], they have paid for their sins" (8.4). And it is true of Job. If he is punished, it is because he has sinned, despite his sincerest denials. "For God detects the falseness in man, he sees iniquity . . ." (11.11). This is why Zophar asserts: "These were your words, 'My way of life is faultless, and in your eyes I am free from blame.' But if God had a mind to speak, to open his lips and give you answer, were he to show you the secrets of wisdom which put all cleverness to shame— you would know it is for sin he calls you to account" (11.4–6). Slight doubts concerning the nature and the precise hour of the sin, but not the sin's existence. Alongside such conditionals as, "If you renounce the iniquity that stains your hands" (11.14), one finds: "If you lay gold down on dust, and Ophir among the the pebbles of the torrent" (22.24; *hence Job has stolen*); "If you return, humbled, to Shaddai" (22.23; *hence he has been proud*); "Is that not *for your manifold wickedness* (that God revisits as judgment against you), *for your unending iniquities*? You have exacted needless pledges from your brothers, and men go naked now through your despoiling; you have grudged water to the thirsty man, and refused bread to the hungry; you have narrowed the lands of the poor man down to nothing to set your crony in his place, sent widows away empty-handed, and crushed the arms of orphans" (22.5–9; cf. 22.12–15). Job is impious.

Hence the friends recommend what the Law prescribes with respect to sins: prayer and purification. "Come, you must set your heart right, stretch out your hands to him. Renounce the iniquity that stains your hands, let no injustice live within your tents. Then you may face the world in innocence" (11.13–15). "Well then! Make peace with him, be reconciled. . . . Welcome the teaching[11] from his lips, and keep his words close to your heart.[12] If you return, humbled, to Shaddai and drive all injus-tice from your tents, if you lay gold down on dust and Ophir

---

[11] Dhorme: "instruction"; Osty: "lesson." The Hebrew word is *torah*, which is often translated as "Law."

[12] "Welcome the teaching from his lips" resonates with "Then do not refuse this *lesson* from Shaddai" (5.17), and "*Heed* it, and do so to your *profit*" (5.27). The Law is material to be taught. The idea that "God" is the

among the pebbles of the torrent . . ." (22.21–24). "Keep your hands unstained, and you will be saved" (22.30). "As for you, if you are pure and honest, seek God, plead with Shaddai" (8.5–6). "As for me, I would appeal to God, and lay my case before him" (5.8). To God, and not to his saints: "Make your appeal then. Will you find an answer? To which of the saints will you turn?" (5.1). Finally, this paradoxical piece of advice: "Does not your piety give you confidence, your blameless life give you hope?" (4.6), which probably means, not that Job has avoided sinning, but that his guilt, unique in a life which has been good on the whole, can still be repaired. *good balances bad*

This mixture of remedies promises to be efficacious, and that is technique's *raison d'être*. Job will straightaway recover his happiness: "*Without delay* the light of Shaddai will shine upon you, he will see that the good man's house is rebuilt. Your former state will seem to you as nothing, so great will be your future" (8.6–7). "Then you may face the world in innocence, unwavering and free from fear. You will forget your sufferings, remember them as waters that have passed away" (11.15–16). This will mark the end of anxiety as we have described it. As there is no common standard of measurement between a normal state and the sick state of anxiety, the rupture between the sickness and the recovery will be total. Job will remember nothing, as if waking from a nightmare. The contraction of time and the disappearance of projects caused by anxiety will undergo dilation, and time will open up anew. Then: "great will be your future." Thus moral technology claims to have overwhelmed what was most serious in evil. The caesura separating the moment in which the ground of the world is still firm from the moment when it falls away like rotten floorboards is regarded by moral technology as a problem that has been pinpointed, bypassed,

prophetic

The sick & the healthy

---

teacher comes to mean, in the modern context, that the technician must learn to read the Law as it is inscribed in the book of the world.

erased. The world, almost completely transparent to knowledge, is a degree of order superior to all conceivable disorder. No doubt there is a "residue" of opacity: we do not rightly know what "God" is going to do, which is why Job is called upon to "beseech" God; science does not know everything. Yet we do know that this "residue," this grain of folly, this Game, does not contradict the Law.

Technique's ambition is displayed in ample imagery. "Once again your cheeks will fill with laughter, from your lips will break a cry of joy. Your enemies shall be covered with shame, and the tent of the wicked folk shall vanish" (8.21-22). Even joy and its brief delirium returns to order. Technique masters and computes emotions, pleasures and pains, and the human existence that feels them. It dominates the whole Earth. "In time of famine, [Shaddai] will save you from death, and in wartime from the stroke of the sword. You shall be safe from the lash of the tongue, and see the approach of the brigand without fear. You shall laugh at drought and frost, and have no fear of the beasts of the earth. You shall have a pact with the stones of the field, and live in amity with wild beasts. You shall find your tent secure, and your sheepfold untouched when you come. You shall see your descendants multiply, your offspring grow like the grass in the fields (cf. 27.14, "If the descendants of the wicked multiply, it is for the sword"). In ripe age you shall go to the grave, like a wheatsheaf stacked in time" (whence death will no longer show up *"before its time"*) (5.20-26). "Your life, more radiant than the noonday, will make a dawn of darkness" (11.17). (Indeed, the archetypal cases of anxiety are rooted in an underlying anxiety. Apart from anxiety, even the most frightening situations can remain on the surface of a total serenity without disturbing it. For those who are truly anxious, on the contrary, as Job has said, everything redoubles their anxiety, day as well as night, solitude as well as crowds. . . .) "Full of hope, you will live secure, dwelling well and safely guarded. No one will dare disturb you [cf. "When I lay down on my bed, I ask myself:

'Until when . . .'"], and many a man will seek your favor"
[cf. "My relatives work to avoid me . . ."] (11.18–19). "Your happiness will be restored to you" (22.21). "Then you will find
Shaddai worth bars of gold or silver piled in heaps. Then
Shaddai will be all your delight, and you will lift your face to
God. You will pray, and he will hear; you will have good reason
to fulfil your vows. Whatever you undertake will go well, and
light will shine on your path" (22.25–28; cf. "Darkness is in his
path.") The previous situation will be restored. The wheel of
justice will have made a full turn and returned all things to
their ordered place. The situation will be even better secured,
since Job, having absorbed the lesson of divine "corrections"
and having acquired more know-how, will have attained a higher
rank within the order of world.

That is the religious-moral view of Job's three friends. They
are the specialists of this view and they put it to work as a
technology founded on a knowledge of rules of conduct. To these
rather schematic rules, for the sake of completeness, it is ad-
visable that we join the ritualistic rules of religious Law. To the
latter set of rules the text refers implicitly, even if it stays clear
of the Torah proper, which it probably does. With this assort-
ment of "technical" procedures ready to hand, the friends intend to "save" Job, not in an absolute sense, but in the sense of
pulling him back from making a bad move, so that he may rejoin the world in its order and stop "blaspheming."

Will Job agree to it? One should think not. For in his dizzy
fall into the abyss, Job has already been touched by an altogether different truth. Does he agree to it in the epilogue, then,
at least, when all is assuaged and returned to order? Even
then it is not certain. After all, Job has lost his children. The
epilogue tells us that he receives *other* children, not the same
ones; technique, as we said, cannot reverse the order of the
world. Can the beauty of the daughters of Job's new beginning
(42.15) make him forget the faces of the daughters he lost? The
school of the world-order, the school of technique, the school of

"corrections," is an apprenticeship in renunciation and oblivion. It teaches one to bridle one's horror and hold it back from running free, to tie it up to a post before scandal can deploy the stream of effects that we shall observe.

But such a reserved attitude, silence welcoming horror, was announced in the prologue. "Looking at him from a distance, [the three friends] could not recognize [Job]; they wept aloud and tore their garments and threw dust over their heads. They sat there on the ground beside him for seven days and seven nights. To Job they spoke never a word, so sad a sight he made" (2.12-13). For Job, this silence, letting horror and memory run free, is a clean slate on which one can come to write the truth. Often in the Bible, silence is a prelude to revelation.[13] After seven days of silence, Job too will receive a revelation, in the enigmatic chapter 3 which we will look at in a moment. By contrast, the friends do not speak from the depths of silence; their speech is a response to Job who has spoken first. Silence *says* nothing to them. For they have decided to stave off the approach of what is beyond the world, be it horror or joyful vision, by conceiving the Beyond as a pleat to be unfolded from this world. Instead of being silent in the face of Job's anxiety and his fulminating hopes, they congregate into the chatter and traffic of technique.

It may be interesting for us to meditate on the similarity between this reductive enterprise, this blunt refusal of everything that comes from the heart of silence, and the procedures

---

[13] Cf. Jer. 42.7: "Ten days later the word of YHWH was addressed to Jeremiah." Ten days of silence—and yet Jeremiah is in a hurry! And let us recall how God speaks to Elijah in a "thin silence," the "sound of a gentle breeze," instead of the hurricane, the earthquake or the fire (1 Kings 19.11–12). The silence that "speaks" of God is the special theme of André Néher's *l'Exil de la Parole* (Paris: Seuil, 1970), where these and other examples are taken up.

of psychoanalysis and civil justice, even though Job's critique of technique still holds more general implications, as we shall later see. The comparison will allow us to understand certain passages from the dialogues which we have deliberately put in reserve.

On the one hand, we have the "moral" interpretation of Job's anxiety: Job has sinned by perpetrating violence against individuals protected under the Law: the poor man, the widow, the orphan. This violence now turns back against him because "God," who is the Law itself, has made sure to return to him violently. He will not understand what is happening to him so long as moralists do not make him see his wrong and set him on the right path again. On the other hand, we have the psychoanalytic interpretation: Job's anxiety is a psychic force that has not found a normal external outlet, having made the error of seeking a forbidden object in the normal horizon of libidinal investments, and that now, consequently, turns back against the subject. The subject does not discern anything, does not know what he is afraid of. But by means of the cure, he is involuntarily led back to the memory of the trauma. If he accepts the interpretation, the "symptoms" subside. Through confession, anamnesis, and through "renouncing the pleasure principle" and "accepting the difference between the sexes," he, too, duly "corrected," will accede to normal life.

A neat parallelism, as we can see. At least in principle. We may pursue it further: Job's rejection of the analysis of the friends is interpreted by them as an *a posteriori* proof, and as an augmentation, of his wrongdoing, just as the patient's rejection of the analyst's interpretation is classified by the latter as "resistance" and only serves to confirm the accuracy of the interpretation.

That is what we find here. As Job declares his innocence, the friends wrench an unexpected argument from his protests: the asseveration of innocence is itself a sign of guilt. "You do worse: you flout piety, you repudiate meditation in God's presence.

A guilty conscience prompts your words, you adopt the language of the cunning. Your own mouth condemns you, and not I; your own lips bear witness against you" (15.4–6).[14] "See how passion carries you away! How your eyes roll when you thus loose your anger on God and utter speeches such as these!" (15.12–13). Job is guilty of insolence; or rather, of insubordination; or rather, of being too thick-skinned to be branded by the Law: "Tear yourself to pieces if you will, but the world, for all your rage, will not return to desert, the rocks will not shift from their places" (18.4). The basic dissymmetry between the individual and the Law is impossible to rectify, the individual can never revise the Law: "Can a man be of any use to God, when even the wise man's wisdom is of use only to himself? Does Shaddai derive any benefit from your integrity, or profit from your blameless conduct?" (22.2–3). "Can you claim to grasp the mystery of God, to understand the perfection of Shaddai?" (11.7). "Can God deflect the course of right or Shaddai falsify justice?" (8.3).

Which means: You *were* innocent perhaps, but see how you render yourself culpable as soon as you make protests on behalf of your innocence; this shows why your punishment is deserved. Justice is broken here, in so far as justice implies a strict logic; the argument makes the accusation into a pure paralogism. For one of two things must be the case: either Job is innocent, in which case he would not be deserving of punishment and, hence, he would not have blasphemed; or he is guilty, and his crime is necessarily *other* than blasphemy and *anterior* to it. The paralogism takes place at the point where the friends say that it is Job's "mouth"—the words he is *presently* uttering—that "condemns" him. Here again we are confronted with a technique for managing disorder, a technique

---

[14] This argument is pointed out by Job in an ironic way: "What provokes you that you answer?" (16.3).

which is introduced in judicial procedures when doubt arises. The paralogism is basically a procedural shortcut whereby the judge evaluates the suspect's normalcy in order to remove this doubt. One arrests the suspect for a misdemeanor, a peccadillo, perhaps mistakenly. But this at least affords an opportunity to gauge how well this individual has internalized the norm. The indices informing this diagnosis as well as the prognosis about future conduct are precisely the suspect's reactions before the judicial apparatus. By denying *all* culpability, Job confirms his dissidence. Even if the flawless onager, the donkey domesticated by divine "corrections," does not reproach himself for any crimes—he cannot recall any—this does not prevent him from considering the possibility that he committed crimes which he has forgotten, or which he did not recognize as crimes perhaps. What he must now acknowledge is the superior perspicacity that belongs to the representatives of the Law. If, instead, his denial is absolute,[15] what he denies is that the Law should prevail in any situation. He says to his friends: "Whatever you know, I know too . . ." (13.2), to which they retort: "What knowledge have you that we have not, what understanding that is not ours too?" (15.9). If Job repudiates the *gap* constitutive of the situation that calls for technical intervention, they make this very repudiation an object of interpretation: in speaking as he does, Job "adopts the language of the shrewd" who, without either acknowledging or knowing the Law, are bound to transgress it sooner or later, even if, perchance, they have not done so yet. For this reason Job's speech is a symptom, a matter for reinterpretation. He says *nothing true*.

For a psychoanalytic technique, likewise, Job's *insistence* that

---

[15] In fact, we will see how in several places Job confesses to having sinned. But we will see that this confession appears only after a "revelation" the friends could never anticipate. In their eyes, he denies everything, both the guilt and the help that the Law can provide: "Do you scorn the *comfort* that God gives?" (15.11).

he is innocent would signal *a contrario* an unresolved inner conflict. The "mouths" of neurotics condemn them, as we know, well before the details of their case histories are examined. Without knowing it, and believing themselves to be speaking about something else, they speak of their neuroses, and their neuroses speak through them. "How (their) eyes roll when (they) thus loose (their) anger on (their object of transference) and utter speeches such as these!" Job's friends take his obsessions as seriously as a therapist takes the parapraxes of his patient. The therapist sits in complete neutrality before the patient, the object of therapeutic intervention, and continues to be "calm" whenever the patient blows up.

The friends turn the same deaf ear to Job's complaints. They are not analysts, to be sure, and the rules of their technology oblige them to speak and to argue, instead of being reserved and of intervening merely stingily. But they display the same "therapeutic" calm which allows them to return again and again to the same kind of argument with a stubborn confidence. They are not really affected, only somewhat irritated, by Job's arguments. They had decided from the outset that they were justified in not taking Job's arguments seriously. Job's words mean the contrary of what they say, they are "a wind from the east" inspired by disarray. Their very disorder demonstrates that Job does not accede to the order of the world.

This is how any *gap* in a discussion is ratified. The gap becomes law as soon as one party *interprets* the other instead of listening to him; this holds for the "grey heads heavier with years than his father" interpreting Job, the therapist interpreting the patient, the judge interpreting the defendant, etc. In each case, technique is founded on a non-reciprocity: "Will you probe the depths of Shaddai?" Will you probe the depths of psychoanalysis, of society, of politics? Technique transforms all things into objects which are integrated into the world, the closed horizon of technical operations. Closed: because it excludes, outlaws, the word that breaks with the Law. An object cannot speak; only the system in which the object is found can appoint it a place in the order. We shall see exactly which *word* Job opposes to a technique that invokes words in general as objects which can be computed, counted and counted upon.[16]

One possible source for the Book of Job from Ancient Near Eastern literature, or one such text with which it resonates,[17] is the Egyptian *Book of the Dead* dating from the New Kingdom (1580–1085). The text tells us of a funeral cult, which has been called "negative confession," consisting of a litany recited by someone who prepares to be judged by the gods. It is a systematic exoneration of every conceivable sin which a person might be accused of, and for which his judges watch him and lie in wait for him. The list is extensive:

> I have not committed iniquity against men.
> I have not mistreated people.
> I have not committed sins in the Place of Truth.
> I have not (sought to) know what is not (to know).
> I have not done evil.
> I have not begun the day having received a commission from among the people who had to work for me, and my name has not reached the functions of a chief of slaves.

---

[16] It is necessary to avoid a misunderstanding here. What we are condemning is not technique but technique's intention to enclose the world within the horizon of thought. As Heidegger says, we wish to pose, not a *technical* question, but the question of the *essence of technique* (cf. "The Question Concerning Technology" in *Vorträge und Aufsätze* [Pfullingen: Neske, 1954]). To the enterprises of moral technology, to psychoanalysis, or to civil justice, we do not oppose (with Job) a pretechnical way of life, a more "humane" manner of embarking upon human relations, a *word* that is simply more "spirited." Such a "traditional" approach, however well-meaning, would *still* be, in essence, *technique*, and would never show us anything of the essence of technique. Moreover, it would probably be useless.

[17] See Jean Lévêque, *op. cit.*, Vol. I, pp. 71–75.

I have not blasphemed God.
I have not impoverished the poor man of his goods.
I have not done what is abominable to the gods.
I have not disparaged a slave in his master's presence.
I have not harassed anyone.
I have not starved anyone.
I have not killed.
I have not ordered to kill.

. . . .

I am pure, I am pure, I am pure, I am pure!

(There are 36 asseverations of innocence.)

It is virtually identical to the litany that Job will unravel before his speakers. He will meet their accusations item for item:

He is not violent in the least, nor proud: "My hands are free of violence" (16.17). "Do you think I bear a grudge against man?" (21.4). "Have I ever laid a hand on the poor when they cried out for justice in calamity? Have I not wept for all those whose life is hard, felt pity for the penniless?" (30.24–25). "I made a pact with my eyes, not to linger on any virgin" (31.1).

I freed the poor man when he called
  and the orphan who had no one to help him.
When me were dying, it was I who had their blessing;
  if widows' hearts rejoiced, that was my doing.
. . . .
I was eyes for the blind,
  and feet of the lame.
Who but I was father of the poor?
  The stranger's case had a hearing from me.
I used to break the fangs of wicked men,
  and snatch their prey from between their jaws.

(29.12–17)

His litany enumerates the points of his innocence like rosary-beads: "If my feet have wandered from the rightful path, or if my eyes have led my heart astray, or if my hands are smirched with any stain, let another eat what I have sown. . . . If I ever lost my heart to any woman, or lurked at my neighbor's door . . . If ever I have infringed the rights of slave or maidservant in legal actions against me . . . If my land calls down vengeance on my head and every furrow runs with tears, if without payment I have eaten fruit grown on it or given those who toiled there cause to groan . . . Have I been insensible to poor men's needs, or let a widows eyes grow dim? Or taken my share of bread alone, not giving a share to the orphan? . . . Have I ever seen a wretch in need of clothing, or a beggar going naked, without his having cause to bless me from his heart, as he felt the warmth of the fleece from my lambs? Have I raised my hand against the guiltless, presuming on my credit at the gate? . . . Have I put all my trust in gold, from finest gold sought my security? Have I gloated over my great wealth, or the riches that my hands have won? Or has the sight of the sun in its glory, or the glow of the moon as it walked the sky, stolen my heart, so that my hand blew them a secret kiss? . . . Have I taken pleasure in my enemies' misfortunes, or made merry when disaster overtook them, I who allowed my tongue to do no wrong, by cursing them or vowing them to death? The people of my tent, did they not say, 'Is there a man he has not filled with meat?' No stranger ever had to sleep outside, my door was always open to the traveler. . . . Have I ever stood so in fear of common gossip, or so dreaded any family's contempt, that I have been reduced to silence, not venturing out of doors?" (31.7–8, 9, 13, 38–39, 16–17, 19–21, 24–27, 29–32, 34).

He has neither lied nor spoken ill of anyone: "Is falsehood to be found on my lips? Cannot my palate tell the taste of misfortune?" (6.30). "Who can prove me a liar, or show that my words have no substance?" (24.25). "Have I been a fellow traveler with falsehood, or hastened my steps toward deceit?" (31.5). "I who allowed my tongue to do no wrong" (31.30). "Have I ever hidden my sins from men, keeping my iniquity secret in my breast?" (31.33). "Come, I beg you, look at me, as man to man, I will not lie" (6.28). "I swear by the living God who denies me justice, by Shaddai who has turned my life sour, that as long as a shred of life is left in me, and the breath of God breathes in my nostrils, my lips shall never speak untruth, nor any lie be found on my tongue" (27.2–4).

He is not impious in the least: "My prayer is undefiled" (16.17). "This thought at least would give me comfort (a thrill of joy in unrelenting pain), that I have not denied the Holy One's decrees" (6.10). "My footsteps have followed close in [God's], I have walked in his way without swerving; I have kept every commandment of his lips, cherishing the words of his mouth in my breast" (23.11–12).

Job is innocent of every single transgression he is accused of. "Put me right . . . show me where I have been at fault" (6.24). "How many faults and crimes have I committed? What law have I transgressed, or in what have I offended?" (13.23). "I do not see myself like that at all" (9.35). "You know very well that I am innocent" (10.7). "I am guiltlesss" (13.18). "[God] would see he was contending with an honest man" (23.7). "I had dressed myself in righteousness like a garment; justice for me was cloak and turban" (29.14). "If he weighs me on honest scales, being God, he cannot fail to see my innocence" (31.6). "Let him test me in the crucible: I shall come out pure gold" (23.10). "Far from ever admitting you to be in the right: I will maintain my innocence to my dying day. I take my stand on my integrity, I will not stir: my conscience gives me no cause to blush for my life" (27.5–6). "When my adversary has drafted his writ against me I shall wear it on my shoulder, and bind it round my head like a royal turban. I will give him an account of every step of my life, and go as boldly as a prince to meet him" (31.35–37).

Not only can he account for every step of his particular existence; he also possesses a general knowledge of the Law. It is not, therefore, by virtue of some kind of accident that he is innocent; he is innocent in essence, by virtue of his conscience, just like his judges. And like them, he "speaks with experience": "I have seen all this with my own eyes, heard with my own ears and understood" (13.1).

He contends with them in full knowledge of the penal code: "Now, what shares does God deal out on high . . . if not disaster for the wicked, and calamities for the iniquitous?" (31.2–3). "Let another eat what I have sown, and let my young shoots all be rooted out" (v. 8). "Let my wife grind corn that is not mine, let her sleep between other's sheets" (v. 10). "Let brambles grow where once was wheat, and foul weeds where barley thrived" (v. 40). "Let my shoulder fall from its socket, my arm be shattered at the joint" (v. 22).

And he knows the code of rewards just as proficiently. He describes his past happiness in the same language used by the friends in their characterization of the remuneration which he could expect for his penitence:

> Who will bring back to me the months that have gone,
>   and the days when God was my guardian,
> when his lamp shone over my head,
>   and his light was my guide in the darkness?
> Shall I ever see my autumn days again
>   when God hedged round my tent;
> when Shaddai dwelt with me,
>   and my children were around me;
> when my feet were plunged in cream,
>   and streams of oil poured from the rocks?
> When I went out to the gate of the city,
>   when I took my seat in the square,
> as soon as I appeared, the young men stepped aside,
>   while the older men rose to their feet.
> Men of note interrupted their speeches,

and put their fingers on their lips;
 the voices of rulers were silenced,
 and their tongues stayed still in their mouths.
They waited anxiously to hear me,
 and listened in silence to what I had to say.
When I paused, there was no rejoinder,
 and my words dropped on them one by one.
They waited for me as men wait for rain,
 open-mouthed as if to catch the year's last showers.
If I smiled at them, it was too good to be true,
 They watched my face for the least sign of favor.
In a lordly style, I told them which course to take,
 and like a king amid his armies,
 I led them where I chose.
My praises echoes in every ear,
 and never an eye but smiled on me

. . . .

So I thought to myself, 'I shall die in honor,
 my days like a palm tree's for number.
My roots thrust out to the water,
 my leaves freshened by the falling dew at night.
My reputation will never fade,
 and the bow in my hands will gain new strength.'
                    (29.2–10, 21–25, 11; 18–20)

A remarkable picture, as we can see, of a man who lives well, having secured every delight that human know-how is supposed to be able to procure.

At the same time, Job still shares with the specialists an exact knowledge of the *reasons* for punishment and reward. He, too, has scrutinized the Law, "God," and his demands. He

is just as good a "theologian"—just as good a technician. He
knows that God knows everything: "But surely he sees how I
behave, does he no count all my steps?" (31.4). He knows that
God inquires: "What shall I say when God inquires?" (v. 14).
That God does not remain inactive, and that one cannot expect
God not to react: "What shall I do when God stands up?" (ibid.).
He knows that God has a plan mapped out in advance so that
he is not caught unprepared whenever human beings transgress and become guilty: "What shares does God deal out on
high, what lots does Shaddai assign from heaven?" (v. 2). Shaddai
possesses a justice that is equipped with a secular arm capable
of disbursing death: "For I should have committed a sin of lust,
a crime punishable by the law, and should have lit a fire burning till Perdition, which would have devoured all my harvesting" (vv. 11–12). "God's terror would indeed descend on me, how
could I hold my ground before his majesty?" (v. 23). "That too
would be a criminal offence, to have denied the supreme God"
(v. 28).

We see then that Job possesses the same vision of the world
that his friends vaunt. There is nothing they know that he
does not know equally well.

He states this in clear terms: "Whatever you know, I know
too; I am no way inferior to you" (13.2). "I can reflect as deeply
as ever you can, I am no way inferior to you. And who, for that
matter, has not observed as much?" (12.3). "How often have I
heard this before!" (16.2). "I know well what is in your mind,
your thoughts . . ." (21.27). Elsewhere, in chapter 4, Eliphaz
had carelessly admitted that Job once numbered among the
technicians: "Many another, once, you schooled, giving strength
to feeble hands; your words set right whoever wavered, and
strengthened every failing knee" (4.3–4). He engaged other
"Jobs" in technical discourse with the expertise of Eliphaz himself. Job has undoubtedly proven his point.

With nothing else springing up to refute it, Job's discourse is liberated, given over to the dawning of the truth. He is free to make the following challenge: "Is this not so? Who can *prove me a liar*, or *reduce my words to nothing?*" (24.25).[18]

As Job's view of the world coincides perfectly with the view of the friends, we do not have a *discrepancy* in views which alone could have corroborated the pretensions of technique.

Let us take up the problem one more time. Job wants to articulate the horror of evil. This horror he attributes to the Wholly Other, to a madness that ravages every order. Technique presents itself. It claims that he is mistaken, because, from where he stands, like one cog in the world-mechanism, he cannot perceive the order which contains him. If he could perceive the order in all its dimensions, in the complete transparency of its structure, it would not occur to him to say what he says. Contrary to what he thinks, evil is located well within the order. The impression of madness which he has received from his confrontation with evil is itself utterly contained within the order; it falls frequently upon those who are suffering.

The levels of order of the world become visible in their totality only by means of a protracted effort of cognition, the same effort carried out by the sages (judges, physicians, psychoanalysts, or religious specialists of the Law, for all of these present themselves under the same rubric: "those who are supposed to know"), an effort which cannot be carried out by invalids and by madmen blinded by their suffering. The crux of the proof, therefore, lies in this discrepancy between views. Hence the friends parade their science before Job at great length, in order to prove their view to be fundamentally less limited than his.

It is the utter failure of this attempted proof that we have just witnessed. The two views are perfectly identical and interchangeable. Job is as competent as any technician and his world

---

[18] Chouraqui: "Who would *discredit* me, reducing my word *to nothing?*"

is as complete as their own. Their reduction of the scandal of evil to an event that is immanent in the world and is accessible to thought and to human technique—a scandal that Job can only see as a rupture of the world—appears henceforth, from their perspective, like a pure begging of the question. By the same token, Job's interpretation is thrown into relief.

It is probably for the sake of producing this effect of meaning that the author of the book, intuitively or deliberately, gave his work the rather original form of long static dialogues in which no properly dramatic development can be detected. For as the dialogue progresses and makes the failure of technique more and more evident, a certain space is depicted where Job's mad discourse, contrary to all expectations, and albeit in a negative manner, assumes meaning.

The author could not really be satisfied with saying: evil is a madness, an unspeakable thing. For once one has given a name to the Ineffable, one can expect to receive the common answer of all technicians: You call ineffable and incomprehensible that which you do not understand. But to fail to understand is an everyday fact for human beings in general, and for sick and weak souls in particular. The Ineffable which they invoke is an illusion, an untruth par excellence. This reduction is made by every positivism, including what may be called religious positivism.

If the author was to give an adequate articulation of the ineffability—the "transcendence"—of the phenomenon perceived by Job, he had to think beyond technique. He had to present the best side of technique, and then to put the structural limits of its power in plain view. This is what he succeeded in doing by letting Job's speeches refute the speeches of the friends right down to the smallest detail. What became manifest is, not the *things* which the friends do not see and which Job affirms, but the sheer fact that the friends *do not see or do not want to see* an extraordinary dimension of evil.

We can formulate this philosophical approach of the author

of the Book of Job in the following manner. We may call the world in which Job has his experience: *Scene I*. The friends appear and tell him that the cause of the evil under which he suffers is a set of events belonging to an Other Scene, a *Scene II*, which he does not see, but which they see and master. Together, the two scenes belong to the world and convene under a unique logic, that of the Law. But, by his exhaustive refutation of his friends' arguments, Job shows that nothing of significance takes place in Scene II. The evil that he suffers is independent of the sins imputed to him, or at least it is, by any standard, infinitely disproportionate to such sins. The alterity of evil that Job wants to discuss is really other than Scene II and Scene I both. Therefore the Other Scene whence, according to Job, evil comes, cannot be a simple other scene, a Scene II in relation to a Scene I, but must be yet more *other*, an "other Other Scene," a *Scene III*.

The latter cannot be thought of as yet another stratum in the order the world. For *who* could articulate such a thing? Certainly no character in the Book of Job. No landmark can be found within the plan of the text where any one of the protagonists might *situate* what Job says. No vision of the world exists to which one might re-join what Job un-joins, what Job shows to be ab-solute.

In order to elicit the radical alterity of Scene III, the author first invoked a simple alterity between Scene I and Scene II. Only after this first alterity was "reduced to nothingness" by the dialogues could the strange alterity of the Wholly Other become visible at the heart of this nothingness, *the invisible finally becoming visibly absent* and, in this sense, "visible." Only as the attempt of the reductive interpretation was itself reduced could the sense of Job's discourse emerge.

We can see now, to some extent, that Job does not really speak *with* the three friends throughout the dialogues, but rather, over their heads, in a space which the friends have closed off so completely that it is impossible to find so much as a *trace* of it.

He speaks with the enigmatic presence that reveals itself in the Other Other Scene.

To sum up: the author of the Book of Job does not simply name the Ineffable—the madness of the world—with one name, like "God." As such this word means nothing. In order to name the Ineffable, the author has deemed it best to compose a long and complex discourse, the dialogues of the Book of Job. Indeed, it is this book, taken as a whole, that is a "divine name."

amazing.

3. The Excess of Evil

JOB'S DISCOURSE CAN NOW SPEAK TO US, in a very stark disclosure of sense, of an *evil*, a madness, an Other Scene that *exceeds* the Law of the world, exceeds the scene of the world as a technical world.[1] Indeed, if from here onward Job remains standing before an impasse, at least the blame for this can no longer be imputed to him. He is up against an external bulldozing necessity, a Master more powerful than every conceivable technique. This does not exempt him from doing battle, to be sure: man is to resist man. That is the task proper to a will armed with technique. Resisting other human beings, one resists the passions attaching one to them, and, consequently, one resists oneself and gains power over oneself. If one shies away from the task, one invites reproach for failing to exhaust the range of all that can be willed, the range of feasible techniques.

---

[1] The term *excess* is meant to correspond with precision to the alterity of the Other Scene. Indeed, when we speak of an evil in excess, we do not wish to signify an extreme evil. The term is not simply intensive or superlative; technique can often overcome evils that are altogether "extreme." It is comparative: evil is in excess when it *overtakes* that which technique has overcome, and hence, considered as such, it may be benign, indeed quite imperceptible, only thinkable.

But, again, the possibility of blame ends there. For what could possibly be expected of us in those times when we are confronted by what truly resists, by the Master whose power continues far beyond the exhaustion of the human will?

Our author had to distinguish this Master, the one with whom Job has a set rendezvous, from the more familiar "inner master" who overpowers human beings from within as their own *weakness*, making them shy away from the lesser confrontations with other human beings. Roman law states as a principle that justice may give no audience to those who put forth their own depravity as an excuse. In order to be heard, one must be able to proffer the misconduct *of another* as an excuse. For Job, this other must be something other than the world dominated by technique.

Evil as Other-than-the-world, the Other as Master: that is what Job presents as the guilty party in a critical moment in his discourse and his thought: "But have I the strength to go on waiting? What use is life to me, when doomed to certain death? Is mine the strength of stone, or is my flesh bronze? Is not my power to help myself as nothing, has not all help deserted me?" (6.11–13). This is the Master we are looking for as he is outlined in his earliest contours: "stone" and "nothing." This Master is no point of weakness in Job's will. Job has worked assiduously to overcome such weakness, not just by eschewing evil whenever it might present itself, but by never slacking in that greater effort which Nietzsche demands of humanity, the demand to surpass oneself, to rule over others, to become prince. He had taken every opportunity to make life intrinsically good. Hence the descriptions of Job's resplendent "months of autumn" (chap. 29): he was the man of maximal robustness and vitality. The fact that it is *this* man who is defeated by evil in the end shows that the evil in question belongs to a different species of Mastery: "So I thought to myself, 'I shall die in honor, my days like a palm tree's for number'" (29.18). If he thought himself capable of standing on firm ground, by virtue of his own strength, his own technique, this ground, alas, erodes under the darkness of evil. Looking now for ground to stand on, what he finds instead is "nothing." This nothing—is his Master.

It is not just a nothing of death. Job would throw himself into death's nothingness quite willingly and with relative equanimity if this act would annul his own being without compromising the whole of universal being. The nothingness of Job is, so to speak, still less than that, less than nothing, as it has even less to offer than the minimal support one needs in order to confront the nothingness that is death.

This nothingness, which has more consistency to it than a stone, is wholly the Master, a Master who wants to suspend Job in nothingness even if the man is free of guilt (free of error, of transgression, of turpitude, of weakness, of exhaustion of the will to power, etc.), which means, effectively, that it is this Master's intention that the human being should never be free of guilt. This is why the discussions about Job's guilt, ultimately, lack a real object. If he is guilty, he has voluntarily handed himself over to that which wills a superior necessity. But likewise if he is innocent, and suffers on account of a sin he could not have avoided committing, this unavoidable sin itself is the superior force that subjugates him. To avoid guilt, he would have to possess a power he does not possess: "Am I the Sea, or the Wild Sea Beast, that you should keep me under watch and guard?" (7.12). The ironic thing about these accusations which condemn Job in principle is that they would make him out to be as great as God himself. Inadvertently, such accusations detract from God's greatness by imputing an impossible power to Job. Protesting these same accusations, then, Job is the first to affirm the unequaled magnitude of a God who is Master. Opposing the shut-eyed obliviousness of the friends and their technique, he begins to recognize that *there is* a Master. And he persists in the work of recognizing this Master by painstakingly taking into account all the *incommensurabilities* that Mastery implies.

Between human sin and divine wrath, he attests, there is no common measure: "Suppose I have sinned, what have I done to you, you tireless watcher of mankind? Why do you choose me as your target? Why should I be a burden to you? Can you not tolerate my sin, or overlook my fault?" (7.20–21). Why would God pretend to be vulnerable, why would God affect an attentiveness toward the sins of humans if not for the purpose of justifying a vengeance which presents itself as a *response* to an attack but which is actually an *original attack*, one that Job cannot hope to oppose? "Have you got human eyes, do you see as mankind sees? Is your life mortal like man's, do your years pass as men's days pass?" (10.4–5). This is the only possible explanation for the wickedness of God: God . . . *would be a human being*. A rather brazen explanation, too audacious for Job to accept here. Later, we will see how this very explanation will be verified by a sudden, lightning-flash intuition affirming that God is in fact commensurate with humans and possesses the same thing God bestows upon humans: a soul capable of wickedness. Here, however, Job's concern is to underscore the impossibility of measuring the dissymmetry between God and himself. Whether God is infinite and incapable of revenge, being infinitely protected from every assault, or God is vengeful and wicked like a man, he remains the Master, and no human initiative can affect him: "Even if I have erred, my error lies with me alone" (19.4). In other words: "This concerns me alone, it does not concern an infinite God who knows his way and who will not be misled by my own straying." To suppose that Job is capable of standing up to that which exceeds every one of his faculties, is, *mutatis mutandis*, to bring Job's adversary down to Job's size. It is to shrink God to human smallness. Which is inconceivable. And which in turn makes it inconceivable that Job was truly successful in having resisted sin.

The evil suffered is disproportionate to whatever sin may have been committed, and, correspondingly, the innocence is not proportionate to whatever happiness can be expected. "Suppose I am in the right, what use is my defense? For my accuser is also my judge" (9.15; T.O.B.). "Indeed, I know it is as you say: how can man be in the right against God?" (9.2). My justice, which would have stood in proportion to an original state of innocence, is necessarily always inadequate, always too late and in retreat when it comes to erasing an equally original state of suspicion. "I know it: you do not take me for innocent" (9.28). No sin can justify such suffering; and, at the same time, no innocence is justified in demanding the infinite happiness necessary to compensate and counterbalance an infinite suffering. Evil is *beyond*. It is in excess.

As the status of his innocence, or of his guilt, has no effect on the incommensurate, excessive evil he suffers, Job, holding nothing back, concludes with the explicit admission that it is conceivable that he sinned: "But am I innocent after all? Not even I know that" (9.21). "You tax me with the crimes of my youth" (13.26). "My sin . . . my transgression . . . my wrong" (14.16–17). But it changes nothing: "Woe to me, if I am guilty; if I am innocent, I dare not lift my head" (10.15). "Who can give lessons in wisdom to God, to him who is judge of those on high?" (21.22). "Though I think myself right, his mouth may condemn me; though I count myself innocent, it may declare me a hypocrite" (9.20). Being what we are, we human beings cannot but sin: "Who can bring the clean out of the unclean? No man alive!" (14.4). "And if I am guilty, why should I put myself to useless trouble?" (9.29).

Nothing can be controlled and nothing can be understood in the face of evil as it reveals its essential excess: "What wonder then if my words are wild?" (6.3). "Have I no reason to be out of patience?" (21.4). Again we find the unhinging and plummeting characteristic of anxiety, except that we no longer need to speak of "anxiety" specifically. It is evil in general that unhinges all human know-how and hurls it into the abyss, precipitating

the appearance—a veritable apparition—of the abyss in which
the whole world sinks.

The friends have described the mechanics of things and actions which they attribute to "God." Job responds by evoking a
deranged mechanics, claiming to have "seen with his own eyes"
how it obeys no laws. First this magnificent passage:

> In him is strength, in him resourcefulness,
> 　beguiler and beguiled are both alike his slave.
> He robs the country's councillors of their wits,[2]
> 　turns judges into fools.
> His hands untie the belt of kings,
> 　and bind a rope about his loins.
> He makes priests walk barefoot,
> 　and overthrows the powers that are established.
> He strikes the cleverest speakers dumb,
> 　and robs old men of their discretion.
> He pours contempt on the nobly born,
> 　and unties the girdle of the strong.[3]
> He robs the depths of their darkness,
> 　brings deep shadow to the light.
> He builds a nation up, then strikes it down,
> 　or makes a people grow, and then destroys it.
> He strips a country's leaders of their judgment,
> 　and leaves them to wander in a trackless waste,

---

[2] Cf. "When a country falls into a tyrant's hand, it is he who blindfolds the judges" (9.24), and *infra*. A frequent biblical theme, but punctuated here. Cf. 5.13, 18.7.

[3] This was the case with Job himself, one-time great lord. Cf. 19.9: "He has stolen my honor away, and taken the crown from my head."

> to grope about in unlit darkness,
> and totter like a man in liquor.

> (12.16–25)

This echoes a good number of biblical texts about the inscrutability of the Almighty. Yet there is an essential difference between the above passage and, for example, the song of Hannah (I Sam. 2.3–10), which is recalled in the Magnificat (Lk. 1.45–55): "YHWH gives life and death, brings down to Sheol and draws up; YHWH makes poor and rich, he humbles and also exalts." There, God also brings down the proud, *dispersit superbos, deposuit potentes de sede*, but does so in order to raise up the humbled, *exaltavit humiles*. Hannah says: "The sated hire themselves out for bread but the famished cease from labor; the barren woman bears sevenfold, but the mother of many is desolate." The paradox of a God who "lowers and raises" is thus defined more sharply as a wheel of justice that turns inexorably.

In the mouth of Job, the paradox, instead, amounts to a *fundamental inconstancy*. Even "old men," and he probably has his three friends in mind, cannot count on their powers of "discretion." The "country's councillors," the "country's leaders," the "judges," the "nobles," the "strong," the "kings," the "priests," the "established powers," the "cleverest speakers," those who "mislead," all are susceptible to losing their "soul," their "wits," to becoming "fools," lost, naked, mute. All human certainty, all knowledge, all power, all technique is perverted, inexorably, by the one whom the friends call "God."

That technique is finite rather than infinite does not mean that it has a finite domain where it can achieve mastery. The infinite that stretches beyond it also turns back into it, returning to the very interior of the domain that technique believes itself to govern in order to plant an essential disorder there. Job's speech may have to be interpreted in the way certain psalms are interpreted: as a jeering that inspires the vain ambition of the human being confronted by a transcendent will. But before anything, it is the expression of a fear that has nothing to lean on, a continual astonishment at the disorder of things. To the friends' positive morality, which is worth something only if it can build an ordered and enduring society, Job contrasts a God who "builds a nation up, then strikes it down." The governors of all human affairs, whether they know it or not, "wander in a trackless waste." And perhaps they did the most "groping about" and were most "drunk" when they believed they could govern according to order. Something is always in excess of every management of human affairs, and to the extent that the management orients itself toward a good, this excess, this gap, this original "straying," is Evil.[4]

The same thing is expressed from a more positive angle. "Have I raised my hand against the guiltless, presuming on my credit at the gate?" (31.21), asks Job, indicating that the abuse of power is a daily issue for all those who, like Job in his time of grandeur, are the guardians of order and the living guarantors of a viable social arrangement. By this he means that transgression, the first "straying," is prior to all technical correction, prior to all justice. If the evil-doers end up being punished, in the meantime, they possess every license for perpetrating their crimes. Even if their sole territory is night and shadows, at least, this territory is theirs. Anomaly pitches its tent there, and the putative reign of Law is at once compromised:

> Others of them hate the light,
> know nothing of its ways,
> avoid its paths.

---

[4] Job prefaces the description of evil thus: "Hear what I have to say, and you will be dumbfounded, will place your hands over your mouths. I myself am appalled at the very thought, and my flesh begins to shudder" (21.5–6). The mere *thought* of evil is enough to reveal its excess.

When all is dark the murderer leaves his bed
  to kill the poor and the needy.
All night long prowls the thief,
  breaking into houses while the darkness lasts.
The eye of the adulterer watches for twilight,
  "No one will see me" he mutters
  as he masks his face.
In the daytime they go into hiding,
  these folk who have no love for the light.
For all of them, morning is their darkest hour,
  because they know its terrors.

(24.13–17)

To speak of *excess* with respect to the Law is not to indicate that the Law merely fails to normalize everything, that technique merely fails to repair all that is in disorder. For to speak thus is to suppose that a closed domain exists where the Law reigns all by itself. As if it were only outside this domain—outside the "realm of the possible," as the philosophy of technique calls it—that we find the reign of disorder, disproportion, impossibility, excessiveness. Such a restricted conception of the excess is still too frugal. It acknowledges that this other region, exterior to the domain of the Law, cannot be reached. But then it assumes that the only ones who would want to reach it are those madmen preoccupied by the strange decenteredness of *utopianism*. The utopians alone are said to be excessive, always asking for more than what technique can accomplish. It is their own fault, their own *faux pas*, if the world, which they measure against what exceeds it instead of simply measuring it against itself, is like an absence for them. They should climb down from their excessive aspirations and reenter the common measure: they would inherit a respectable share of a world which is no longer absent.

This restricted concept of the excess relative to the Law

depends on a queer forgetting of what is being conceived, and precisely on a forgetting of *the Law itself*.

For what is the Law but a representation whereby man tries to rectify the crooked effects of the unforeseeable, of madness, of evil's excess? But why does evil exist to begin with, prior to this rectification? We know what Eliphaz was told in his dream-revelation: evil is the result of an original *impurity* of human-kind. But now we are obliged to ask: What is hidden behind this impurity? In classical political theories, which impute the origin of disorder and the consequent institution of Law to a state of nature imbued with an intrinsic disorder, the question translates as: Where does an intrinsic natural disorder come from? In psychological theory: How is it that all psychic proc-esses do not undergo normal development? The fact is, *there is always* disturbance, and always more disturbance than the amount needed to disturb the disturbance and thus return it to order. So that disorder reappears, and with it the Law that has to bring it to an end. Technique, the human effort to dominate the world, is a response to the human impotence that is always already there.

This observation is not made by the forgetful technical think-ing which, wholly occupied and entertained with its affairs and operations, never wonders how it is *that there is a place*, a work-shop, as it were, for it to perform any operation whatsoever. That technical thinking takes pride in all that it accomplishes, without remembering that the very success of its operations attests to a more original defeat, that of *having* an evil to begin with which it must combat.

But Job remembers this. Not by an actual effort of memory, but because of a revelation that consists in evil's truncation of his affairs and operations (cf. "My initiatives are cut off"; 17.11, Chouraqui). This "memory," thrown upon him in the advent of personal misfortune, opens his eyes to the misfortune of the whole of humanity, unveiling a picture of the accursed share of the innocent and the madness of the world.

What Job is given to remember is that disorder, because it is essential and not accidental, endures forever, even under the appearance of order. The Law is not delimited by an exterior space which stretches beyond it, and where it has no jurisdiction. It fails to legislate in any space, because everywhere, even in the space where it reigns, it is always already *too late* to intercept the transgression. It is the Law that is *utopian*. *So* *not "valid"* *in the* *real* *world.*

The perspective flips around: the excess changes camps. No longer is the excess to exceed the world and its Law; it is to give the world as Law, as we come to realize that the Law of another master always reigns there first, a master whom Nietzsche denies and whom Job bears witness to: the one who has sent us evil. It is under *his* Law that we live. *built in loosing direction*

We ourselves witness its distinctive appearance in every transgression where it humiliates the Law of the world.

The wages of crime are the sufferings of the innocent, here described in political terms: the Law's impotence to establish a society of Law is the triumph of the outlaws.

> The wicked move boundary-marks away,
>   they carry off flock and shepherd.
> They drive away the orphan's donkey,
>   and take away the widow's ox for a security.
>
>   (24.2–3)

Hell, therefore, is the lot of the innocent, and Job would like to depict this hell, responding feature for feature to the allegations of the friends. Where they said: "God plucks the wretched man from the mouth of the wicked," "lifts up the downtrodden," "raises the afflicted to the height of felicity" . . . Job responds:

> Beggars, now, avoid the roads,
>   and all the poor of the land must go into hiding.

Like wild donkeys in the desert, they go out,
  driven by the hunger of their children,
  to seek food on the barren steppes.
They must do the harvesting in the scoundrel's field,
  they must do the picking in the vineyards of the wicked.
They go about naked, lacking clothes,
  and starving while they carry the sheaves.
They have no stones for pressing oil,
  they tread the winepresses, yet they are parched with
  thirst.
They spend the night naked, lacking clothes,
  with no covering against the cold.
Mountain rainstorms cut them through,
  shelterless, they hug the rocks.
Fatherless children are robbed of their lands,
  and poor men have their cloaks seized as security.
From towns come the groans of the dying,
  and the gasp of wounded men crying for help.
  Yet God remains deaf to their appeal!

(24.4–12)

God is complicit why?

The unhappiness of the innocent obliges them to labour for
the wicked. It is not simply an "objective" unhappiness, the result of a universal penury. It is a direct effect of the wickedness
of the wicked. Hence the terms of the Law are inverted: evil for
the just, good for the unjust. Job gives a refutation, term for
term, of the legalistic theories and of the "God" who authorizes
them. "Deaf" to the "appeal" of the just, "God" indulges the
unjust:

Do we often see a wicked man's light put out,
  or disaster overtaking him,
  or all his goods destroyed by the wrath of God?

How often do we see him harassed like a straw before the
wind,
    or swept up like chaff before a gale?
God, you say, reserves the man's punishment for his
children.
    No! Let him bear the penalty himself, and suffer under it!
Let him see his ruin with his own eyes,
    and himself drink the anger of Shaddai.
When he has gone, how can the fortunes of his House
affect him,
    when the number of his months is cut off?

                        (21.17–21)

But the most incisive refutation of all is the following picture of the wicked proudly rejoicing in their savvy ability to
turn the groundlessness of the laws to their own advantage.
Theirs is long life, ever-swelling power, laughter at home, security, luck, urbane festivities, inner serenity:

Why do the wicked still live on,
    their power increasing with their age?
They see their posterity ensured,
    and their offspring grow before their eyes.
The peace of their houses has nothing to fear,
    the rod that God wields is not for them.
No mishap with their bulls at breeding time,
    No miscarriage with their cows at calving.
They let their infants frisk the lambs,
    their children dance like deer.
They sing to the tambourine and the lyre,
    and rejoice to the sound of the flute.
They end their lives in happiness
    and go down in peace to Sheol.

                        (21.7–13)

Not only do they descend to Sheol with their hearts at peace; throughout their lives, they receive an external peace from their victims. In this extraordinary political picture,[5] the author of Job has also taken note of the feebleness, the fear, the apathy, and the alienation that make victims adulate their victimizers. Not only does the political portrait of the world refute the analysis of the Law's partisans and profiteers, it removes the last semblance of truth from their words, showing how happiness on earth belongs to the stronger animal, for whom the Law is essentially a means to be employed or to be rejected, but never a serious obstacle:

> "What has become of the great lord's house," you say
>> "where is the tent where the wicked lived?"
> Have you never asked those that have traveled,
>> or have you misunderstood the tale they told,
> "The wicked man is spared for the day of disaster
>> and carried off in the day of wrath"?
> But who is there then to accuse him to his face for his deeds,
>> and pay him back for what he has done,
> when he is on his way to his burial,
>> when men are watching at his grave.
> The clods of the valley are laid gently on him,
>> and a whole procession walks behind him.
>
> (21.28–33)[6]

---

[5] Which does not even miss a reference to the absurd suffering of the soldier, the slave, the worker: "Is not man's life on earth nothing more than pressed service, his time no better than hired drudgery? Like the slave, sighing for the shade, or the workman with no thought but his wages . . ." (7.1–2).

[6] Qoheleth makes the same disillusioned observation: "And I then see

God's "deafness" presides over this order of things. Since God does not create the Law that orders things, or—what amounts to the same—since his Law is neither omniscient nor omnipotent, this Law of God guarantees nothing more than a general *laisse-faire*: it promises to leave the disorder of the world at its play. Yet by choosing to make himself absent in this way, God actually imposes an implacable law on the world, one of illegality and disorder. The world bends and breaks under the law of evil, a law which is precisely absence of law, a neutrality, an atony and apathy of the world, a gift of neutrality given to the outlaw, a license permitting some individuals to crush other individuals, sometimes followed by resources to these other individuals to take vengeance, a legalized lawlessness that is simultaneously helpful and pitiless, in a word, pointless. Contrary to what the Doctors of the Law would have us believe, in this world there is no Law at all, no providence, no reward and no punishment:

> And again: one man dies in the fullness of his strength,
>   in all possible happiness and ease,
> with his thighs all heavy with fat,
>   and the marrow of his bones undried.
> Another dies with bitterness in his heart,
>   never having tasted happiness.
> Together they now lie in the dust
>   with worms for covering.
>
> (21.23–26)

---

the wicked brought to burial and people come from the Temple to honor them in the city for having been the men they were. This, too, is vanity" (Ecc. 8.10).

It is all one, and this I dare to say:
innocent and guilty, he destroys all alike.

(9.22)

The world is a coliseum for multilateral competition among egoisms; there are no rules, everything goes. The key is to know this and to shrug off any belief in a Law. That is how the wicked prosper, by having liberated themselves from this servitude: "These were the ones who said to God, 'Go away! We do not choose to learn your ways. What is the point of our serving Shaddai? What profit should we get from praying to him?' Is it not true, they held their fortune in their own two hands, and in their counsels, left no room for God?" (21.14–16).

None of this is a secret. No one believes in the wages of virtue and vice. Consider the following biblical text which seems to say, surprisingly enough—surprising for the Bible— that communal consciousness is instinctively "atheistic," that it has long known the true law of the world, the law that is inconsistency and free Play abandoned to its excesses. The communal consciousness harbours a distaste for the feeble, and interprets religion as a rather poor strategy invented by this feebleness. The consensus is: it's all a matter of luck.

A man becomes a laughing-stock to his friends
if he cries to God and expects an answer.
The blameless innocent incurs only mockery.
'Add insult to injury,' think the prosperous,
'strike the man now that he is staggering!'
And yet the tents of the brigands are left in peace,
and those who challenge God live in safety,
and make a god of their two fists!

(12.4–6)

But now we must again take up what has provoked this reversal of perspective and caused the madness, the excess, to step from the Other-than-the-world into the world itself. We return to the most excessive evil that Job suffers from: not death, but the impossibility of dying.

Death, to be sure, is a constant presence in the Book of Job, and might easily be taken to represent the extreme degree and perfection of evil. If life is the characteristic and natural goal of technical labors, death is a fitting image for technique's failure. Yet there is still one more technique, one last avatar of technique, which death does not exceed: causing death, or letting die, as an escape from evil.

From a Nietzschean perspective, which in effect banks on technique as human power and radicalizes it, to provoke death, or to accept death without revolt, is a last possibility given to us whereby we may reconcile ourselves to the world and conquer our resentment, in obedience to the call of the will to power. Thus, by contradistinction, it will be the impossibility of dying that will appear as an image of evil in infinite excess.

Death, at first, seems present, it stands on the horizon of every description of misfortune. "He who goes down to Sheol never ascends again" (7.9). "[The evildoer] has no hope of fleeing from the darkness, but knows that he is destined for the sword" (15.22). "Death's First-Born gnaws his limbs" (18.13). "Driven from light into darkness, he is in exile from the earth" (18.18). "But he who lays mighty hold on tyrants rises up to take away that life which seemed secure" (24.22). "A sword awaits his sons, however many they may be . . . Plague will bury those he leaves behind him, and their widows will have no chance to mourn them" (27.14–15).

Job repeatedly imagines his own death: "It will not be long before I lie in earth" (7.21), "before I go to the place of no return, the land of murk and deep shadow, where dimness and disorder hold sway, and light itself is like the dead of night" (10.21–22). "For the years of my life are numbered, and I shall soon take the road of no return" (16.22). "My breath grows weak, and the grave diggers are gathering for me" (17.1). "I know it is to death that you are taking me, the common meeting place of all that lives" (30.23). Death, as sudden disappearance of lingering time, is here an image of anxiety.

We will presently see how even in other texts, which seem to contradict this, where death is presented as a desirable deliverance, anxiety always reappears in order to place itself opposite this desire. For if death, in Job's case, could be desirable in some way, it could obviously be desired only as something that might put an end to his suffering, which in Job's case means an end to anxiety. But we should recognize that such an instrumental approach to death—letting oneself die, killing oneself—assumes a detachment, a full and broad perception of the world, and an indifference opposite oneself, as preconditions, as vital resources and necessary technical tools. It is just these resources that are most lacking in the situation of anxiety.

According to the disposition of the anxious soul, death, far from being conceived as the end of anxiety, deposits the end of anxiety beyond the farthest conceivable reach, and makes the soul maximally anxious. Death im-mortalizes anxiety; redoubles it, multiplies it to infinity, makes it extreme. This slipping, which prevents technique from laying a hand on the root of evil, is precisely what we mean by excess. When one can represent oneself as an object in the world, nothing prevents one from treating this object like any other. But if the world, together with all objectivity, collapses and becomes a "nothing," as it does in anxiety, then this "nothing" itself takes on the density of "stone" in as much as one cannot treat it as an object in the world. The world is no longer there to offer any action a hold on any object.

This is what happens to Job. Something within him, the nothingness that he is, possessing infinite force—like a stone that cannot be lifted up—resists being taken as an object of a technical operation, and cannot be drowned in the deepest ocean. Evil forces him to cling to his own skin, forbids him to forget himself, to pull the plug and let himself sink into death. While death would probably bring everything to a quiet end and a perfect peace, suffering continually awakens Job and obliges him to stay alive despite himself.

"Oh may my prayer find fulfilment, may God grant me my hope! May it please God to crush me, to give his hand free play and do away with me!" (6.8–9). If God were essentially the metaphor for the world as Law, he would have either rehabilitated the criminal Job or somehow removed him from the world. But God does neither. God keeps Job under his heavy hand without settling anything. "Strangling I would welcome rather, and death itself, than these my sufferings" (7.15). "As for my life, I find it hateful" (9.21). "I have lost all taste for life" (10.1). "God has made my heart sink . . . because I am not annihilated before darkness" (23.16–17). Job nevertheless foregoes "silencing" himself and annihilating himself, even as this is what he desires most. He sighs: "All I look forward to is dwelling in Sheol, and making my bed in the dark. I tell the tomb, 'You are my father,' and I call the worm my mother and my sister" (17.13–14).

What is this eternalization of evil, which even death cannot bring to an end, but that thing that the religions have called "hell"?

Hell is not death; it is eternal life within suffering. Conversely, death would be a paradise if it were a result that could be attained by a technical operation. One would simply be a thing in the world that became transformed into another thing, a thing that changed position and became dislodged. Who has suffered extreme evil and has not dreamed of quickly falling asleep into death? The religions deny the evil-doer this dream. The evil that Job suffers is *eternalized*.

4. The Intention

FROM THE DEPTHS OF A WORLD-NOTHINGNESS, the personage of Job suddenly appears as eternal, truer than the world. It is only now that we can turn our attention back to chapter 3, to Job's introductory lament which breaks a meditative silence of seven days and seven nights; the proper beginning to the verses of the fifth century author. We have not mentioned or cited this chapter until now because it has remained too veiled-over, even as it has placed the body of the dialogues under its essential and enigmatic sign. From its very outset, there arises the question of Job's person considered as a kind of *insistence*, the question of Job's inexplicably singular existence in a world that can just as well do without him and that could very easily have denied him the opportunity to see the light of day.

Far from considering Job as an object in the world, the question attempts to see the absolute difference between Job and the world. The world has ceased to be a whole of which the human being is a part. Now, instead, it adumbrates itself as a thing standing at an infinite distance from something within the human being. As we shall see, the operator of this enigmatic distancing will be the "God" who personifies an evil in excess of the world, the "God" whom Job addresses. The chapter begins quite brusquely:

In the end it was Job who broke the silence and cursed the day of his birth. This is what he said:

> May the day perish when I was born,
>   and the night that told of a boy conceived.
> May that day be darkness,
>   may God on high have no thought for it,
>   may no light shine on it.
> May murk and deep shadow claim it for their own,
>   clouds hang over it,
>   eclipse swoop down on it.
> Yes, let the dark lay hold of it,
>   to the days of the year let it not be joined,
>   into the reckoning of months not find its way.
> May that night be dismal,
>   no shout of joy come near it.
> Let them curse it who curse the day,
>   who are prepared to rouse Leviathan.
> Dark be the stars of its morning,
>   let it wait in vain for light
>   and never see the opening eyes of dawn.
> Since it would not shut the doors of the womb on me
>   to hide sorrow from my eyes.
>
>   (3.1–10)[1]

Job imagines that the night which conceived him "waits in vain for light," that the sun has arrested its course, that the laws of the world suddenly have been suspended; that the world,

---

[1] The exegetical commentaries contain all the necessary information on the mythological context and the literary materials of this admirable text. See Jean Lévêque (*op. cit.*, Part I, pp. 333–44) who rightly compares the present passage to the parallel text of Jer. 20.14–18.

in short, has ceased to be the world. Why does he imagine this? In order to "shut the doors of the womb" upon himself, so that they may "hide sorrow from [his] eyes." If it is necessary to eclipse the world in this manner, seeing how it has nothing to offer but the spectacle of suffering, this is because suffering, it would seem, comes from the world. At the same time, however, because it is not up to the world, but up to "God," "on high," to eclipse the world, so as to allow Job to be delivered from suffering that originates from beyond the world, the whole situation suddenly appears to be played out between "God," on the one hand, together with the world that God can turn about in his fingers according to his own caprice—that is to say, without Law—and, on the other hand, Job, who suffers and imagines that his suffering could have been evaded if only God had not set in motion the wheel of the world that presently crushes him.

The world and its laws are relegated into the background for the sake of a confrontation between Job and something he calls "God." But this God, to be sure, is not the "God" of the Law. The "God" of the Law is not one to be entreated. It would be impious of any human being to ask this "God" to suspend and eclipse his own creation. Technique does not ask the laws of the world to change. No, Job finds himself confronted with a "God" who is Other-than-the-world-as-Law.

For the meantime, this Other is a pure negative, a "nothing." That Job should not have been born means that he should never have emerged from the "nothing." By posing the wish, "May the day perish wherein I was born . . .," Job evokes the depths of the nothingness from which a thing like his own troubled existence has been able to emerge into daylight. His existence, therefore, is not an event *of the world*, demarcated by an internal difference within the world; his existence *and* the world are both demarcated in relation to "nothing." It is from this "nothing" that everything emerges, and emerges in accordance with an essential contingency rather than by necessity of some Law.

Nevertheless, Job does not speak of "nothingness," but of

"God." "On high," what we find is not a "nothing," but the very Contingency, the Caprice that disburses the world, or holds it back, according to its pleasure; in any case, something capable of deciding something. This is why Job, instead of silencing himself as would be seemly before a "nothing," can *address* the Other. He poses questions to the Other, and with a rather prosaic "you" at that:

> Why did I not die new-born,
>   not perish as I left the womb?
> Why were there two knees to receive me,
>   two breasts for me to suck?
> Had there not been, I should now be lying in peace,
>   wrapped in a restful slumber,
> with the kings and high viziers of earth
>   who build themselves vast vaults,
> or with princes who have gold and to spare
>   and houses crammed with silver.
> Or put away like a still-born child that never came to be,
>   like unborn babes that never see the light.
>
> (3.11–16)

> Why did *you* bring me out of the womb?
>   I should have perished then, unseen by any eye,
> a being that had never been,
>   to be carried from womb to grave.
>
> (10.18–19)

This is no longer the celebrated metaphysical question of Leibniz and Heidegger, "Why is there something rather than nothing?"[2] Job's question, as an address, straightaway puts the

---

[2] See Martin Heidegger, *An Introduction to Metaphysics*, trans. Ralph

emphasis on the addressee's capacity for caprice and intention: "*You*, why did you take me out from the nothing?" To the nothing, which according to Heidegger is Being itself in its first disclosure, Job immediately gives a name: "You." In fact we should not even say that the nothing is *called* a "you." What arrives in the opening of the nothing, in the game of contingency, in the very absence of Law *is*, before any name, *you*.

The Capricious, that which decides by challenging the Law and which arrives as the Law departs, in order to be, must be a *you*; that is, not just a pure Intention, but an Intention that stands in essential relation to me. For the text says: "Why *me*? Why must I be born to know a suffering that eternally reveals my 'I'?" The Caprice is not pure contingency, it takes an *interest* in me, and, being interested, it *desires* my suffering.

Job does not ask, "Why something rather than nothing?" He asks, "Why do *you* make *me* suffer rather than granting me an eternal beatitude, like that of the 'kings and high viziers of the earth' who lie in their tombs, 'wrapped in a restful slumber'?"

> Down there bad men bustle no more,
> there the weary rest.
> Prisoners, all left in peace,
> hear no more the shouts the of the gaoler.
> Down there, high and low are all one,
> and the slave is free of his master.

> (3.17–19)

This passage brings on images of the excess of evil where every effort of the human will, including the one that reaches the point of "exhaustion," ends up in failure, so long as evil has

---

Manheim (New Haven: Yale University Press, 1959), chap. 1; *The Principle of Reason*, trans. Reginald Lilly (Bloomington: Indiana University Press, 1991).

its resources. The wicked perpetrate their crimes, and hence we get "the high" and "the low," the "gaolers," the "prisoners" and the "slaves." This is the mad manifestation of the Law's absence. Job conjures up a world where these examples of evil would no longer exist, a conjured world in place of which this world has taken place. That is the world whence we come, to which we belong, where we find the "you" who has capriciously decided to hunt us down. Such a world, a world where beatitude reigns, Job can imagine only in the "tomb," which is not a place in the world like a tomb in the ground. It is the problematical place where Job was "before" he was "conceived" and "born."

Where were we before we were conceived? That is the question God will thrust upon Job as a challenge, "Where were you when I laid the earth's foundations?" (38.4). Here we see Job meditating on it already. The place whence we come lies outside the world. It must lie there, for it is not our biological source of origin. We are not born into a world that preexists us. Biologically, to be sure, an individual life is nothing but the seed of the species passed like a baton in a relay, a fact that belongs to the organization of the world. And if we wish to define ourselves as terrestrial beings, we must say that we are as old as the Earth, since the ground from which we are drawn and fashioned is as old as the Earth itself. But then if we inquire into our "prenatal" location, we must designate an elsewhere-than-Earth, an elsewhere-than-the-world, and we must designate ourselves as being beyond-the-world.

With this Beyond we have an essential kinship and an essential affinity. Once our being-in-the-world dawns upon us as a question, once our suffering assumes the form of a why-lessness that demands a reply, once the world which houses suffering appears as something unthinkable, then, talk of an other-than-the-world, a "before" and an "elsewhere," ceases to be unthinkable. If we suffer in this world beyond what is reasonable, the evocation of a beyond-the-world is fittingly *un-reasonable*, and the other-than-the-world is just as real as the world.

We have an essential kinship with the You who has decided to deprive us of beatitude. The question this You poses to us is the same question we ourselves pose as soon as we perceive our suffering as something abnormal, incredible, *problematic*: Why this suffering, why am I in suffering, why am I not elsewhere in beatitude, *why is there evil rather than good?*

[handwritten margin note: how do we know about? Sorrow... Life is Hell]

> Why give light to a man of grief?
>   Why give life to those bitter of heart,
> who long for death that never comes,
>   and hunt for it more than for a buried treasure?
> They would be glad to see the grave-mound
>   and shout with joy if they reached the tomb.
> Why make this gift of light to a man who does not see his way,
>   whom God balks on every side?

(3.20–23)

"Why make this gift (of suffering) to man?" Why this world where there are slaves and taskmasters, why this non-Law, why this why-lessness?

It is necessary to listen to the question *Why?*, and to do so in order to displace its accent, as Heidegger does in his treatment of the "principle of reason."[3] "Nothing is without reason" can be accentuated: *nothing* is *without* reason. Which sounds like: everything has a reason. This is a proposition concerning beings (*Seiende*). But it can also be accentuated: nothing *is* without *reason*. This time we hear: to be is reason. This is a proposition concerning Being (*Sein*). Is it possible to make an equally thoughtful move with the question *Why?*

---

[3] Martin Heidegger, *The Principle of Reason*, pp. 46–49.

If one asks "Why this why-lessness?" and understands the two "whys" in the same way, namely in the simple speculative manner of a question concerning beings, then one runs around in circles. The absence of any conceivable reply is already contained in the absurd form of the question. But if one poses the question as Job does, from within the context of the encounter that reveals the excess of evil, where Law-lessness immediately opens into a Beyond that transcends beings and Why-lessness reveals a world-lessness that frees up a space where Job can interrogate the Intention, then something very different happens.

Then the question must be accentuated as: *With a view to what?* This puts us somewhere before, or after, speculative questions. Speculation speculates on a world (even if this is "another" world) *as world*, that is, *as Law*. The question "why," heard as speculative question, investigates the Law of a world, its reason. But Job's encounter with the excess of evil brings us to the Other-than-the-world, to an essential and enigmatic bond with a "giver" who has "given suffering to man."[4]

---

[4] We must here invoke the Heideggerian *Es gibt*. Here indeed, when Job experiences the "touch of Being" as he raises the question of Being as "given," there is something that joins up with Heidegger's thought. To juxtapose this thought with a religious *Denkenweg* would obviously require a whole separate study. Here we can only make a quick note of one point where the two ways of thinking seem to intersect.

The experience of Job takes place on the occasion of anxiety. And this is the same point of departure in *Sein und Zeit* and in the lecture "Was ist Metaphysik?" Anxiety is the *Grundstimmung* and "fundamental affective modality" (*Befindlichkeit*) in which we *encounter* nothingness and can evoke the depths of nothingness wherein the question of Being is posed. The nothingness (of beings) *is* Being. To think that Being is, it is necessary to have met nothingness. But here is the peculiarity of the Joban problematic (and, no doubt, of other mystical paths of thinking) in relation to this schema: what Job meets is not nothingness, but evil. He does not question Being, but goodness. For at the bottom of the madness of evil

Now, someone who "gives" something must have an idea, an intention, a project; or, at least, he can have this. In the moment that it becomes apparent that the world does not exist by itself, that it does not carry within itself a legitimacy and a necessity to be, but is created, or is not created, according to the Caprice of Someone, in that moment, the nets of the Law fall apart in tatters. We see, in that moment, that *nothing is*

there can appear, as an enigma, the idea of an Intention that governs the madness, without rendering it reasonable. The Game of the soul of God is an *Abgrund* that is the *bottom* (*Grund*) of the *Abgrund* of evil, without being a "reason" or a "cause" of evil in the sense that a technique aims to discover a reason or cause of a being. This *Grund* remains *Abgrund* in the sense of a Game, a lawlessness that springs from a spontaneous Intention, impenetrable in itself. In order to be, this Intention has to reply to another Intention, Job's, to the difference of Being; it is never "alone." It plays a role where it originally has to deal with us and where we originally have to deal with it. The very notion of the soul (God's, Job's) implies this mutual Game, while the Game of the *Abgrund*, of Heidegger's Being, is one that seems to exclude our personal being, even if according to many Heideggerian texts it does not exclude the being of "man," in whose thinking, properly speaking, Being happens. But if it excludes "us" in our "authentic ipseity" eternalized by the hell of evil, the Game of Being would therefore be for us only a pure, indifferent chaos, hence another embodiment of the Law of evil (cf. Heidegger, *The Principle of Reason*, pp. 111–13). For us, this splendid Game of Being, likened by Heidegger, quoting Heraclitus, to the Game of the child, would appear as a constraint, since the "pleasure" and "rest" which Heidegger evokes belong to Being itself, not to us. The Game returns to Law. Chance does not contradict the Law, it is an aspect of it. The Intention alone, as it abandons all "neutrality," is the Other who is other than the Law. What is the Non-neutral for us? Or as Job will say, who is the "Non-stranger"? It is that which is linked to our soul in a common history (eschatological only in the sense that eschatology does not concern the world or an abstracted humanity, but the soul) in such a way that it is *interested* in the lot of this soul, whether it wishes evil upon it or wishes its beatitude.

Therefore the Game, in the sense that Job understands it, is not lacking a Partner. Now with Heidegger, in the early works just mentioned, we find *Dasein*, which is certainly endowed with an "authentic ipseity," even if it is not like the "ego" of psychology or the "subject" of metaphysics.

written, that the future lies open. This Giver, to the degree that the purpose and meaning of his gift is unfathomable, immediately appears as Someone who is free to make other decisions, free to give other gifts. These decisions and gifts may well be more frightening, more "twisted," than the first; but they also

---

More expressly, in the lecture, there is a "personal being": "Without the original revelation of the nothing, no selfhood [*Selbstsein*] and no freedom" ("What is Metaphysics?" in Heidegger, *Basic Writings*, ed. David Farrell Krell [New York: Harper & Row, 1977], p. 106). "Personal," or self-identical, *Dasein*, in the encounter with nothingness in anxiety, is "transcendent," just as we would say of a soul: "Holding itself out into the nothing, Dasein is in each case already beyond beings as a whole. This being beyond beings we call 'transcendence'" (ibid., p. 105). But these notions begin to disappear from Heidegger's later writings, due to a critique of the metaphysical subject-object dualism (cf. the very fine article of Michel Haar, "La pensée et le moi chez Heidegger," *Revue de métaphysique et de morale* 80 (1975): 456–483, where this disappearance is taken up as something quite telling and is held responsible for the Heideggerian bankruptcy on the question of ethics).

By contrast, in Job, the encounter or "revelation" is indiscriminately that of God and the soul, in the tension of a "With a view to what?" that does not pose a metaphysical question, but an eschatological waiting.

Heidegger, then, first thought the question of Being as different from that of beings, and the question of the human person as "transcendent," emerging from a crucial experience, namely anxiety, being-toward-death, the recognition of which is the necessary condition of "authenticity" of *Dasein* and of the "personal being." Thereafter he continued to pose the question of Being by putting the accent on Being without beings, forgetting this being that is *Dasein*, which was nevertheless indispensable at the start. Human beings are indeed not absent from Heidegger's later thinking; but only as carriers of thinking and language, and no longer in their "authentic ipseity."

Nevertheless, Heidegger in one sense continues to rub shoulders with the question that, according to us, Job confronts face-on, the question of the "gift" of the world, when, continuing his meditation on Being as Being, he comes to the question of the *Es gibt* (in the 1962 lecture *Zeit und Sein*, in *On Time and Being*, trans. Joan Stambaugh [New York: Harper & Row, 1972], pp. 1–24). We know that Heidegger dethrones Being and time from their ultimate position in questioning. Acknowledging that he may call everything into question, and may even return to the moment before the gift of life was made, when the gift might still have not been made, and so, *a fortiori*, when it might still have been made otherwise, perhaps better.

The question of Job, "Why this gift of suffering to man?" posed to "You," "Giver," is not a theoretical, speculative, detached question, any more than it is a morose and vain deploration. It is a fundamentally open and "engaged" question involving several meanings all inextricably meshed together: *With a view to what did you make this gift? What was on your mind? What terror and what injustice do you still keep in reserve for me? Or what pity, perhaps, and what grace? And if my lot in life has not already been inscribed and sealed, what can I do, what ought I to do? What do you expect of me?*

Such questions are not theoretical, we say, because they are not posed by a "cognizing subject," that is, by someone who would be able to remain outside that which is at stake. They are posed by an existent who is exposed and who exists only within this exposure. The question of Job is what creates "Job"; hence "Job" cannot escape it. In contrast to the "metaphysical" (simply speculative) question of Leibniz and Heidegger, it is an "existential" question. It is posed not by a *subject*, but by a *soul*. It cannot be solved as a simple "problem." Job himself strongly suspects that there will be no reply other than one implicating his entire existence and that, perhaps, he himself, in part, holds the key to the reply. The extraordinary overture of chapter 3

---

cannot say that time "is," or that Being is "temporal," he decides to speak in a more original manner: *Es gibt Sein, es gibt Zeit* ("There is Being, there is time"; literally: "It gives Being, it gives time."). The *Geben* of *Es gibt* ("There is"; "*Il y a*") is a *giving*. *Es*, it, or he—gives. For Being, to disclose is to give, and to let Being be; for the human person, it is to receive a gift. Now the same idea of *giving* interests us in that it effectively evokes the gratuitousness of the spontaneous gift, and breaks with relations that metaphysics counts on: producing, making, causing.

has placed the totality of the book under the sign of a very peculiar *freedom.*

The dialogues now have to be reread in light of this first revelation which Job receives after seven days and seven nights of silence, the revelation of his creatureliness and contingency. We henceforth can be more alert to the way that Job, right from the beginning of the dialogues, speaks above the heads of the friends whenever he argues and complains—speaks to the "You" who has brought him out of nothingness.

The *intentionality* of a "you" who has intentionally hurled a world of suffering against a soul is something that will become visible everywhere. It is this that Job is going to *see* in evil and that he is going to decipher in the world as its formerly hidden and now unveiled *sense.*

If evil were strictly an operation of the blind world-machine that crushed him by the laws of its mechanics, a machine that consolidated all its parts into one all-inclusive motion, then Job *would not know such evil.* He would not know an evil *in excess.* So Job concludes. The world would kill him, certainly, but only in passing, in the manner that an earthquake happens to engulf human beings together with beasts, plants and stones. In principle, one can escape a blind catastrophe, if one has survived its first shock-wave and then has managed to put some distance between the catastrophe and oneself. This is the very principle of technique, namely, to act in accordance with a knowledge of the neutral constancy of laws.

Job, however, encounters an evil that is not neutral. This evil is not satisfied with killing him. Yet it does not desire to kill him either; indeed, it even forbids him to die. It is an evil that tortures him, eternalizes his pain and makes it into a hell. This evil does not reach him in a neutral manner, its madness is not that of chaos. It *looks for* him.

And when it catches up with him, it does not continue down

its path toward other victims with a locomotive-like necessity, or an indifferent caprice, but stops and sets up house around Job. Not only does it endure and persist: it insists. This insistence is evil's eternity. For were it content to eternalize him in some kind of sleep, he could still hope to reawaken and shrug it off like a bad dream. A nightmare can at least be apportioned to us as something destined.

But for Job evil is no Destiny, as Destiny is neutral and blind. Destiny is not cruel, it favours everyone equally, hence, no one. The evil that Job experiences is not "blind." If anything, we should say it had eyes. It pursues Job, corners him and encircles him in order to get a better look at him. His suffering is machinated and prepared by some mastermind as an aim and a wish. The torture does not take place without a torturer, without cause, without an Intention.

While other beings do not become the objects of any special objective,[5] Job, if he tries to anticipate danger and take flight, can get nowhere, proof that Destruction keeps a special eye out for him. "No use to wash myself with snow, or bleach my hands pure white; for *you will plunge me in dung*, until me very clothes recoil from me" (9.30–31). "And if I make a stand, like a lion *you hunt me down*" (10.16). "You have grown *cruel* in your dealings with me, your hand lies on me *heavy and hostile*" (30.21). "Terrors attack him one every side, and *follow behind him step for step*" (18.11). Evil is redoubled, repeated, insistent: ". . . you hunt me down, *multiplying* your exploits on my account. You attack, then *renew* your attack, *redoubling* your fury against me, *relentlessly* your fresh troops assail me" (10.16–17).

---

[5] Cf.: "There is always hope for a tree: when felled it can start its life again; its shoots continue to sprout. Its roots may be decayed in the earth, its stump withering in the soil, but let it scent the water and it buds, and puts out branches like a plant new set" (14.7–9).

Somewhere there is a scrutinizing intention that "counts every step" Job takes and "spies on [his] sins" (14.16). This gaze and this intention is "you": "you tireless *watcher* of mankind" (7.20), you who "have put my feet in the stocks, *watching* my every step, and measuring my footprints" (13.27), "You who *inquire* into my faults and *investigate* my sins" (10.6), you who "*surveys* me if I should sin" (10.14), you who "*keeps an eye* on [man]" (14.3).

This "you" is an intention that has dedicated itself to the task of rallying evil against the human individual, and with carefully devised tactics: "Distress and anguish close in on him, *as though some king were mounting an attack*" (15.24). "He has made me a *target* for his archery" (16.12). "Why do you chose me as your *target?*" (7.20). "He *knows* of every step I take!" (23.10). "Turn *your* eyes from [man], leave him alone, like a hired drudge, to finish his day" (14.6). "Turn *your* eyes away, leave me a little joy" (10.20). "What is man that you should make *so much of him*, subjecting him to your *scrutiny*, that morning after morning you should *examine* him and at every instant *test* him? Will you never take your *eyes* off me, long enough for me to swallow my spittle?" (7.17–19).

What is the human individual that the Intention should make *such an issue* of him? The Intention is interested in the individual more than in the rest of the world. That it should be so interested shows that the human individual must be radically other than the world.

If evil is in excess of the world, this is because an Intention sustains it beyond the penalties established by the Law. If the soul is other than the world, wherein it would like to submerge itself, this is because something, something with an infinitely more imperative will, wants to prevent the soul from plunging into the nothingness of the world and the blur of neutrality and wants the soul to take notice of itself and to pose itself as a question. To that end, so much evil is brought down upon the soul that it can no longer forget itself. Unremittingly, and deep in the bones, the Intention etches the *proper name* that the soul tries to efface in order to forget itself and to vanish into the love of Destiny and of the Earth.

The Other Scene ceases to be a pure negative. It now appears as the Intention that dedicates itself to being the adversary of a soul, the very soul which the same Intention creates and re-creates unceasingly by its insistent infliction of evil upon it.

The Intention *reveals itself* in its insistence on hurting us. If we did not suffer, or if we suffered according to the algebra of a Law of pleasures and pains, we would undoubtedly content ourselves with existing as world and as Earth. But would we exist? We would be without evil and without excess, but our "we," our soul—which is nothing but this very excess, subsisting above the world and the fusion and the mutual acceptance of all the world-parts as that which does not accept the world but opens up an other-than-the-world to make room for the horror of the world—our soul would not exist.

Evidently, the Intention "looks for" us, like a thug looking for a fight at the end of the local dance. And like the Angel who "looked for" Jacob in order to pick a fight with him. He blocked his path, he harassed him, he poked his chest, until it was clear to Jacob that the Angel (the "Other") intended to fight him. *We are sought, we are interrogated.* Evil, excessive and mad, is the *word* of a soul that wants something from our soul and will even give our soul existence to begin with just so that it knows that someone wants something from it.

If there has ever been such a thing as revelation, a "Word" of God, it is something that has been heard in this *clearing* that opens up within the being of the soul in its encounter with evil. In this sense, a "revelation" suffers no haziness. But that which is revealed is only You and Me and the world thrown in my face like a question. That which is revealed *is* the question. To the question, "With a view to what?", addressed by a soul to a soul, one still owes a reply that is a commitment. And there is the haziness. What commitment? Whose commitment, and whose "with a view to what"?

The reply still needs to be deferred. First we see the *world* reveal itself. The Intention insists that we distinguish it, the Intention, from the world which we have long grown accustomed to regarding as our unique partner, as the sole being on whom we can count, on whom we have counted to such an extent that we have come to pronounce the "great Amen" upon it, a partner who has granted us intimacy, albeit in a relationship of reciprocal utility that could have ended up confusing us. It is this intimate fusion that is compromised by the caesura of evil in excess. Overtaken by evil, then, I am suddenly separated from the world, and the world itself shifts from something embodying ultimate power and inclusivity to a second-rate reality, passed into the hands of a will that is obviously *much more interested in me than in the world.* In this way, the world together with its Law becomes an instrument of the Intention, a mediation, the open arena of my confrontation with the Intention. Ontology is upset.

Being is not the world. The soul and its question are not illusions that one part of the world, incapable of objectively knowing the world in its totality, engenders by way of disease, of pathology, by way, in general, of a privation of Being. On the contrary, the world, ceasing to be Being, appears in retrospect to have been *the veil and the illusion that prevented the seeing of Being in its truth,* that is, as my soul's questioning confrontation with the Intention that wants something from my soul. Ontologically, what is primary is the debate between myself and evil. It is the struggle with the Angel that is the truth of Being. The world is there, it seems, only to serve as an arena for this struggle, though the soul may sometimes forget it.

I can no longer see myself as a part of the world. The world,

world as we "know" it keeps from The Truth of our existence

on the contrary, is the veil that in ordinary times conceals from me the absolutely essential truth I would like to forget, to wit, that I stand face to face with an Intention that "looks for" me. In which case the world is not Being, and my self is not a being for the sake of being a part of the world. I *am* in so far as I am sundered by this hostile confrontation that ceaselessly announces itself and ceaselessly differs and delays itself, that surfaces at certain moments when the veil of the world, too violently shaken by a too insistent intention, is suddenly thrown out.

Within the interval of these moments in which the truth of my being is revealed, what can happen, by some false, inessential and distracted circumstance, is that I fail to see myself as the risk of a question, and, consequently, conceive myself, falsely, because always provisionally, as a neutral thing in a neutral world.

The insistence, and the repetition, and the excess of evil are one revealing instant. There is no "Revelation" other than in this sense. If there is such a thing as Revelation and Word, it does not take place in the midst of the world, as one voice among a thousand other worldly voices, a voice that one can choose to hear or to ignore as one pleases. The very disappearance of the world into the excess of evil, abandoning us to a debate where we are required to "put our flesh between our teeth" (13.14) and to "step forward" (31.37), is what reveals to us, unveils for us, our true being by giving the world over to its truth as veil.

For proof that all this is the thought of Job, we may turn to the *intention* that Job, for his own part, demonstrates almost everywhere in the text: the intention *to make contact*, to cross paths, with that Intention whence everything seems to materialize.

"Oh may my prayer find fulfillment, may God *respond* to my patience!" (6.8). "No wonder then if *I cannot keep silence*; in the anguish of my spirit I must *speak, lament* in the bitterness of my soul" (7.11). "Nonetheless, I shall *speak*, not fearing him: I do not see myself like that at all" (9.35). "I will give *free rein to my complaints*; I shall let my embittered soul *speak* out. I shall say to God, 'Do not condemn me, but *tell me* the reason for your assault'" (10.1–2). "My *words* are intended for Shaddai; I mean to *remonstrate* with God" (13.3). "Silence! Now I will do the *talking*, whatever may befall me" (13.13). "But grant me these two favours: if not, I shall not dare to confront you . . . Then *arraign* me, and I will *reply*; or rather, I will *speak*, and you shall *answer* me" (13.20, 22). "Why do you hide your *face?*" (13.24). "Then you would *call*, and I should *answer*, you would want to see the work of your hands once more" (14.15). "If only I knew how to reach him, or how to travel to his dwelling . . . Then I could learn his *response*, every word of it, taking note of everything he *said* to me. Would he use all his strength in his debate with me? No, he would have to *listen* to me" (23.3, 5–6). "Who can get me a *hearing* from God?" (31.35).

Let us reflect on the meaning of these demands. Asking "God" to *speak*, Job recognizes *ipso facto* that this "God" whom he addresses is totally other than the "God" of the three friends. One only addresses someone who is capable of reply, that is to say, someone who can *say something other than what has already been said*. Thus Job considers God to be a *free* being, not subject to necessity—unlike the Law, which, for the same reason that it is not harmful, can no longer exceed itself and render the impossible possible. His "being sought" gives some rationale to the idea that the One who seeks him must be able to reply to him, with a reply to which he could then reply in turn, so that a dialogue could ensue and the story could continue.

On the other hand, this dialogue *must necessarily* take place. There is no question of letting the gap reclose yet again on the slumber and on the lie: "Cover not my blood, O earth, *afford my cry no place to rest*" (16.18). "Ah, would that these words of mine were written down, *inscribed on some monument* with iron chisel and engraving tool, *cut into the rock forever"* (19.23–24).

Job's need to make contact with God is imperious, feverish, almost unseemly—shall we not say that he wants to *force* God to speak, as if seizing him by the collar like a felon and brutalizing him until he "talks," until he "coughs up the truth"? Such a need is paradoxical, in any case, for a man with a bankrupt earthly will. Elsewhere he is reproached by Eliphaz for having a swollen head: "Are you first-born of the human race, brought into the world before the hills?" (15.7). But we already know it is not his head that swells here from the pressure of a will to power that would have its source in this same head. The thing within Job that steps out in search of God's face is neither Job's will nor his intelligence, it is what we have called his "soul." This soul, far from constituting itself either within the world as a will to power or in front of the world as a cognizing subject, emerges from the disappearance of the world in the experience of the madness of the Law and the appearance, at the heart of this nothingness of the world, of a "you" who is as responsible for the world as he is for its disappearance, an absolute master of the Game who preserves the soul in an eternity of awakening. The soul, then, is the "daughter" of this "you." It is that which "you" see behind the nothingness, and *which exists only in this being seen.*

The soul exists only as a response to an always anterior Intention, and this is why this soul is not mad, but on the contrary, is supremely logical *when it imagines that it could speak to Him from whose word it receives existence.*

According to what modalities can this "debate" be resolved in a tie?

Apparently it is a judicial debate, a *trial.* Which is what Job seems to want after all. He wants to speak to the supreme judge: if only he could appear in person, by-passing the counsel of bad lawyers, he would be able to plead his case, which is a good one, which appears bad only when it is badly defended. And as the judge is just, the whole affair would be fairly arbitrated and concluded.

But now the author of the dialogues takes a certain crafty pleasure in demolishing this perspective in the same way that he enjoys creating it. It may well be that the dialogue with God is described in *terms* of a judicial procedure, a legal debate where the innocence or guilt of the soul is at stake. But if we look closer, we will notice that it is an *impossible* trial.

Legalistic terminology abounds. "I hold on to my *justice* and will not relax . . ." (27.6). "He would see he was *contending* with an honest man, and I should surely win my *case*" (23.7). "You shall see, I will *proceed by due form of law*, persuaded, as I am, that I am guiltless. Who comes against me with an *accusation*? Let him come! I am ready to be silenced and to die" (13.18–19). "I should set out my *case* to him, my mouth would not want for arguments" (23.4). God replies on the same note: "Do you really want to reverse my *judgment*, and put me in the *wrong* to put yourself in the *right*?" (40.8). All of this is a natural progression of Job's trial as formulated by the friends and during which Job already put together his defense.

At this point, nevertheless, the proceedings appear rather strange. In a "normal" trial, which proceeds in accordance with the Law, in a technical fashion, there are distinct roles: a defendant, a (prosecuting) judge, or inquisitor, witnesses, a defense attorney. That is what we had in the trial conducted by the friends: Job was the defendant, God was the judge, and the friends were witnesses assisting the judge's inquisition. There was no defense attorney, true, but the defendant took the defense upon himself, and vigorously so.

Here the entire arrangement is upset. The being whom Job addresses continues to be *judge*, omnipotent and omniscient, and everyone knows that his sentence will be executed. But because he penetrates Job's soul and life in all transparency, he becomes *witness* at the same time, at once testifying to his own injustice and acquitting Job of any injustice. On the other hand, as he does not exercise any judicial power to give Job what is right, even as he is familiar with Job's absolute innocence, he is the principal and sole *defender.* In the end, without any break in continuity, by a sudden metamorphosis of his being, without nuance or reservation, God will reveal himself as the ultimate defender of the same soul that he has afflicted with evil.

God is judge: "My *judge*" (9.15). "You pass *sentences* against me" (13.26). "You bring [man] into *judgment* before you" (14.3). "Once he has decided, who can change his mind? Whatever he plans, he carries out. No doubt, then, but he will carry out my *sentence*, like so many other *decrees* that he has made" (23.13–14).

God is witness: "You count every step I take" (14.16). "Will you never take your eyes off me?" (7.18). And there are many other texts in which God is said to "scrutinize" Job (e.g., 10.14; 7.17–20).

God is the accused: as we know from all the passages where Job imputes the initiative of evil to God. "Or if it is not he [who sends evil] then who?" (9.24; cf. 10.3). Job just as explicitly transfers his own guilt onto God: "It is still true, though you think you have the upper hand of me and feel that you have proved my guilt, that it is God, you must know, *who has done me wrong*, and his is the net that closes around me" (19.5–6; cf. 19.21).

Three texts underscore the divine *wicked intention* as such:

"When a sudden deadly scourge descends, *he laughs at the plight of the innocent*" (9.23).

"Yet, after all, you were dissembling, biding your time ... *to let no fault of mine go uncensured*" (10.13–14).

"From the towns come the groans of the dying and the gasp of wounded men crying for help. *And God remains deaf to their appeal*" (24.12).

But we must pay very special attention to the texts where God appears as defender.

This incredible possibility is implicitly assumed in passages such as these, where Job imagines that his very torturer, contrary to all expectations, would interrupt or suspend the torture: "If only you would hide me in Sheol, and shelter me there until your anger is past, fixing a certain day for calling me to mind . . . day after day of my service I would wait for my relief to come" (14.13–14). How so? Is the angry one, in the very midst of anger, supposed to shelter his prey from the blows of his anger, as if he knew in advance that his anger was soon due to abate? Is he to make an act of clemency without yet ceasing to be angry? Is the left hand of God to stop his right hand from hitting?

Other passages formulate this paradox quite clearly—although by a light that is still pale, to be sure. Job has the feeling that there is a secret affiliation between himself and the Intention that tortures him, a tenderness, a predilection, a compassion, a form of attachment at once both vigilant and distant, which he compares to a relationship of *paternity*: "I, whom God has fostered *as a father*, from childhood, and guided since I left my mother's womb" (31.18). This quasi-paternity is again connected to the idea of *creation*: "They [my servants], no less than I, were *created* in the womb by the one same God who *shaped* us all within our mothers" (31.15).

This creation cannot be understood as a mechanical manufacturing that links nature to so many of its parts. Rather, Job's formulations make one think of the relationship between an "artist"-creator and his "finest works": "[I am] *the work of your hands*" (10.3). "Your own hands *shaped me, modeled me* . . . You modeled me, remember, as clay is modeled . . . Did you not *pour me out* like milk, and *curdle me* then like cheese, clothe me with skin and flesh, and weave me of bone and sinew? And the you *endowed me with life, watched each breath of mine with tender care*" (10.8, 9, 10–12).

According to Job's sketch, then, the creator is far more fascinated with his work as something that leaves his hands, than he is determined in advance to give that work such and such a shape. God exerts no power over it, in the sense of an ascendancy, but lets human beings be, yet without releasing us. And we, for our part, know whence we come, by what "hands" we have been "shaped." A unique relationship: dependence of the creature on the creator, yet, at the same time, game, freedom, distance.[6] We might say it all comes down to *an incredible reciprocal interest*: God's "solicitude" for human beings, as irksome as it is discreet, testifies only to an Intention intent upon us, which God intends for us never to be relieved of.

To be God's "handiwork" in this way, to have each of his steps "watched" in this way, according to Job's suggestion, would give Job a sort of *right* on God, a right that cannot demand anything with exactness, in the way that human justice demands exact penalties for breeches of contract, but at least a right to demand "solicitude," if not more besides.

Since God has intentionally created human beings, and since we do not remember ever having existed without the creator, the entire human adventure would be an affair which essentially concerned God and which God could not forget without, in a sense, ceasing to be himself. That is Job's repeated injunction toward heaven: "Remember!" (7.7; 10.9). There is also the invocation of a past when their relationship was ideal: "Who will bring back to me the months that have gone, and the days when God was my guardian, when his lamp shone over my head, and his light was my guide in the darkness? . . . when God hedged round my tent; when Shaddai dwelt with me" (29.2–5). Since God is the one who made the first gesture without having been compelled by anything or anyone, and since God only "exists" for us in the sense that God is the one who took the initiative with regard to this entire remarkable adventure which

---

[6] "Distance" is precisely the notion whereby Jean-Luc Marion (*L'Idole et la distance* [Paris: Grasset, 1977]) tries to think the rapport between human beings and God.

might just as easily not have taken place, *no more can God forget us than we can forget God.*

God is the one who had an "idea," a "project"; all of this must have a meaning for him too. Therefore if God has forgotten what he has made, he must confess to an error, a fatal inattention. Unless this very inattention is intentional, his project still needs to be completed. It still remains for God to *return* to humankind. This is why Job's hope, that he will some day come to *see God*, has for him a very essential and very striking coherence. It explains these peremptory affirmations: "then *you will look for me*" (7.21). "*Your eyes will turn my way*" (7.8). This hope is a waking dream that stands in perfect dream-continuity with the intuition at the end of the seven days and seven nights of silence expressed in chapter 3: "Why has not Shaddai his own *store of times*, and why do his *faithful* never see *his Days?*" (24.1).

Whence, to return to the problematic of the trial, we get a reversal which is stupefying and yet completely natural in the context of the texts that we have just quoted: "You *yourself* must take my own guarantee, since no one cares to clap his hand on mine" (17.3). Apparently an absurd request. How could God, as judge, do without the guarantee of another, and offer *himself* as guarantee, as if God were at the same time the defense attorney? And yet, this is just what God becomes for Job's soul in two other celebrated passages where Job, in a rather startling tone of triumph, affirms his certainty at being defended by God.

We will begin with the most triumphant of the two (the second in the order of the book), which, due to the mistranslation of St. Jerome, and consequent Latin theology, has come to serve as a principal Old Testament text announcing the resurrection of the flesh. Here is the translation of Larcher:

This I know: that my Defender lives,
   and he, the Last, will take his stand on earth.
After my awakening, he will set me close to him,

and from my flesh I shall look on God.
He whom I shall see will take my part:
he whom my eyes will gaze on will no longer be a stranger.[7]

(19.25–27)

Despite philological uncertainties,[8] one thing is certain: Job here envisages his entire salvation, the resolution of the human adventure, the end of evil, and more specifically the beatific encounter with the Master who has taken the initiative. He *will see* God, instead of simply being *seen*. They *will regard one another.* The soul will be returned to its essential affinity, to its affiliation with the one "who will not be a stranger."

---

[7] *Will no longer be a stranger*: the ultimate formula of the Joban eschatology, which thus signifies the return to the affinity and the memory of what was once a communion and now only waits for communion again. Like a hundred other formulas in the Bible, this one evokes the admirable visions of Isaiah and Hosea, both of whom embody the eschatological wait: "[Jerusalem, you are] no longer to be named 'Forsaken,' nor your land 'Abandoned,' but you shall be called 'My Delight' and your land 'The Wedded'" (Isa. 62.4). "When that day comes . . . the heavens will have their answer from me, the earth its answer from them . . . I will love the Unloved, I will say to No-People-of-Mine, 'You are my people,' and he will answer 'You are my God'" (Hosea 2.23–24). And the most constant formula of the Covenant: "Then I will be their God and they shall be my people" (Jer. 31.33).

[8] They are numerous. Cf. the exhaustive exposé of Jean Lévêque, *op. cit.*, Pt. II, pp. 449–97, a lengthy study basically devoted to our two passages (and to verse 17.3, on the "guarantee"). At the end of the study the author proposes the following translation: "But I myself know that my *go'el* is alive and that he will be the last to rise on the earth. And if one rips the skin from my flesh, even after that I will see Eloah. He whom I will see will be for me [will take my side], and he whom my eyes will behold will not be a stranger! My kidneys languish in my trunk . . . [verse unfinished]." Neither the *go'el* nor the final vision of God present a problem. The disagreement lies in the mode of this supreme happiness: is it to be a resurrection of the flesh, or a disappearance of the body? Here is the text of the Vulgate, in any event, substantially resumed by the theology of

The *go'el*, or "Defender," is the blood-avenger. He is the family member who was nearest in blood to the murder victim, and who now assumes the latter's rights and responsibilities: he has to avenge the death of the victim, he may marry his widow, purchase his wealth. He is in the fullest sense of the term the "Defender" of children who, thanks to him, do not have to be alone in the world. God will be called the *go'el* of the oppressed in general: "Do not displace the ancient landmark or encroach on orphans' lands, for he who *avenges* them is strong and will take up their cause against you" (Prov. 23.10–11); and the *go'el* of Israel in particular: "Thus says Israel's king and his *redeemer*,[9] YHWH Shabaoth: I am the first and the last, there is no other God besides me" (Is. 44.6). Thanks to God, Job is no longer alone in the world.

God the Defender then! But Defender against whom? In Isaiah, against the wicked. But in Job, it could only be against the wickedness *of God himself*. The formula, "The Last will take his stand on earth" (v. 25: he will take the stand, as in a trial, to speak on behalf of the defendant), as well as, "He whom I shall see will take my part" (v. 27), imply a Defender God who mounts his defense *against* an Accuser God. Like the verse about the "guarantee," this delivers us over to the rather outrageous idea of a *split God*.[10]

_____

the resurrection (e.g., St. Thomas of Aquinas, *Summa theologica*, suppl., question 75.1, *et passim*) and by the liturgy of the dead: *Scio enim quod redemptor meus vivit / et in novissimo die terra surrecturus sum / et rursum circumdabor pelle mea, / et in carne mea videbo Deum meum . . . / reposita est hæc spes in sinu meo.*

[9] We must stress that "redeemer," which translates *go'el*, means "he who buys back," and not, as common usage would have it, "he who *revives*." To be *repurchased* is to be returned to one's original condition, to one's kin, after having been excluded by an oppressive law of slavery or by a death that has made a kinsman disappear.

[10] The theme of the schizoid God is key for Martin Buber in his exegesis of the Book of Job; see *The Prophetic Faith*, trans. Carlyle Witton-Davies

It is this same idea that the other passage puts forward:

Henceforth I have a witness in heaven,
my defender[11] is there in the height.
My own lament is my advocate with God,
while my tears flow before him.
Let this plead for me as I stand before God,
as a man will plead for his fellows.

(16.19–21)

Who is this mysterious "witness" and "defender"? To Job's mind, he would have to be the *go'el* that we know from verse 19.25, the same one who "stands surety" (17.3). Here, however, the witness-defender resides "in the height," "in heaven," while what is said of the *go'el* is that he will take his stand "on earth." The "witness in heaven" must be an Angel therefore.

It is another mode of the "splitting of God." For an Angel is a divine being, even if it has a human form, and even if the text insists on its anthropomorphism. Moreover: here, for Job, the "witness in heaven" is manifestly divine *just because* he has a human form, that is to say, as the author makes clear, just because he is human enough to understand the significance of "tears." This Witness, therefore, will be able to defend us *with full knowledge of the facts*, "as a man will plead for his fellows," against the accuser God. In his case, as in that of the *go'el* who "will take his stand for us upon the earth" (19.25), the thought of Job evokes Christian messianism. The passage seems to say that if God can be Mediator against his own justice, it is because God, or something in God, or someone in God, is *like*

(New York: Harper Torchbooks, 1960), pp. 192 ff. Cf. Arthur S. Peake, *The Problem of Suffering in the Old Testament* (London: Bryant & Kelly, 1904), pp. 94–95; and Paul Volz, *Hiob und Weisheit* (Göttingen: Vandenhoeck & Ruprecht, 1911), p. 62.—Tr.

[11] "He who testifies on my behalf": *sahad*.

a human being, similar to us. God has this irreplaceable affinity with us—which the neutral world does not have—of *intimately knowing good and evil, of knowing how and at what point evil actually hurts and causes pain.* Now how could God have this knowledge which is reserved for the *happy few*, the "chosen," for the "choicest" of sacrifices, if not because, being Creator of everything, he is the one who possesses the virtuosity of having created evil? Torture is only administered by someone who knows *how* to cause pain.

By the same token, however, like the poisoner who also knows the remedies, God is not helpless in the face of evil, not if God does not wish to be helpless. The text spells this out without ambiguity: the witness in heaven knows the meaning of our "tears" "flowing before him"; it is upon seeing these tears that he interjects himself as Mediator between us and evil. The God that Job catches a glimpse of is so much so a defender that he is not afraid to contradict himself, to interpose himself between himself and his own decrees, to have commerce with humans and to transform his omnipotence into an omni-impotence to this end. The *go'el* and *sahad* of Job is actually difficult to tell apart from Jesus crying Lazarus!

Job thus imagines what is, strictly speaking, an *impossible* trial.

Every procedure is *upset*: a trial where one and the same authority is judge, accused, witness and defense attorney! We are at an infinite distance from technique. The God of the friends could not be the accused and the defense attorney, he was content to record the declarations of witnesses and to scrutinize them with his omniscience, and then to mete out punishment by his omnipotence. God was only a judge, a "divine" and "infinite" judge, to be sure, but one who was in his essence, unambiguously, a judge. Here, on the contrary, God is the *assembly* of the authorities of technical procedure. God is never truly *an* authority, since he also very quickly steps forward as a *counter-authority*. He is certainly not a "supreme" judge, the instrument of a "supreme" justice. If anything, he smashes justice, ruins it and derides it.

This is what Job emphasizes with a force that sounds like despair. God, too contradictory to be able to be grasped, is decidedly *absent*. "If any were so rash as to challenge him for reasons, one in a thousand would be more than they could answer" (9.3). "If I protest against such violence, there is no *reply*; if I appeal against it, judgment *is never given*" (19.7). "I cry to you, and you *give me no answer*; I stand before you, but you *take no notice*" (30.20). "If I go eastward, he *is not there*; or westward—still I *cannot see him*. If I seek him in the north, *he is not to be found, invisible* still when I turn to the south" (23.8–9).

We have already looked at these texts on the absence of God. They were, when we looked at them, in God's *care*, revealing an essential aspect of the wickedness of the Master of existence: God's refusal to let human beings access the secret of existence as a formula of a Law, as a world, that can be mastered. Now we read these texts in another light. We see in them indubitable testimonies to the *radical alterity* of the Other Scene. An authority that rejects the ordinary categories of the trial and manifests itself to human beings in such a manner that we cannot count on its neutrality, or its assistance, or its culpability, such an authority stations itself before us at a *distance* that is all the more cryptic and fascinating.

Job has measured this distance only in and by the excess of evil. This has opened up the question of good and evil—*Why, with a view to what, is there evil, rather than good?*—a question which still has no answer at this stage. That God, then, as it has been said for centuries, is the object of "faith" and not of "reason," that God is in "heaven" and not on "earth," that God is infinite and obscure and not clear and distinct in an apprehensible finitude, that God is silent when human beings speak, that even when he does "speak" this is still by some always escaping discourse or sign, that, lastly, there is nothing "certain" about God in any sense of the term, *all this results from the fact that God is, for us, nothing other than the excess of good and of evil incomprehensibly confused.*

The sphere of good and evil is where we find the soul and God, and where their dialogue unfolds, if it finally reveals itself as possible. This sphere includes the world, contrary to technique's belief that the world is all-inclusive and that good and evil together form a marginal phenomenon within the world. Technique is convinced that the world would continue on its course with its chain of causes and effects, even if nobody suffered evil or desired good. Job is now convinced of the contrary: he sees that the question of good and evil is more serious, more severe, more urgent than every technical question that can concern the existent. He concludes that the sphere of being of good and evil is *denser* than the sphere of being of the world, that it dictates the world's gravitational pull, deciding how heavy or light things are in the world.

The problem is that nothing, up until now, has penetrated this sphere of good and evil. Job has not spoken to God. God has not replied. God has "sought" Job, indeed, and Job has "sought" God. The question of their dialogue has been posed. But there is still no reply. Why is there evil rather than good? Are we in the world . . . with a view to evil? . . . with a view to good? And is God ultimately . . . an impassive judge, an accuser, a defender?

Now, we shall see that Job, precisely because he will have renounced a certain type of reply, the kind that would correspond to the question "Why?"—that is to say, a "scientific" reply pertaining to the existent—for the sake of another type of reply corresponding to the question "With a view to what?"— that is to say, a reply putting existence at stake independently of the existent and even in sovereign indifference toward the existent and his Law, posing an *a priori* challenge to every calculation—*Job will end up effectively obtaining a reply, one that is in some sense certain and secure, dazzling like the day.*

We read the passage where he announces his highest hope:

> I put my flesh between my teeth,
>   I take my life in my hands.
> Let him kill me if he will; I have no other hope
>   than to justify my conduct in his eyes.
> This very boldness gives promise of my release,
>   since no godless man would dare appear before him.
>
> (13.14–16)

And the words that conclude the dialogues:

> I have spoken my last word; now let Shaddai answer me.
> When my adversary has drafted his writ against me
> I shall wear it on my shoulder,
>   and bind it round my head like a royal turban.
> I will give him an account of every step of my life,
>   and go as boldly as a prince to meet him.
>
> (31.35–37)

A startling reversal! One might say that Job suddenly and by a single movement all at once becomes sure of himself and sure of God, as if all the former vagueness is removed. How does this "princely" certainty represent itself? By a process comparable to the juxtaposition of two separate parts of a coded message suddenly rendered legible. Of the fact that he will be "saved," Job is certain, by virtue of a reasoning that, although starkly intuitive and lacking in discursivity, carries an overwhelming logic. God does not love the impious; an impious man would not dare to show up before God. If I act in a way that makes me deserving of appearing before God, then God will love me. But I *am* ready to make this appearance, I can in fact "defend my conduct" before God and give God "an account of all my steps." Therefore I *am* saved.

Let us attend to this "innocence." The issue is not Job's *past* innocence. With regard to the past, Job, as we have seen, has come to concede that he may be guilty of however many sins, however often committed, as one pleases. He has understood that this is not the important thing, not for someone who has the least inkling of God, someone who has a fear of God. Whether innocent or delinquent according to the Law, we are all equally innocent, or equally guilty, before a God who is infinitely above the Law.

Thus the innocence that Job avers is of another order: it is the *present* innocence of his heart, that is, the innocence of his *intention*. This innocence, which is of a very special purity, consists in a resoluteness for the future: *a will to sin no more*, to evermore *struggle against evil*, to make this struggle *the orientation of his entire life*.

Job speaks as if he knew that he is bound to be essentially pleasing to God so long as he has this intention and to the degree that he has it. As if he knew that *this is the manner in which God too sees things*, that *God too, God especially, hates evil*. As if, consequently, his allowing the horror of evil to be in his soul and to orient his entire life suddenly placed Job in company with God. As if, from then on, God could only welcome him in a "princely" fashion, in a light of glory, as the father in the parable welcomes the prodigal son.

In other words, it seems to Job that everything that has happened to him will make sense *if, and only if, what he comes to have for his own intention is the very intention of the Intention*; if the two intentions *coincide like two fragmentary communications of one and the same message*.

How can Job be so certain? He has explained his certainty: the "hand" of God has "fashioned" and "created" him. He is therefore essentially made in God's image. The heart of God is

an analog of his own heart. Hence, the deeper he digs into the
depths of his heart and lets this heart speak directly, authenti-
cally, sincerely, the more he *must* find God. He knows that God
is in no way a "stranger" to this horror of evil and this unexpected new energy to fight evil, and that these somehow belong
with God. And because the excess of evil has revealed God as
Master, as Creator, Job perceives that an intimate fellowship
with God will immediately dispatch a force, a life, an overabun-
dant ("princely") future shattering the barrier of the world and
negating death ("He may kill me . . ."). The coincidence of intentions will *produce* this "miracle," the complete reversal of
the situation, the end of anxiety's upheaval and the unfolding
of infinite perspectives.

Every time that he will decide to commit himself, every time
that he will be certain of his "piety" and dare to step forward,
every time that he will fight the madness of the world for at-
tacking other Jobs, every time that he will allow the horror of
evil to assail him without trying to deduce it or calculate it,
every time he does these things, he will know that he stands in
a full communion with God, he will see the Law disappear and
open onto the Infinite, so that a new Possible will reduce death
to nothingness.[12]

We see from the tone of the passages quoted above, however—
and in fact from the tone of Job's remarks in general—that this
adherence to the Intention of God involves something extremely
paradoxical.

---

[12] [Note of 1995] The soul will be guided and constantly inspired in this
respect by the revelation that has been for this soul the excess of evil.
Having suffered evil in excess, it will know *how to recognize it unmistak-
ably everywhere in the world whenever other souls are attacked.* The void
that evil will have dug out in the soul henceforth will be like an enduring
breach through which compassion for others will enter without restraint,
a windy draught that breathes the souls of others into us and makes us
enter into a total communication with them. Thus, what the fight against

Although Job claims to have an intimate knowledge of God's real intention, he is not content to passively await salvation. He feels the need to "take his flesh between his teeth," and to "step forward," in other words, to *force the hand* of God. Everything happens as if, inverting the gesture made by the Angel toward Jacob, Job plants himself in God's way and "looks for" God, like the pugilist who "looks for" his adversary by the exit-doors in order to settle some old score.

Indeed, this behaviour of Job's is already, as we think we have shown, a reply to the God who "looks for" him. Yet there is a fundamental vagueness surrounding the *beginning* of this dialogue. Who speaks first? Who takes the initiative? To speak, one must be sure of one's interlocutor, one must have him in one's confidence. But no one, to begin with, is sure of anyone. Human beings are alone. God is only an hypothesis. Does one speak to a dream?

Job has no *guarantee* therefore. When he addresses God, he "exposes himself." That does not prevent him from stepping forward, but, if he does step forward, he must step onto an open field like a duelist in shirt-sleeves exposing himself to the gunfire of his adversary.

With this gesture, the true meaning of Job's challenge suddenly becomes clear: he will oblige God to *revoke the equivocation*, to *convert his wickedness back into love*. "More kingly than the king," we might say, Job *would force God to be God*.

---

evil asks of Job, and what Job accepts, is—we understand this better to-day—the mystery of charity found in the suffering servant of Isaiah 53, and in the Sermon on the Mount. This is the "responsibility for others" and the "responsibility for the responsibility of others," magnificently elucidated, in our days, by Emmanuel Levinas. What allows us to say this is the picture that Job and the friends paint throughout the book of the forms of justice that would exonerate a man in the eyes of God: it is always a matter of defending the widow, the orphan, of helping the pauper, of making truth triumph against the hypocrisies of the powers of the world. The relationship to the other is always the first issue—and in this sense, the Book of Job hardly differs from the other great texts of the Bible.

A peculiar attitude, but one that we think truly belongs to Job, whose conduct would be absolutely inexplicable without it. Job behaves as if he believed that the commitment of human beings is indispensable to God, that God needs this human gesture in order to be emancipated from his own ambiguities,[13] that God even awaits this commitment anxiously.

Only the choice of human beings, the choice to love, would release God from the pain of his quest, would "save" him, in a way, even God!

To put the matter in yet another way, the adventure of God and of humans, hell or salvation, must be essentially interdependent. When humans and God fight shoulder-to-shoulder against evil, then Love can happen. If either one of them fails, then horror triumphs. *Alone, neither one of them holds the key to the entire situation, and this very departmentalization is the mystery of Love!* The encounter between Job and God, therefore, can take place *only if they step forward together, if they walk a stretch of the road together.* It is only then that the two fragments of the message can converge.

It would be misleading, however, to push the comparison with a human "love story" too far. For the event in question is truly *salvational* for Job. When the adversary becomes a defender, he is an *unconditional* defender. In retrospect, he appears to have made the first step. He appears to have *always held everything in his hand.*

---

[13] This emancipation is the antithesis of what Robert Frost had in mind in his poetic exegesis, *A Masque of Reason* (London: Routledge & Paul, 1945), where God says to Job (ll. 69–78): "My thanks are to you for releasing me/ From moral bondage to the human race./ The only free will there at first was man's,/ Who could do good or evil as he chose./ I had no choice but I must follow him/ With forfeits and rewards he understood—/ Unless I liked to suffer loss of worship./ I had to prosper good and punish evil./ You changed all that. You set me free to reign./ You are the Emancipator of your God". It is more in line with Carl Jung's exegesis in *Answer to Job*, trans. R. F. C. Hull (New York: Holt, 1945).—Tr.

The explanation of this paradox is nothing other than the divinity of God, here glimpsed in a veritable theophany. The Creator is capable of everything. God uproots mountains like piles of straw, subverts Law and Time. It is thanks to God that Job, who might not have existed, exists. God can do everything, undo everything, redo everything. If God is responsible for this horrible business of *killing* by *love*, it is because, within his love, he houses a profusion of lives. Whence Job's certainty that *he will be saved from the depths of every conceivable hell, provided he manage to strike a harmony of intention with God.*

Under this light everything becomes clearer. God desired Job's innocence for the sake of this harmony. It is for this reason that God has "killed" him, excluded him from the world; that being the only way to make him yield to his free Game and to open up a horizon for him where no Law would put limits upon either mercy or salvation. And Job has *accepted*: he has "put his flesh between his teeth," he has stepped forward, he no longer makes the pursuit of life in this world a condition for replying to God. He has *taken upon himself* the responsibility of the fight. He no longer makes his innocence into a reason, or a pretext, for hiding. He has agreed to take responsibility for something over which he had made no earlier contract. He has turned his back to the plan of the justice of the Law in favor of another plan, that of the "injustice" of mercy. From this moment and by this very gesture he has been saved, effectively, and he knows it— as the Christ will know it—indubitably. Whence the "princely" confidence he has displayed, this tranquil audacity, this unforeseeable end of tears.

We notice the radical nature of this "certainty" of Job, which we have called "dazzling as the day." It is dazzling in its irrefutable logic: God is the supreme Possible. But this light shines only after the night ends. It has been necessary for Job to expose himself to the fire of the adversary, to his ambiguity, to his absence, to his wickedness. It has been necessary for him to decide to be good *even if God, this adversary, is wicked.* It has been necessary for him to decide upon love *independently of all perspectives and all calculations of salvation.* And then—*salvation has come!*

We can see that in this situation the moment of fundamental uncertainty is never to be circumvented. *Night is the unique path of day.* And this night falls again upon each instant. None of our previous replies has value for the question posed today by the excess of evil. Nothing can take the place of a decision to commit. Nothing can save one from the necessity of passing through the unveiled, through the *nada.* Job, before St. John of the Cross, experienced the dark night of the soul.

God is found only in the *nada.* This is the dazzling certainty of Job.

It is—if we wish—*faith.* The excess of evil has produced this fruit.

And yet—is this not a last "ruse of reason"? Does all of this not amount to saying: if you want your salvation, you, soul, commit yourself to fighting, at God's side, against evil—hence—in this commitment, give yourself evil—hence—you will not receive good except at the price of evil—hence—take up technique, again and as always, which calculates a Law in a world?

Not an impossible scenario. How shall we recognize it? No doctrine as such can put an end to the wavering of the soul before a decision to commit. Here, we are at the absolute limit of knowledge. The commitment alone will decode the message.

In any event, the text allows us to follow the thought of the author of the Book of Job intimately enough to know that it is in this commitment to fight evil that he has suspended the wavering of his soul, and that a spiritual wellspring has overflowed into his heart. Otherwise he would never have dared to conceive the book and its final resolution. The paradox of a Defender suddenly springing up in the very heart of distress would simply be *derisory.*

5. The Difference

WHAT THEN, IN THE END, IS THE CONTENT OF THE JOBAN *revelation?*

The thing about God that is equivalent to the Law is in fact not God at all, but rather is equivalent to the world.

Conversely, there is something which exceeds the world and which is God, the one whom Job addresses, and that is:

– evil, as an insistence beyond everything that technical thought can render reasonable,

– good, as an open possibility beyond every failure of technique.

This "something" wants to make itself recognized (which is why it insists), but recognized as that which our intention will not dominate so long as our intention is not engaged in a resolute fight against evil.

If the word "soul," instead of signifying the object of a psychology, is heard in its evocation of that which is masked, impenetrable, and nevertheless—because the soul remains behind when everything disappears and because everything disappears—excessively existent, then we can say that the projected Intention reveals itself as soul, at the same time that it reveals us to ourselves as souls, souls whose intentions must come into agreement with it: beings given the immemorial task of resonating with this being, without in any way resonating with the world, and therefore beings that are as masked and as impenetrable to the eyes of our own technical reason as the Intention itself.

Thus, again, what exceeds the world is what concerns a soul's waiting.

Thus, lastly, God is a soul related to our soul, or God is nothing. God is like a human being, or is nothing.[1]

---

[1] God is a "personal" being, God has nothing to do with a Law, with an order of things, with a world. As a soul, God is ambiguous, uncertain, inconstant, as long as the eschatological wait is not concluded in some final resolution. We have other signs of this everywhere in the Old Testament around the incredible relationship between God and Israel. The jealousy of God, his tenderness, his powerlessness before the inconstancy of his well-beloved (Ezekiel, Hosea . . .), hence God's *omni*-im-*potence*. Conversely, God's anger, cruelty (the dreadful curses of Deut. 28.15–68), further indices of his omni-impotence, which Job indirectly takes note of ("Do you have eyes of flesh . . .?"). All these biblical texts show that in God's testing of Israel, that is to say, in the very revelation whereby Israel believes, wrongly or rightly, that God is testing it, Israel perceives God as a "person," absolutely a person, one *like* a human being, as mysterious, as unpredictable, as "gracious," we might say by a play on words, as human. Should we recall again the Lover of the Song of Songs? The only difference is that this "person" is not of this world, but is the Partner of the whole world, standing outside it or behind it. Apart from that, God is not different from what is properly the humanity of the human being, namely the soul. We see only the body of the neighbour, and if we know the neighbour's soul, this is never by a direct and uncluttered view, but always only to the extent that our soul has to deal with the neighbour's soul in an engagement that is a Game and that is always in abeyance, always waiting of something, good or evil, benevolence or horror. In the relation between two human souls, the Game involves wickedness, ruse, deceit, cruelty, revenge, distrust, indifference, or esteem, love, pride, affinity, kinship, pardon and desertion. And the same goes for the relation between the human soul and God's soul, to judge by the climate of the biblical texts. Except that we do not see the body of God. Yet we also do see it: the world is God's body. The world is the organ by which God makes signals in the direction of souls, it is the opaque element that prevents souls from seeing God if they do not want to know God, but that remains transparent to those who read the signs.

God is at once perfectly near (both God and we are other than the world, and we share an essential removal of the world for an essential mutual proximity) and infinitely distant (in no way do we have God while we have the world).[2]

But now we must develop a thesis which was a watermark beneath all that has preceded: the Being that reveals itself in the opening of the Other Scene is indistinct. Our souls, extreme evil, the absolute benevolence of the memorial soul of God are all one and the same thing. *Evil, God, and humankind are the data of the same revelation, the fallout of the same original event.*

Does the prologue of the Book of Job not present God and Satan as being in collusion? The strategy deployed for putting Job to the test is devised by the two of them *together*. They are

---

[2] That God reveals himself in and by means of the excess of evil forcefully challenges a constant thesis of metaphysics, namely, that God is Being first of all, and is the *summum bonum* only as a *consequence* of this, the concept of the supreme good being eminently understood in the concept of "God." But initially this consequence cannot be exhibited, it can only be signified by dint of the ultimate vagueness of the concepts of infinity and eminence. More importantly, we have already seen that any existent that does not have for its being that which concerned good and evil in excess would still belong to the world. This is why the idea of such a supreme being has been able to give rise to calculation, in a theology conceived as a metaphysics, that is, a technique whose dominion is, by definition, the world.

The result of this is that it becomes necessary to invert Nietzsche's formula, "The moral God alone is refuted" (*The Will to Power*, trans. Walter Kaufman & J. R. Hollingdale [New York: Random House, 1967], frag. 5 [71]), a formula which he thought he adequately established with his doctrine about how human resentment invents alternate worlds; it becomes necessary to say: *The moral God alone* is not *refuted.* Any other "God" is refuted, since he is a being of the world. And if the Being that Heidegger opposes to beings, or even the *Ereignis* that he opposes to Being and to beings as a more original "there is" (*Es gibt*), had nothing to do with good and evil, these would all be equally refuted. Heidegger claims that "Being" and "*Ereignis*" are different from beings. Yet this cannot be so, we say here with the Bible, if they have nothing to do with the difference between good and evil (to which we shall return).

partners in the same enterprise, their Intention is common. In fact, there would seem to be no reason to distinguish them. The Divinity is the Devil—God *is* Satan, and Satan *is* God, and Job would not be Job except by way of the Game of God-Satan.

One of the most powerful arguments of atheism is: if God existed, God would not permit all this evil. We state, with Job, that, on the contrary: without all this evil, God would never exist. It is evil that places us on the path of something like "God," and that opens up an Other Scene for us. Evil "demonstrates" God.

Now, in one sense, the atheistic argument is irrefutable: in effect, yes, if God "existed," that is, if God "existed" as a being, evil would surpass him infinitely and thus refute his "existence," seeing how evil, in as much as it opens up an Other Scene which surpasses, envelops, and overturns every being, must also surpass a God who exists like a being. This is both the first thought and the constant inspiration of Job in his confrontation with evil: if God existed as a being, as a metonymy of the world which the thought of the friends fashion idolatrously, God would not permit all this evil; but evil exists, therefore God does not exist.

Yet this only signifies: the being God, the God-"thing," who "is" before revealing to us his expectation, the God for whom Being is *by itself* and *without our souls*, this God, as magnificently as we may conceive him, whatever attribute we might affirm of him, is compromised, rendered contradictory and unintentional, annihilated, by the evil in excess of the world. Failing to offer salvation, God is annulled to the same degree that salvational techniques emerge. Whence the death of God in the epoch of the universal advent of technique. This annulled God is very much the God of religions in as much as these proceed along a technical-metaphysical discourse which posits and situates God, evil, and humans, as beings, within an technical conception of the world.

We know that by positing God at the beginning, right from

the very beginning, religious doctrines are hard pressed to explain how evil comes into the world *afterwards*. Is it humankind that welcomes evil? If so, it is only because evil already exists of itself, as something that can consequently come to human beings; and that is so because God, who created everything, created evil. Besides, was it not God who created human beings so poorly, as creatures obtuse enough to welcome evil with open arms or to invent it by themselves? The creative power of God, no matter how we look at it, contains a flaw: How could God have created an Adversary for himself?

But the three incompatible moments—God, evil, human beings—do not fall into contradiction except when we posit them separately as isolated beings. In fact the error lies in positing them separately, in a space, as if they constituted a world.

When they are in fact *revealed* to us, in their truth, they are of such a nature that they exist *one through the other and one at the same time as the other*, within the questioning rift of the waiting: we, human beings as soul, exist through the evil that touches us and reveals to us the inalterability of our souls; God exists through our soul which addresses itself to a "you" as to a Non-Stranger who has majestically taken the initiative and who remembers us within the same moment that we respond to his own waiting; finally, evil exists through God who allots it to us as an enigma.

Whatever the case may be with regard to this "ecstatic" tripartite relation among the three moments and its possible resolution in the soul's involvement with God against evil, what is established in the disclosed truth of the revelation is that these moments do not sanction a description of Creation as a series of successive appearances *following* God's eternal existence, such that human beings in the world are followed by evil (or vice versa).

Whence, then, does the *distinction* arise? In what way is God *not* evil? And are we ourselves not the indistinct mixture of pleasure and pain, slipping within the madness from one extreme to the other? The answer lies in the revelation that unveils evil for us as that which our soul loathes, and unveils our soul as that which emerges only in and by the decision to fight evil. From then on, the soul of God distinguishes itself from the Satanic soul *as the soul that is the parent of our soul,* the soul that awaits our commitment to fight Satan in order to join us in celebrating the memory of the eternal kinship of Satan's adversaries. God waits for us to "return"

Such a commitment was realized by Job when, avowing his innocence—not the innocence of his life in the past, which he doubts, but the innocence of the intention that presently engages him—he saw the ambiguity of God suddenly resolving itself on the side of benevolence in the texts on the Defender.

Here, unexpectedly, technique, human power in the world, takes on a meaning. For if evil comes from beyond the world, it encounters us within the world, the arena in which we fight it. But there is no fight without power over the world. It is necessary to find the means to combat evil in the world. Before the revelation, technique was the will to dominate the world for the purpose of coming into agreement with it. Now, after the revelation, technique is the *will to disagree* with the world. To find the means to combat evil is a task for knowledge, and hence this becomes the significance, the second exigency, of science and of every class of know-how.

On the other hand, a certain speculative practice is effectively emptied of its meaning. As speculation has lost its bearings, it must stop trying to define itself as something other than a denial, a diversion, a distraction, and a refusal to fight against evil. It is the slope on which knowledge in general slips, disoriented in a world where the Other Scene no longer surfaces.

In the capsizing of ontology and the conversion to the self-revealing Intention, a fight breaks out which mobilizes technique as a means, which challenges speculative thought for being a diversion and an accomplice to the adversary, and which must consequently raise its battle cry in a discourse of the toughest sort, the sort poorest in mundane determinations but also the most forceful, a discourse of which we take the Book of Job to be an example and which we qualify as *mysticism.* Other discourses commonly qualified as mystical often say similar things and orient the same fight. But there too, amid the great wealth of other discourses, other texts or other signs, even outside religious contexts, the same conversion to the Intention will sometimes be illuminated for the eyes of the soul engaged in the fight.

This is why we will have to seriously consider the final silence of Job: "I knew you then only by hearsay; but now having seen you with my own eyes, I retract all I have said and in dust and ashes I repent" (42.5–6). That is to say: while I knew you then only by yes-saying (and much is affirmed about you), I, in my own turn, piled speeches atop of speeches about you. As these speeches unraveled, I found you contradictory and null. Now I have seen you in the profound coherence of your Intention, and I know that in order to continue seeing this Orientation, it is up to me not to compromise your coherence by new speeches, but to tarry here silently as I render my soul homologous to your Intention. Perhaps then will all the acts of all those who have been inspired by Job's experience join up and converge with the signs of the revelation—so that the Other Scene will make an indirect appearance, by what signals it, on the scene of the world.

The "meanings" of these "signs" serve to unveil the Other Scene, and the "meaning" of the alterity of the Other Scene is: good and evil in so far as these exceed the world and orient it. The "difference" between the one scene and the other is the difference between good and evil. Any other "difference" is internal to the world, no matter what any all-too-speculative philosophy may think. And every other "meaning" is an effect of language. The positivisms then can maintain that since language is a thing of the world, the meaning that seems to fly above language actually continues to belong to the world, and that when language appears to have this alacrity and this self-evidence to the eyes of the subject who busily exchanges signs with other subjects for the sake of communication, this only marks a subjective phenomenon which the objective analysis of science very happily rethinks.

Everything changes if one defines *meaning* thus: *meaning is that which concerns a waiting soul with respect to the alternative between good and evil in excess.*

A thing has more or less meaning according to how much it impinges on the sphere of Being of good and of evil. It has meaning in so far as it is oriented toward the Other Scene, in order to rejoin it or to escape it.

The meaning of an event, of a text, of a word addressed to us, is what, in all these signs, signifies something for the good or the evil of our soul. There is no meaning, therefore, when one objectivizes words as simple media of communication between two subjects in the world. It is always *for a soul*, torn between good and evil and floating before the engaged commitment, that there is, or there is not, a meaning in a sign.

If a landscape, a work of art—to take examples that appear farthest removed from ethics—have meaning, it is for the sake of revealing a certain possibility of abandon to our soul, an open perspective of an infinity of joy in excess of the technical world, *and hence, it is for the sake of participating in the revelation of the world as a veil that hides something else.*

Thus, to non-meaning or non-sense, to the general equivalence of everything that neither *has* nor *makes* any difference, to the entropy that modernity—age of the universal advent of technique—tends to slip into, there stands opposed the meaning of good and evil as the absolute duty to fight the oblivion of evil's horror and as the commemoration of the eternal alliance in which our soul puts its trust in order to expose itself in this fight.[3]

---

[3] This is the tearing of good and evil that "makes" the difference. This,

We can henceforth secure the meaning of two passages in the Book of Job: one—which is in fact a collection of dispersed texts—usually goes unseen by commentators; the other—the celebrated "YHWH speeches"—is, on the contrary, too abundantly commented on for us not to suspect that a fundamental obstruction to interpretation lies in this very prolixity.

---

and nothing else. This is the point of departure for every effective critique of the *neutrality* that makes up the very worldhood of the world and shuts it in on itself. It is all the more necessary to stress that it is also at this point that, for us, Heidegger's thought loses its force, precisely because the doctrine of difference that is formulated by him does not seem to do justice to the most original truth in the biblical thought of Job. Emmanuel Levinas expresses it with perfect clarity, precisely apropos Heidegger: "Materialism is not in the discovery of the essential function of sensibility, but in the pre-eminence of the Neutral. To place the Neutral of Being underneath the beings which Being will somehow determine without their knowing it, to place essential events without beings knowing it—this is to profess materialism" (*Totalité et infini* [The Hague: Martinus Nijhof, 1961], p. 275). What alone delivers us from "materialism" is a thought of the Non-Neutral, that is to say, a thought of the difference between good and evil.

This difference, Heidegger would say, is "ontic" and not "ontological." It concerns beings. In so far as good and evil *are*, they are (indifferently) governed by Being. Now we have already seen that the first thought of the ontological difference, contemporary to the first thought of Being, intervened with respect to *Dasein*, which "emerges out of beings" in "transcendence," on the occasion of an encounter with evil in its madness. At the other extreme of the Heideggerian itinerary, Jean-Luc Marion in his own way notices the same deficiency in his subtle comments on the conference *Time and Being* (in *l'Idole et la distance*, pp. 294–315). Taking the relationship "of the Son to the Father in the Spirit," according to Christian theology, as an image of the relationship of man to God, he names this paradoxical relationship of extreme separation within the most extreme connection, "distance," and qualifies this distance as "difference of differences." Then in the *Ereignis*, the concept whereby Heidegger attempts to think the "gift" of Being and of time insofar as the one is appropriated to the other by this gift for humankind, Marion pinpoints traits of distance as well. Like distance, Heidegger's *Ereignis* is at once definable and not representable; like it, it is a "gift that abandons what it gives by withdrawing"

In the first passage, or group of texts, Job formulates a judgment on the attitude of the friends. As soon as Job shows, by his demarcation of the Other Scene, that he is no less knowledgeable about God than his friends are, and is at least their equal in this respect, their presumption of superiority, so essential to their technical enterprise, becomes absurd, and hence intolerable. Its *violence* suddenly shows itself, and begins to unveil the true nature of the friends' will to power, which is also technique's will to power.

"What sorry comforters you are!" (16.2). "You are only charlatans, physicians in your own estimations" (13.4). "So what sense is there in your empty consolations? What nonsense are your answers!" (21.34). "To one so weak, what help you are, [Bildad,] for the arm that is powerless what a rescuer! What excellent advice you give the unlearned, never at a loss for a helpful suggestion!" (26.2–3). "Is there never to be an end of

---

and that "discloses with insistence in this very withdrawal"; both are an "advance of absence." Marion does not deduce that the *Ereignis* and distance are identical, and even less so that *Ereignis* "is" God; Heidegger's analysis and the concept in which it culminates are only, in his view, an "icon" of distance, which allows distance to be seen only to those who seek to read something else altogether through it. What is missing in this *Ereignis* that is responsible for the fact that it can only be an *image* of the distance or difference between humans and God? It fails to be, as distance, a dimension where "praise" and "goodness" interplay. For this failure, Marion says that the *Ereignis* must be forgiven: Heidegger's analysis of Being is indeed "vain" because it is "devoid of charity." But what are charity, goodness and praise—if not words that receive their meaning from the abyss of evil, and from it alone? The ontological difference has to be exceeded not on the conceptual plain, but at a "depth," by the loving knowledge of St. Paul (1 Cor. 8.2, 13.12; Eph. 3.19), that is to say, at the price of a hermeneutic that reads the difference with "love." Which is a way of saying that love alone differs, and properly allows—with Heidegger or undoubtedly with any other thinker—a hermeneutic relation: for what does it mean to *interpret* if not to discern, to "make a difference" in a discourse between what engages one in love and what is "devoid of love," precisely where objective readings have an eye only for the identical?

airy words?" (16.3). "I wish someone would teach you to be quiet—the only wisdom that becomes you!" (13.5). "But who are they aimed at, these speeches of yours, and what spirit is this that comes out of you?" (26.4). So much for their useless technique—even if the people do believe in it: "Doubtless, you are the voice of the people, and when you die, wisdom will die with you!" (12.2). Job mocks their "wasted breath in empty words" (27.12). "Your learned maxims are proverbs of ash, your retorts, retorts of clay" (13.12).

As we know from the phenomenology of anxiety: in the face of the assaulting "armies" of darkness, words that shut things up, like those of the friends, are "retorts of clay." These words have been "learned," they have not been revealed in an encounter: they cannot save one from the excess. What is learned from the world and comes from the world is not proportionate to the danger that opens up under our feet and sunders the world apart. Their "empty consolations" "signify" just that: the vanity of all consolations of human strength when they have to confront the "void" itself; this "nothingness" is harder than "stone."

Now these magicians, duped by their own incantations, do not want to recognize this. This is why Job adjures them: "Have you never asked those that have traveled, or have you misunderstood their testimonies?" (21.29), namely the testimonies that everywhere verify the excess of madness over the enterprises that count on the Law.

They misunderstand these testimonies, effectively. Then what do they want?—Hell. For by refusing to recognize the Master, they submit themselves to the Law of their own impotence in the face of evil. Unfortunately, that only shows why they *do not* abhor evil.

Which shows why Job is no longer simply equal to the friends in his approach to the truth, but is actually superior to them. For Job abhors evil, abhors it as something horrible. Evil tells him about an Other whom the friends do not see. Therefore it is Job who is authorized, by his vision of the truth which is unveiled in this horror, to interpret the discourse of the friends, to deny its truth, and to call it *horrible*: "Why do you hound me down like God, will you never have enough of my flesh?" (19.22). "Ten times, no less, have you insulted me, ill-treating me without a trace of shame" (19.3). These vain discourses, which are oblivious to evil and incapable of doing good, nonetheless do evil, by increasing the anxiety and the dereliction of Job, as we have already indicated: "Will you ever stop tormenting me, and shattering me with speeches?" (19.2). Indeed, the friends actually augment the horror of evil and are partisan to it, since, having shown up "to pity him and to console him," they embody the living proof that human knowledge cannot save. Unjust justice is a monster, impotent medicine an abyss of iniquity. They have betrayed him moreover: "Have I said to you, 'Give me this or that, bribe someone for me at your own cost, snatch me from the clutches of an enemy, or ransom me from a tyrant's hand'?" (6.22–23), and yet, "Soon you will be casting lots for an orphan, and selling your friend at bargain prices!" (6.27). They make fun of him: "you may jeer when I have spoken" (21.3).

Worst of all, they attempt, in the name of their certainties, to suppress the salvational thought that has been given to Job. They come to cast doubts on the progress of this thought: "Fair comment can be born without resentment, but what is the basis for your strictures? Do you think mere words deserve censure, desperate speech that the wind blows away?" (6.25–26) Finally, their presence becomes intolerable, and Job must dismiss the very ones in whom he had placed his hope, as he says: "Come, I beg you, look at me . . . Relent, and grant me justice; relent, my case is not yet tried" (6.28–29). "Pity me, pity me, you, my friends!" (19.21): vain cries showing how the friends are mingled in with the rest of the world, with which they cooperate in anxiety's rampage: "Grudge pity to a neighbour, and you forsake the fear of Shaddai" (6.14).

In the same spirit of these many remarks, Job finally pronounces a few decisive words on the subject of the friends, to be confirmed in the epilogue (a matter which we nevertheless will not take up directly) when God will say that Job, unlike Eliphaz and his two companions, has "spoken truthfully about me" (42.7). These final words go well beyond those earlier remarks which were inspired by pure anger and pain, and were formulated in the style of the curses often employed by the Psalmist addressing his "adversaries." Job's new words are stronger than those curses: "May my enemy *meet a criminal's end*, and my opponent *suffer with the guilty*" (27.7).[4] Is this not a veritable legal *condemnation*, which is rather paradoxical, seeing how it comes from someone who has denounced the Law as madness?

To understand this paradox, we must again turn to Job's words. He says: "I shall not find a single sage among you" (17.10); and still more, ascribing the opposite merit to his own science, against the total ignorance of the friends: "*I am instructing you on the mastery of God*, making no secret of Shaddai's designs. And if you all had understood them for yourselves, you would not have wasted your breath in empty words" (27.11–12). They who are specialists in the mastery of the Law fail to recognize the Master of mastery. Let us for a moment consider this: "I am *instructing* you." It certainly has nothing to do with the teaching of a technique. The "science" of Job is a lightning revelation that fulminates again in this imprecation:

Kindly listen to my accusation,
  pay attention to the pleading of my lips.
Will you plead God's defense with prevarication,
  his case in terms that ring false?
Will you be partial in his favour,
  and act as his advocates?

---

[4] Cf. "Yes, God has handed me over to the *godless*, and cast me into the hands of the *wicked*" (16.11). But what Job has in mind in this last text is his entourage in general.

For you to meet his scrutiny, would this be well?
    Can he be duped as men are duped?
Harsh rebuke you would receive from him
    for your covert partiality.
Does his majesty not affright you,
    dread of him not fall on you?

                                        (13.6–11)

Job has suddenly cast off doubt. Although he is not sure what will happen with him, not knowing to what extent he will manage to do what is asked of him, he nonetheless knows by a sure science that the friends have strayed. For he ignores God, but knows his "mastery." He knows what distance God has put between himself and us, and this is what others have not measured: they have not seen the "terror" and the "majesty" of God; and when God is unpredictable, they have considered themselves capable of counting on him. Henceforth Job is the man to "instruct" them: he sees what they do not see, or rather, he sees *that* they do not see.

You, then, that mutter, "How shall we track him down,
    what pretext shall we find against him?"
may well fear the sword on your own account.
There is an anger stirred to flame by evil deeds;
    you will learn that there is indeed a judgment.

                                        (19.28–29)

Strangely enough—Job repays the friends in their own currency: the language of sin and punishment! Yet this language is equivalent only in appearance. What has taken place in the meantime, within the excess of evil, is the revelation of how the Law is derided and how the imputableness of sins really works. The friends, for their part, had not *reproached* Job. They had declared a state of affairs, the facts. They said that men have a tendency to stray, and that when they lose their way and are far removed from the Law, this constitutes an error. An unfortunate error, indeed, for the author of the straying who has to undergo suffering; nevertheless, this suffering is a simple repair in the world-machine.

Whereas here Job actually does reproach them for a *sin* of which they are *guilty* and which no repair-procedure will fix or eliminate. A sin is a distance, not from a state of affairs that one knows, but from a demand that calls you. Because the wait— the wait which the sin frustrates—comes from beyond the world, from an unidentifiable place which had opened this very wait-ing, no sin can be repaired, ever. Once committed, it is too late.

What veils the Law more than anything else, like a lie tossed over the truth of the world, is the fact that the world passes away, in accordance with time. This is why the contraction of time, time which always grows too short and appears in its very essence as a passing-away without return, is a revelation *par excellence* of the Other Scene. The Other Scene reveals itself as time's in-calculability by a Law. It is because the ex-istent's calculations never provide us with the ability to go backwards and to redo what we did not do, that we see, *par excellence*, that the world is madness. But then, if the sin of the friends is irreparable, and we point out this irreparable thing to them by way of reproach, do we not thereby reveal the Other Scene to them?

This would be the meaning of reproach. One can, in all co-herence, reproach a soul for failing to be responsible. *By such a reproach, one informs the individual of this very responsibility. One teaches him his freedom.* The paradoxical violence of Job with regard to the friends is meant to make them see, besides their sin, the fact that it was in their power not to sin to begin with. In daring to condemn the three friends for their oblivion to the horror of evil, Job executes an about-face on the oblivious indifference wherein the world annihilates itself.

The response of YHWH is particularly enigmatic—particularly if it is meant to constitute the awaited response all by itself. Yet how can that be? After questions that were so precise, considerations that were so complex, a game so subtly played among various attitudes in the face of evil, can it be that a tardy reply arrives to entangle all that had been disentangled, to annul everything that Job has said and to constrain him to silence? God shows Job the wonders of his power, puts him to shame, and would even, it seems, poke fun at the poor fellow! Given these circumstances, one understands how Elie Wiesel could compare the unexpected and coerced "retraction" of Job's "confession," too total and too quick to be sincere, to the retractions of those who were accused in the great Moscow trials.[5] They confessed, says Wiesel, so that the international community, with which they could not otherwise communicate, would be surprised by their attitude, would reflect on it and come to uncover the truth. They confessed in order to better disavow. Precisely by surrendering, they continued the struggle under a most radical form. Similarly, the retraction of Job would be a signal sent from the very interior of the Bible warning us not to extend God too much credit and not to acquit him of his infinite ruses.

We can understand why a certain theology, on the other hand, remains satisfied with the outcome. The last word belongs to God, and it is Job himself who acknowledges his openly atheistic arguments to be invalid. Hence the invalidation is perfect. Nevertheless that the last word should belong to God is

---

[5] Elie Wiesel, "Job ou le silence révolutionnaire," *Célébration biblique* (Paris: Seuil, 1975), pp. 181–98.

something that Job would never have opposed; far from it, what he embraced as his express hope is that God, himself and in person, should advance and speak. Let us therefore evaluate its success. What does God say? Or rather: what does the anonymous author make God say, what commentary and what conclusion does he make God tote for him in his literary work? For the author, if we have read him properly, has *already* made God speak, *before* chapters 38–41, or has shown how God "speaks"—precisely by his questioning silence, in the excess of his wickedness. It is on the basis of a reply already given and a theophany already transpired that the final theophany emerges "from the midst of the whirlwind" as a new question.

God summons his astonishing power. God has created Behemoth and Leviathan, and many other wonders, which, as he underlines with a rather heavy irony, Job will never dominate. But we already know that the world is not inhabited by fantastical animals alone. The Law itself and the world itself as Law number among such monsters, monsters whose power God renders derisory as he teaches Job that it is God who intentionally set them loose on Job in order to upset the man's dream of solitary power and to restore for Job the memory of God.

To say to Job that the world will forever remain incomprehensible for him is God's way of confirming that human beings must wait out the madness of the world, wait for the One for whom this madness is a project.

We understand the meaning of Job's retraction then:

> I know that you are all-powerful:
> what you conceive, you can perform.
> I am the man who obscured your designs
> with my empty-headed words.
> . . . .
>
> I knew you then only by hearsay;
> but now, having seen you with my own eyes,

I retract all I have said,
    and in dust and ashes I repent.

(42.2–3, 5–6)

The reality of the world is the sign of God's project. But for our soul, this project—and for us, our soul itself—remains an enigma. It is again up to us not to obfuscate the Intention by shutting closed the space of the enigma within us, in other words, by refusing to put our soul at stake. *This opacification of the revelation is what Job retracts*: he does not regret having accused God, or having rebelled against God's cruelty, he does not even regret having counted his sins for nothing. On the contrary, these various sacrileges are responsible for having put him on the path of the Intention, and in having set them forth, he replied to the One who sought him. It is not these that Job retracts, therefore, but something else in his discourse that too often resembled the senseless remarks made by the friends, the remarks that, properly speaking, lacked *sense*: what resembled these remarks too well were the replies he made to *them*, the justification which engaged him in *their* presence. He repents of having spoken with them in their language, the language of the world, instead of reserving his energies for the dialogue between his soul's intention and the Intention of the Other Soul, a dialogue that is not a matter for speculation in this world here, but that takes place in the secret of souls, between silence and struggle.

Eschatology

We are condemned to endure and suffer the horror, not simply until we know beatitude—succession of times, wheel that turns absurdly, neutral time—but so that we may demand a response commensurate with the absurdity of the horror: an eschatological response, which is to say, a response that brings everything together.

A happiness that comes of a chance encounter—neutral—cannot put an end to a suffering not encountered by chance. Only the encounter of encounters can do that, the encounter of the Intention that has wanted every encounter as it has had a project concerning our soul. It wanted our beatitude and wanted us to know that we would receive this beatitude from it as a gift at the end of times, as a gift of the end of time.

Hence, it seems to me, that objection must fall away which says that the duty to fight—the Law—interposes itself between our soul and its beatitude. According to this objection, which is really quite a powerful one, beatitude in its own turn would be the result of an act—the fight against evil—implemented with a view to beatitude. And so we would still have failed to exit technique. We would have to accord ourselves with a Law. And as the fight against evil causes us to suffer evils, we would again be confronted with a ruse of the world, the eternity of evil, with which we would accord ourselves by means of our philosophy of evil, presumably after being duly "corrected" by it in the way Eliphaz thought Job would be. This philosophy would conquer us, and only resentment could be speaking in the kinds of argument Job put forward. Obviously, technique proper is better adapted to this end, choosing and adapting its means by scientific practices, in comparison with the unavowed technique which can only imagine an Other-than-the-world as a means to conquering evil.

But the objection does not stand, as we say, because, for Job, it is not at all a matter of conquering the evil that oppresses him, or even evil in general; evil is not the horizon of his soul's fight. His soul, within this fight, and while he is engaged in it, sees beyond. It is a matter of returning to the memory of God, in order to know everything, understand everything, resolve everything. His soul does not want, negatively, to stop suffering the horror; it waits to "see" God, "in the flesh," in order, positively, to enjoy God.

Technique aims at an end by way of a means. It conceives this end in the same moment that it puts the means to work. Technical thought is nothing other than the thought of the means and the end, how the one emerges from the other, how the one is linked to the other in the space of one world. The will, proffering itself as a means, simply envisions obtaining what it lacks in the end. It does not aim further than that. A thing of the world, having its place in the full world, it has the fullness of the world for its last horizon.

But evil, as it conquers the will and becomes its Master, points to the Other-than-the-world, by contrast with which the world vacillates and appears fractured. In that moment, the horizon ceases to be the full world; it has become the Other-than-the-world. Even if the world was replenished, even if the fracture was repaired, even so, the Other-than-the-world appears, and the soul retains a lasting impression of it. The soul henceforth will never get enough of the seeing which sees all things, including the world, from the height of the Other-than-the-world, in other words, under the eye of God's soul.

The fight against evil in which our soul is engaged from then on does not implement means to ends, not in any technical manner, for there is an absolute incommensurableness between the means put into play and the end which is eschatologically awaited. Henceforth, the soul knows that the end at which it aims, the beatific encounter with God, infinitely surpasses what it aims at. The soul will have more than it waits for. What it waits for is that its waiting should be infinitely exceeded. It cannot think, in a single thought, both the means which it implements—the fight—and the end—the beatitude. It knows that whatever will happen will be given to it by the Master, and that it cannot so much as want it. If the soul received what it waited for, the wait, necessarily, would be disappointed. If it could produce beatitude by its works, this would not be beatitude. It has learnt to be eternally disappointed by its own works. It has unlearned to wait for something that it itself draws from itself.

Any end that it would obtain in this way would not quench the thirst breathed into it by the horror. Only the beatitude that comes from the Master, from eternity destined by God for the soul, will be commensurable with the horror, by an immeasurable measure. Only the excess *of beatitude will be consonant with the excess of evil. It will be up to God not only to obliterate the given evil, but to show himself, by the beatitude given in the excess, in the same measure as the immeasurable excess of evil.*

The one capable of horrifying the soul with the—ineffaceable— excess of evil that he sends it, God, would be going back on his decision, would be failing in what we now know about God and what we will not forget, if he did not grant beatitude with the same profusion, the same madness, the same excess, the same unprecedented and unpredictable manner. God, in revealing himself to be infinitely wicked, is engaged and committed. *God has shown what is excessive about his divinity. In every simple, measured, relative, awaited joy that might now betake us, we would no longer recognize God. We would know with certainty that any pleasure which simply effaces sorrow does not come from God. We will acknowledge God only if God surprises us infinitely by a profusion of beatitude. God is engaged and committed; and in this sense we have a hold on him, not as if God were at our beck and call like a being we cipher out and decipher; we have a hold on God by virtue of his own promise. We have seen God; God is accountable to the memory that we have of him.*

This excess in the gift is the definitive lesson that the horror has taught the soul, in the same moment that it revealed the soul itself as what is in excess of the world and what does not belong to it. The soul will henceforth maintain that everything comes from Elsewhere. It will acquire a predilection for receiving. Every question to which it, and it alone, will respond will

remain for it, in effect, without response. This is why, by allowing itself to acquire a taste for excess, it comes to find measure
distasteful. Measure never saves. Philosophy does not save, as it
knows how to reply to questions that it itself poses. As for
eschatology, it is the confession of the excess of the gift: it opens
itself up to the soul when the souls remembers that an initial
question had always already been posed to it from Elsewhere,
by the touch of the horror, and that the reply must come from
Elsewhere as well, therefore, if it is to be commensurable with
the question, if it is to be a true reply.

Thus, Job here does not (re)discover a technique to which we
would be eternally captive. He does not invent a new technique,
one based on a different plan (a plan more, or less, efficient?). He
confesses that both the question and the response are given by
God. But this too he does not dis-cover, as we have seen, except
in so far as it clears an open field in his soul to the horror of evil.
He is saved therefore by grace and by his works, just like it says
in the tradition which this alternative has torn. Perhaps the
alternative would be less obscure if one did not speak of works,
if one articulated instead, in the singular, the proper work of the
soul: commitment to the good fight. This work whereby the soul
liberates itself from the Law and creates itself as soul is indeed
a necessary condition for grace to find someone upon whom to
bestow beatitude in profusion. It is here that we find what we
call the "wait" of God. For, the fact that this work is necessary is
already an appropriate image of excess: it is excessive, indeed it
is mad, that God should need us in order to save us.

This is quite consistent with the madness of evil, this idea
that God is weak, that God too awaits our return in order to
truly enjoy himself. Could the separation be less heavy on God,
God who is a soul, than on us? In what God reveals to us of
Himself, nothing militates against the idea that, following our
own example, God is currently as if in hell—until we free God
from hell by surrendering to God. Does Job not know (and of
God he knows nothing else) that the soul of God is related to his

own? The paradoxical idea of God's suffering, that too, is commensurable with what is given here for thinking. Our soul likes to think that the soul of God, seeking our soul, suffers hell, like our soul, in this anxious wait. Anxious, because it does not know if our soul is going to surrender to God.

Indeed, why not evoke the anxiety of God? Was it not necessary for God to know anxiety in order for God to think of allotting it to humankind? And in the questions that Job posed to God on account of the scandal, was Job not anxious for God? How can it be, he wondered, that You who are so great, so powerful, take shade from my deeds and gestures; if not because You suffer? If You actually enjoyed the infinite beatitude that one imagines You to enjoy, You would not think of torturing me. Just so, when Job decided to have a pure heart, it was to save God from his own wickedness which encloses God in hell.

God knows dereliction, indecision. God burns to encounter us, we who are His go'el, rising up on the earth for Him. We are God's dream, just as God is our dream. God, like us, must traverse the nada.

In the very ignominy of God, Job has perceived His utter impotence, hence His humanity, hence our divinity. *It is precisely this that the three friends did not understand and that every kind of idolatry is supposed to cover up. It is the "touch" of God. This is what saves us from every kind of hell.*

Such is the Revelation given to Job by the excess of evil, and it is because of it that the Book of Job is truly the Word of God.

Appendixes

Postface: Transcendence and Evil

Emmanuel Levinas

> . . . I establish peace and I am the author of evil,
> I the Eternal do all this.
> —Isaiah 45.7

1. Thought and Transcendence

The attempt to cast doubt on the very significance of words like "transcendence" and "beyond" attests to their semantic consistency, since, at least in this critical discourse that concerns them, we recognize what it is that we are contesting. The reduction of the absolute meaning of these terms to a *transcendence* and a *beyond* which are relative, but which are taken to the furthest and highest pitch by the force of who knows what impulse, already interjects *transcendence* and the *beyond* into this superlative, or gives a transcendent power to some of our

---

This book review first appeared as "Transcendance et Mal" in *Le Nouveau Commerce* 11 (1978) 55–75; it reappeared in *De Dieu qui vient a l'idée* (Paris: Vrin, 1982), pp. 189–207. I have gratefully consulted the previous English translation made by Alphonso Lingis in Levinas's *Collected Philosophical Papers* (Boston: Kluwer, 1987), pp. 175–86.—Tr.

psychological forces. And nevertheless, is something not missing in the intelligibility of these notions if they are to become veritably thought? The problem is that in our philosophical tradition the veritable thought is a true thought, a knowing, a thought referred to Being—to Being designating a being, but also to Being understood as a verb, as expressing the accomplishment of the task or the destiny of Being by beings, without which we could not recognize beings as beings.

In distinguishing idea from concept, reason from understanding, Kant was certainly the first to separate thought from knowing, and to thereby discover meanings that do not rejoin Being, or, to be more exact, meanings that cannot be subsumed under the categories of the understanding, and cannot be subsumed under reality, which is in fact correlative with these categories. But this thought which is distant from Being, and which, nonetheless, cannot be reduced to meaninglessness, is still understood by Kant as being empty of the things-in-themselves that it aims at. It still measures itself against the Being that it lacks. Ideas thus have a dialectical status, in the pejorative sense that Kant confers upon this adjective; the transcendental illusion that plays within this thought is the drama of an aspiration after Being. It is always as if the appearing, and the knowledge, of Being were equivalent to rationality and "spirit"; as if the signification of sense—intelligibility—were due to the manifestation of Being, were ontology, be it only in the guise of intentionality: of a will, or a nostalgia, for Being. Through these novel developments in ontology, to be sure, Kant braved a more radical distinction between thought and knowing. In the practical application of pure reason, he discovers an intrigue that is irreducible to a reference to Being. A good will, utopian in a sense, deaf to any information, indifferent to any confirmation (important for technique and the hypothetical imperative, but of not concern to practice or the categorical imperative) which could come to it from Being, proceeds from a freedom situated above Being and on this side of knowing and ignorance. And yet, after an instant of separation, the relation with ontology reestablishes itself within the "postulates of pure reason," as if it were anticipated on the scene of all these audacities: in their own fashion, ideas rejoin Being in the existence of God who guarantees either, according to the letter of critical philosophy, the agreement between virtue and happiness, or, according to Herman Cohen's reading, the agreement between freedom and nature and the efficacy of a practice decided upon without knowledge. The absolute existence of the Ideal of pure reason, the existence of the Supreme Being, is what matters in the end in an architecture where the concept of freedom alone was supposed to be the keystone.

This capacity of the idea to equal the given, or its obligation to justify its emptiness, this susceptibility of referring itself to Being—perhaps in a fashion that is other than intuitive, but always to Being—this necessity for thought to belong to knowledge, does it remain the measure of all intelligibility? Is the thought that proceeds toward God constrained to this measure under pain of otherwise being taken for a thought in its last quarter, a privation of knowing? Can we not show that, far from being restricted to a pure refusal of the norms of knowing, the thought that proceeds toward God—and proceeds thither otherwise than toward that which is thematized—consists of modalities that are psychic and originary, beyond those demanded by a world of laws without play, with its relations of reciprocity and compensation and its identifications of differences; modalities of the disturbance of the Same by the Other, modalities proper to and original to the *toward-God*, where the ontological adventure of the soul is interrupted, where the idea of Being is *eclipsed* by the Glory (and is perhaps precisely demoted, in God, to the rank of a simple attribute), and where, in dis-inter-*est-edness*, the alternative between the real and the illusory is blurred?

2. TRANSCENDENCE AND PHENOMENOLOGY

How and where in the psychism of experience is the major rupture produced capable of substantiating an *other* as irreducibly *other*, and, in this sense, as a *beyond*—given that every tearing in the tissue of the thematized thinkable conserves or re-knots the thread of the Same? How can a thought proceed *beyond* the world which is precisely the way in which the Being that it thinks is assembled—whatever the heterogeneity of its elements and the variety of its modes of Being may be? How can the transcendent signify "the wholly other," even if it is easy enough to say it, seeing how the common ground of the thinkable and of discourse restore it to the world and restore it as a world? It is not enough that, in the thinkable, a difference becomes more pronounced or a contradiction is unlocked which opens up an interval commensurate with transcendence, or even a nothingness before which the dialectical and logical resources of thought exhaust themselves to the point of impotence. How can a *nothingness* take on a meaning which would not be merely the negation of negation, "conserving" (*aufhebend*) the Being that it repudiates? How can the difference of an alterity that does not rest on some common ground take on meaning?

I think that, on these two points, Husserl's phenomenology has opened new possibilities. It affirms the rigorous solidarity between every intelligible and the psychic modalities *by* which and *within* which the intelligible is thought: it is not the case that any meaning whatsoever is accessible to any thought whatsoever. To be sure, these psychic modalities have intentional implications—repressed or forgotten intentions—but they are irreducible essences, *origins* (whatever the reductive ambitions of the phenomenology called "genetic" may be). Husserl's phenomenology is, in the end, an *eidetic of pure consciousness*. On the one hand, it is a confidence in the idea of the irreducible structure of the psyche, irreducible to any mathematical or logical order, of an irreducibility, more original than all mathematics and all logic, that therefore can only be described: phenomenology is the idea of psychic essences which do not constitute a "definite multiplicity" (*definite Mannigfaltigkeit*). On the other hand, what animates these irreducible thoughts is phenomenology's reference of meaning to the giving of meaning—to *Sinngebung*. With this, phenomenology has disciplined us to resist explicating a meaning in such a way that it is thought uniquely or principally in terms of its relations to other objective meanings, lest all meaning is relativized and all signification is enclosed in the *system* without egress. Phenomenology has taught us to explicate, or to elucidate, a meaning in terms of the *irreducible psychism* wherein it is given, to thus seek meaning in its origin, to seek originary meaning. This method, which emerges from a philosophy of arithmetic and from logical investigations, thus affirms the primacy—the principality— of the nonformal!

From this perspective, we can appreciate the novelty of Heidegger's approach, which, for example, arrives at nothingness by way of anxiety, lived anxiety, a modality of the psyche leading further than negation. But it is also for the notions of the *other* and of a difference-without-common-ground, that contemporary thought seems equally indebted to a Heideggerian concept developed from anxiety, namely the concept of the *ontological difference*: the difference between Being and beings presupposes no common ground other than the paper on which the words designating them are written, or the air in which the sounds that serve to pronounce them vibrates. The difference between Being and beings is *difference itself*. It should not be surprising, then, that it exerts a fascination upon philosophers, who, after Nietzsche's word on the death of God—and outside all ontotheology—still dare to take an interest in the sense of transcendence, guided, undoubtedly, by the conviction that the domain of *meaning* is not limited to that of the *seriousness* of science and the labours devoted to thematizing Being, nor to that of the *playfulness* of the pleasures and the arts which evades Being but, preserving its memory, delights in its images and involves putting up stakes.

We may certainly wonder whether Being, in the verbal sense Heidegger gives it, Being transcending beings, but also giving itself to all beings, remains beyond the world which it renders possible, and whether it allows us to think a transcendent God beyond Being; we may wonder whether the neutrality that proffers itself in the *thought of Being* transcending *beings* can be suitable and sufficient for divine transcendence. But the fact remains that the *ontological difference* serves philosophers as a model of transcendence, and that, even when it is repudiated in investigations that belong to religious thought, it is often invoked. It is enough for us to recall here the profound and subtle essay of Jean-Luc Marion on the divinity of God.[1] A courageous attempt at penetration, an attempt, still isolated among philosophers, to no longer understand God primordially from Being. Even as he recognizes his debt to Heidegger, and even as he fixes his own itinerary by exploring Heideggerian paths, the author places himself in the end "at a distance from the ontological difference."[2]

It is with the same attention given to transcendence and from a certain modality of the psyche—a certain noteworthy "experience"—which interrupts the world (even if psychology, as a science, that is, as a thematization, recovers from this interruption, and always has its recovery period, and takes this interrupting phenomenon to be a psychological state among others,[3] accessible to theory and to treatment), that another

---

[1] *L'Idole et la distance* (*op. cit.*).

[2] Ibid., p. 214.

[3] An interpretation which cannot be dismissed forever; through it, the thematization and the discourse of science are superimposed on every rupture and put transcendence back into question. Without preventing the return of the lived and of the interrupting sense. Can transcendence have more than an ambiguous sense for someone modern? But it is the same with the world. Cf. the lines that end the present essay.

young thinker, Philippe Nemo, recently has written a book on evil as Job knew it. An exegesis of a biblical text. There once again, the *ontological difference* seems to have been the major encouragement. But it is a description of the lived, of experience, as this is ratified by the phenomenon, even if it is suggested by the verses of the book commented upon. The rupture of the Same is there approached from the vantage of a psychic content endowed with an exceptional significance; whatever extreme it involves is investigated not in some superlative, but in the simple given of an experience. We would very much like to exploit this phenomenology and to judge it for itself while forgetting the exegetical intentions from which it emerges, and this, despite the great finesse and the great scrupulousness of this latter hermeneutic. But we do not intend here to take a position on the truth of the ultimate significance that it attributes to the Book of Job. The philosophical language employed by the author to which we are responding seems perfectly justified by the philosophical perspective that is opened up by this work, which itself is not an exercise in piety.

3. The Excess of Evil

In order to describe evil as it must have been lived in the suffering of Job, Philippe Nemo begins by insisting on anxiety as the underlying event. In agreement with Heidegger, anxiety is interpreted as a disclosure of nothingness, as being-toward-death, as the fact of a world that sneaks away and isolates man, and the fact of a human being who closes himself off to words of consolation that still belong to the resources of this sneaking world.

Anxiety thus comprehended cannot be taken for a simple "state of the soul," "a form of moral affectivity," a simple consciousness of finitude or a moral symptom preceding, accompanying, or following a pain which we, no doubt too lightly, call physical. Anxiety is the sharp point at the heart of evil. Illness, evils plaguing the living flesh, flesh that ages, decays, withers and rots, these would be the modalities of anxiety itself. Through them and in them, dying is, as it were, lived, and the truth of this death is unforgettable, unimpeachable, irremisible. In the impossibility of dissimulating it for ourselves, we find nondissimulation itself, and perhaps disclosure and truth par excellence, the of-itself-open, the original insomnia of Being; a gnawing away of human identity, which is not an inviolable spirit burdened with a perishable body, but *incarnation*, in all the gravity of an identity which mutates in itself. Here, we still have not reached, or we are already beyond, the Cartesian dualism of thought and extension in man. The taste and the odour of putrefaction is not added here to the spirituality of a tragic knowing, to a presentiment or to some prevision, howbeit desperate, of death. Despair despairs like pain in the flesh. Physical evil is the very depth of anxiety, whence— Philippe Nemo demonstrates by means of the verses of Job— anxiety, in its carnal acuity, is the root of all social miseries, of all human dereliction: of humiliation, of solitude, of persecution.

But this conjunction of evil and anxiety does not receive, in the analysis offered to us, the sense to which the philosophers of existence have accustomed us, the model of which Heidegger—at least the Heidegger of *Sein und Zeit*—has traced with the neatest lines. There, what is taken to be essential to anxiety consists in an opening of the horizon of nothingness, more radically negative than that of negation, incapable of making one forget the Being that it rejects. The death understood by anxiety announced itself as pure nothingness. What seems to us the strongest and most novel element of Nemo's book is the discovery of another dimension of meaning in the conjunction of anxiety and evil. Evil will certainly signify an "end" of the world, but an end which, in a very significant manner, leads beyond; elsewhere than to Being, to be sure, but elsewhere than to nothingness as well, to a *beyond* conceived neither by negation nor by the anxiety of the philosophers of existence; evil is neither a mode nor a species, nor yet some consummation of negation. Why, then, this insistence on anxiety at the heart of evil? We shall return to this question.

In its evil malice, evil is excess. Whereas the notion of excess straightaway evokes the quantitative idea of intensity, of its own degree surpassing all measure, evil is excess in its very quiddity. A very important notation: evil is not an excess because suffering can be heavy, and thus go beyond what can be borne. The break with the normal and the normative, with order, with synthesis, with the world, already constitutes its qualitative essence. Suffering as such is only a concrete and quasi-sensible manifestation of the non-integratable, of the non-justifiable. The "quality" of evil is this very *non-integratability*, if we may use such a term: this concrete quality is defined by this abstract notion. Evil is not just the non-integratable, it is also the non-integratability of the non-integratable. As if, to synthesis—even the purely formal synthesis of Kant's "I think" which is capable of reuniting *data*, as heterogeneous as they may be—there stands opposed, under the species of evil, the non-synthesizable, more heterogeneous still than every heterogeneity subject to being embraced by the formal which exposes heterogeneity in its very malice. As if Bergson's teaching in *Evolution Créatrice* regarding disorder as another form of order were contradicted by evil, an irreducible disturbance. What is very much noteworthy here is that what is purely quantitative in the notion of excess shows itself in the guise of a qualitative content characteristic of the malice of evil, as quiddity of the phenomenon. In evil's appearing, in its original phenomenality, in its *quality*, there is announced a *modality*, a manner: the not-finding-a-place, the refusal to be comfortable with . . ., a counter-nature, a monstrosity, the of-itself disturbing and alien. *And in this sense, transcendence!* The intuition which consists in perceiving, in the pure quality of a phenomenon like evil, the *how* of the rupture in immanence is an insight that appears as intellectually rich to us as the discovery of intentionality or the dazzling pages in *Sein und Zeit* on *Zuhandenheit* and *Stimmung* appeared in the beginnings of phenomenology. But these are personal impressions, perhaps, belonging strictly to a short and anecdotal history of phenomenology!

The exteriority or the transcendence in evil does not receive its meaning by opposition to psychic "interiority," does not borrow it from some prior correlation of exteriority and interiority, which would make possible the illusion of multiple background-worlds still accumulating in the same space. It is in the *excess* of *evil* that the preposition *ex* signifies, in its original sense, excession itself, the *ex* of all exteriority. No categorical *form* could invest it, could retain it, in its frame. The "wholly other," beyond the community of the common, is no longer a simple word! It is the *other* "other scene," as Philippe Nemo calls it, since it is more alien to the consciousness of being-in-the-world than the scene of the unconscious—which is "other" simply—a withdrawal of alterity that is provisional and that psychoanalysis knows to unpack in the world.

That transcendence should be the unjustifiable, with the malice of evil as its concrete event, is perhaps all that the fatuous theodicy of Job's friends signifies. Their idea of justice would proceed from a morality of recompense and punishment, from a certain order of the world, one already technological. Moreover, is not every attempt at theodicy a way of thinking God as the reality of the world?

Does not the evil wherein Philippe Nemo perceives anxiety have its significance of excess and of transcendence independently of such attempts? Does evil not obtain this significance through the unjustifiable, which is the malice of evil, through the resistance that it puts up against theodicy, rather than through its being-toward-death which anxiety anticipates? This is something we have already asked ourselves. But is it certain, after all, that the essence of death which is accomplished in anxiety must be thought, according to the description of *Sein und Zeit*, as nothingness? Does the secret concerning death not phenomenologically inhere within death? And is the anxiety of dying not a modality, the anticipated sharp point, of suffering, rather than the solution to the dilemma: to be or not to be?[4]

4. THE YOU

The content of evil is not exhausted by the notion of excess. Guided by the exegesis—but claiming to have an intrinsic significance—the analysis, *in its second moment*, discovers in evil an "intention": evil reaches me as if it sought me out, evil strikes at me as if there were a motive behind the bad fortune that pursues me, "as if someone were hounding me," as if there were malice, as if there were someone. Evil, of itself, would be an "aiming at me." It would reach me in a wound wherein a meaning arises and a *saying* is articulated which recognizes this someone who is revealed in this way. "Why do *you* make *me* suffer, why do you not reserve an eternal beatitude for me instead?" A first saying, a first question or lamentation, or a first prayer. In any case, a calling out to a You and a glimpse of the Good behind Evil. A first "intentionality" of transcendence: someone is seeking me. A God who hurts and causes evil, but God as a You. And, through the hurt within me, my awakening to myself. "Awakening of the soul in the excess of evil," says Nemo. From its state of subjectivity in the world—from its being-in-the-world—the I is awakened to the condition of the soul that calls out to God. This idea of suffering as persecution, and of election within persecution, and of the setting apart and the distinction through pain, is of course not an idea coming from a

---

[4] Cf. Our attempt at phenomenology in this regard in *Le temps et l'autre* which appeared in the collection, *Le Choix, le Monde, l'Existence* (Arthaud, 1948), reprinted in a single volume (Montpellier: Fata Morgana).

phenomenology that is as communicable, or as universal, as that of the excess in evil; we have reason to think that it is not inspired by the particularities of the Book of Job alone.

That the original "intentionality" of the relation between Beings is a relationship with God, that it comes from God, that this relationship cannot be described in a neutral and formal manner, that it is instantly qualified as a "hurting me," or "doing evil to me," as the malice within the dark paradox of God's wickedness, that the original—that the principle—is neither the general nor the formal, but *the concrete and the determined* (not to be taken in an empirical sense), is something striking enough here, and continues to conform to the spirit of the analysis which knew how to discover the transcendence and the excess in the concreteness of evil. But then, by the same token, the "element" in which "first philosophy" moves about is no longer the impersonal, the anonymous, the indifferent, the neutral unfolding of Being problematized, even within the humanity that it envelops, as a world of things and of laws, or as a world of rocks, a world supporting every intervention, and as susceptible of *satis*-fying every conceivable desire by the implementation of technique. Technique assumes only the lawfulness of things, their being equal to our desires, and the ruse of thought. The first metaphysical question is no longer Leibniz's "Why is there something rather than nothing?" but "Why is there evil rather than good?"[5] This is the de-neutralization of Being, or of the beyond-Being. The ontological difference is preceded by the difference between good and evil. *Difference itself* is the latter one, it is the origin of the meaningful: "Meaning is that which concerns a waiting soul with respect to the alternative between good and evil in excess".[6] Meaning therefore begins in the soul's relation to God and from its being awakened

---

[5] *Supra*, p. 104.
[6] *Supra*, p. 146.

by evil. God hurts me and does evil to me in order to uproot me from the world and hold me up as unique and exceptional: as a soul. Meaning implies this transcendent relation, "the alterity of the Other Scene" which is no longer a negative concept. "The 'meaning' of the alterity of the Other Scene," writes Nemo, "is: good and evil in so far as these exceed the world and orient it. The 'difference' between the one scene and the other is the difference between good and evil. Any other 'difference' is internal to the world".[7]

A priority of ethics in relation to ontology, we would say, although Philippe Nemo might not like this formula to qualify his path. In fact, despite a notion of difference that is not ontological, the discovery of the You to whom one calls from within evil is interpreted by a recourse to Being: "God who appears in the You has for his Being: being a You." The You in God is not an "otherwise than Being," but a "being otherwise." The reflection on the You does not risk going so far as to think a beyond-Being in the You. It subordinates itself to ontology, recoiling from the supreme infidelity to the philosophy handed down to us, which says beings and the Being of beings are the ultimate sources of sense. To maintain ourselves in relation to the You that in God *eclipses* Being, would be interpreted pejoratively as a manner of complacency with illusion. We do not dare to think[8] that the human psyche in its relation to God ventures as far as significations of the beyond of Being and nothingness, beyond reality and illusion, as far as dis-inter-*estedness*.[9]

---

[7] *Supra*, p. 145.

[8] Such "audacity" is also lacking in Buber, for whom the discovery of the I-You relation at once appears like a new mode of Being—the You of God being only a more intense way of being, the divinity of God thus being lost in the You's mode of existence which would be the final sense of its epiphany, as it is of the unveiled world.

[9] Nemo would not like the formula "ethics precedes ontology" for yet another reason. He identifies the ethical—like almost all philosophical literature of our day—with the Law (which is its consequence), while the

5. THEOPHANY

Evil as excess, evil as intention—there is also a third moment within this phenomenology: evil as hatred of evil. A final inversion in the analysis: evil hits me within my horror at evil and thus reveals—or already is—my association with the Good. The excess of evil, whereby it is a surplus of the world, is also the impossibility of our agreeing with it. The experience of evil therefore would be also our waiting for the good—the love of God.

This inversion of evil and of the horror at evil into a waiting for the Good, for God and for a beatitude in measure or incommensurate with the excess of evil, as expounded in the final pages of this book which is so beautiful and suggestive, raises many questions. This horror at evil, in which evil, paradoxically, is given—is that the Good? There can be no question here of a passage from Evil to Good by an attraction of opposites. That would be just one more theodicy. Doesn't the philosophical contribution of all this biblical exegesis consist in being able to go as if beyond the reciprocal entreaty of terms that negate each other, beyond dialectics? Precisely evil is not some sort of negation. It signifies ex-cess, refusing every synthesis where the utter alterity of God comes to show itself. For Nemo, the Nietzschean warning against the spirit of resentment also is present. He would not want, as the sole result of his hermeneutic, a good that would only signify a compensation for evil or a vengeance, which moreover would also be equivalent to a

---

evil which awakens us to the You of God would be precisely a challenge to the Law and to the technical spirit which, for Nemo, is bound up with it: the morality of the Law would for him be only a technique for securing recompenses and avoiding punishments. We think that, primordially, ethics signifies an obligation before the Other, that it leads us to the Law and to the voluntary service which is not a principle of technique. [The possible French noun *essement* alludes to the Latin verb *esse*, so that *des-inter-essement* would mean both "disinterestedness" and "going beyond being."—Tr.]

return of the technical spirit to the suffering of evil. Whence, in the description of the wait for the Good, the formulation, to our mind very profound, of a thought which would think more than what it thinks. "The soul," writes Nemo, "knows henceforth that the end at which it aims, the beatific encounter with God, infinitely surpasses what it aims at".[10] The soul which, awakened by evil, finds itself standing in relation to the beyond of the world does not regain the structure of a being-in-the-world, an empirical or transcendental consciousness *equal* to its objects, *adequate* to Being, equal to the world, in its desires promised to *satis*-faction. The soul beyond satisfaction and beyond recompense waits for an awaited that infinitely surpasses the waiting. This is undoubtedly the "psychic modality" of transcendence and the very definition of the religious soul, and such that it would not be a simple specification of consciousness. The notion of a "game" which, by contrast with technique, designates for our author the relation of the soul with God is not reduced nevertheless from this disproportion between the wait and the awaited. "Only the excess of beatitude," he writes, "will respond to the excess of evil." Now it is not certain that excess has the same meaning in the two halves of this proposition. The excess of evil does not signify an excessive evil, with the excess of beatitude remaining a superlative notion. If it were in fact necessary to already see an excess in beatitude as such, evil would not have been able to possess the privileged significance around which Nemo's entire book is constructed. Transcendence could pursue less tortuous paths.

This movement that leads from the "horror at evil" to the discovery of the Good, and that thereby achieves, in a theophany, the transcendence that is opened up in the totality of the world by the concrete "content" of evil—does it merely lead to the opposite of evil, to a goodness of simple pleasure

---

[10] *Supra*, p. 158.

howbeit great? Does not the Good awaited in this "wait which aims at infinitely more than this awaited" maintain a less distant relationship with the evil that suggests it, while differing from it by a difference more different than opposition? One is surprised in reading this commentary on the Book of Job, so mindful of the lines of the text and of what is between the lines, of the said and of the unsaid, so refined in ear and intelligence to notice, that the problem of the relationship between the suffering of the I and the suffering that an I can feel of the suffering of another human being never appears in the *foreground*. Even if we could suppose that in this biblical text itself there is never any question of that, would there not be in this very silence some secret indication? And is there really no question of that? Does the "Where were you when I laid the foundations of the earth?" of verse 38.4, at the opening of the speech attributed to God, where Job is reminded of his absence during the hour of Creation, merely reprimand the impudence of a creature who allows himself to judge the Creator? Does it merely expound a theodicy in which the economy of a harmoniously and wisely constructed whole houses evil with a regard limited to a part of this whole? Can we not understand this "Where were you?" as a record of truancy, which can only make sense if the humanity of the human being stands in fraternal solidarity with Creation, that is to say, if man is responsible for what was neither his I nor his work, and if this solidarity and this responsibility for everything and for everyone—which is impossible without pain—is spirit itself?

We shall not propose "improvements" to Philippe Nemo, whose thought is so personal, so new and so ripe. Rather, it is in the context of his thought that we find singularly illuminated an idea which is familiar and dear to us, which is often repeated and with which we would like to affiliate what it is about the ways of transcendence that his book throws light upon, and the manner in which this light is thrown. The manner is that of turning to a "material datum" of consciousness, to a "concrete content," rather than that of reflection on some "formal structure." Thus we find signified a "beyond" transcending the closed dimensions which are delineated by the judicatory operations of the intellect and which the forms of logic reflect.[11] It is in the same way, in fact, that transcendence seemed to us to shine in the face of the other person: alterity of the non-integrateable, of that which does not let itself be gathered into a totality, or which, being in an assembly—barring its being handed over to violence and powers—still constitutes a society and enters into it as a face. A transcendence that is no longer absorbed by my knowledge. The face puts into question the adequacy and complacency of my identity as I, it constrains to an infinite responsibility with respect to the other. An original transcendence that signifies in the *concrete* of the face, the concrete that is *right away ethical*. That the evil suffered by another person afflicts me in the evil that pursues me, that it touches me, as if the other person were calling out to me right there and then, putting into question my *relying upon myself* and my *connatus essendi*, as if before my lamenting over my woes here below, I have to answer for the other—*is it not this that is a breach of the Good into evil, into the "intention" that targets me so exclusively in my woe?* Theophany. Revelation. The horror at the evil that aims at me becomes the horror at the evil besetting the other person. A breach of the Good that is not a simple inversion of Evil, but is an elevation. A Good which

---

[11] These dimensions, according to Husserl's lessons reproduced in *Erfahrung und Urteil* (Hamburg: F. Meiner, 1972), begin with the *position* of an individual substrate wrested from the background of the world, a substrate exposed to the "passive syntheses" of ex-plication and "modalization" of belief where this position is found. These syntheses are then resumed in the *categorical activity* of judgment proper. They are the dimensions of the affirmation of an impetus in its *being* and in its properties, assembled into syntheses and into a system: a coherent universe without background-worlds, reign of the Same without any "other scene."

is not pleasant, but which commands and prescribes. Obedience to prescription—even just listening and understanding, which are the first gestures of obedience—implies no compensation other than this very elevation of the soul's dignity; and disobedience implies no punishment other than this very rupture with the Good. A service indifferent to remuneration! From this responsibility for the evil suffered by the other person, no failure could exempt us. It remains meaningful despite failure. It is the very opposite of technical thinking by contrast with which, to believe Nemo, evil restores us to our life as human souls.

6. THE AMBIGUITY

To be sure, the knowing of the world—thematization—does not abandon its cause. It works towards, and succeeds in, reducing the disturbance of the Same by the Other. It reestablishes the order troubled by Evil and by the Other through the history which it agrees to enter. But the cracks reappear within the established order. Our modernity would be attached not only to certainties of History, or Nature, but to an alternation: Recuperation and Rupture, Knowledge and Sociality. An alternation where the moment of recuperation is not more true than that of rupture, where laws do not have more meaning than the face-to-face with the neighbour. Which does not attest to a simple lack of synthesis, but which would define time itself, time in its enigmatic diachrony: tendency without result, aim without coincidence; it would signify the ambiguity of an incessant adjournment or the progress of purchase and possession; but also the approach of an infinite God, an approach which is his proximity.

To Pursue the Dialogue with Levinas

Philippe Nemo

If, in the text just read, Levinas betokens his fundamental agreement with the method of *Job and the Excess of Evil*—an approach to transcendence through the analysis of a concrete content of consciousness rather than through a reflection on the formal structure of Being—and if, on account of this, he would associate my analysis of evil with his own analysis of the Face, he also formulates a number of reservations that crystallize into a serious difficulty. The notion of the Good that I discern in Job would be a simple inversion of evil, a pleasant Good, whereas, fundamentally, the Good is Law.

In what follows, I would like to take up this question once more, not, to be sure, in order to defend my erstwhile "position," but rather to try for my own sake, thanks to lighting flashes that Levinas has given us here and elsewhere in his works, to see more clearly to the bottom of a problem which, it must be granted, is not of mediocre importance.

I

For Levinas, if there is a "breach of the Good" in the excess of evil (and there is such a breach only to the extent that "the horror at evil aiming at me" can be transformed into "the horror at evil suffered by the other man"), it is not, as I have seemed to suggest, a "simple inversion of Evil." The Good is essentially what "commands and prescribes." It is—as with Kant—a stranger to all reward, other than "the very elevation of the dignity of soul." The Law alone, as categorical imperative, can demarcate a distance from theodicy. This would be the meaning of "Where were you when I laid the foundations of the earth?" (Job 38.4). It is there that God would remind Job—or would teach Job the non-Jew—of the Law.[1] Without that, Levinas seems to say, there would be more of the *sacred* and less of the *holy*[2] in the exegesis that sees the announcement of a salvation in Job 19.25 (the so-translated: "I know that my Redeemer liveth").

To follow the Law, asserts Levinas, "is not possible without suffering." In this sense, the Good is never "pleasant," and that is the precise reason why it is not the contrary of, or symmetrical to, evil. This unpleasantness of the Good goes as far as death. Let us here recall some well-known themes from Levinas's philosophy.

---

[1] This exegesis of Job is expounded in his *Otherwise than Being or Beyond Essence*, trans. Alphonso Lingis (The Hague: Martinus Nijhoff, 1981), p. 122.

[2] Cf. Levinas's "From the Sacred to the Holy," *Nine Talmudic Readings*, trans. Annette Aronowicz (Indiana: Indiana University Press, 1990), pp. 91–197.

The "otherwise than being" who is the human subject is fundamentally a hostage. One cannot respond to the suffering of others without exposing oneself, laying oneself bare, fracturing the *connatus essendi* that sustains the human within being. One knows how far Levinas takes this idea. He goes so far as to say that one is responsible for the very responsibility of others, and that one is therefore, in a sense, responsible for the very persecutions one suffers—the Jew is responsible for Auschwitz, or at least the crimes of his persecutors are not totally strange to him. He could have edified them, converted them, he could have done *something more* than he did. A magnificent attestation to the freedom of the spirit before every putative law of nature and history! But one understands that Levinas's man cannot do more than "take a beating" under these conditions; hostage becomes victim.

In "Transcendence and Evil," Levinas refuses every Kantian "postulate of pure reason" that would guarantee, for the present or for later, an accord between virtue and happiness. He prefers the "hardness of philosophy"—meaning the pure ethics of the Law—to "consolations of religion"—meaning messianic promises, "eternal life": "I was once asked whether the messianic idea still had meaning for me, and if it were necessary to retain the idea of an ultimate stage of history where humanity would no longer be violent, where humanity would have broken definitely through the crust of Being, and where everything would be clear. I answered that to be worthy of the messianic era one must admit that ethics has a meaning, even without the promises of the Messiah."[3]

---

[3] *Ethics and Infinity*, trans. Richard A. Cohen (Pittsburgh: Duquesne University Press, 1985) p. 114. Levinas cannot find sufficiently harsh words for the "aspiration for salvation" that is "egoism" (*Difficult Freedom*, trans. Seán Hand [London: Athlone Press, 1990], p. 47) and against those individuals who are not touched by the divine word only "as Law," who think

Levinas thus seems to want ethics without salvation. But, as he does not affirm his faith in God any the less, the question stands. Do the consolations of religion lack all sense then? Are the salvational verses of Job "vain words borne by wind"?

It is difficult to give an answer to the question by taking our point of departure directly from the Book of Job. Levinas rightly points out that, in this book, the problem of the relationship between the suffering that affects me and the suffering of the other man is never placed in the forefront. It is therefore left to us to discover what in the Bible would be closer to Levinas's problematic, and to see whether pleasure and salvation are excluded as rigorously as they are with Levinas. It seems me that we can invoke the Gospel here and establish an extremely close parallel between Levinas's ethics and the ethics of the Sermon on the Mount.[4]

---

that history is "a perpetual test whose goal is the diploma of eternal life" (*Difficult Freedom*, p. 100). Levinas does not say this only against Christianity, moreover, but also against a certain return of the sacred to the very heart of contemporary Judaism.

[4] Although the question of the relationship between Levinas and Christianity is both psychologically delicate and intellectually complex, I am not wary of raising it here. One will find in Marie Lescourret's *Emmanuel Lévinas* (Paris: Flammarion, 1994), pp. 268–302, some exact and useful information, and, in *Difficult Freedom* (*passim*), minutes, if I may call them that, of proceedings against Christianity initiated by Levinas. Precise accusations, directed at the fundamental immorality attributed to Christianity (and not only to the Church), and carried out both in the name of Reason and in the name of the true God. Levinas has also spoken on Christianity in an audibly different tone, in *Transcendance et Intelligibilité* (Geneva: Labor et fides, 1984), pp. 50–60.

I approach the question without wariness because I am convinced that the philosophy of Levinas, in the perfect universality of its rationalism, by nature seeks both to demythologize and to de-ethnicize Judaism together with Christianity, by honing the sharp point of their common message. I do not see anything in this philosophy that a Jew, a Christian or an atheist could hear differently, if they hear it truly. On the other hand, I myself, in writing *Job and the Excess of Evil*, have not considered myself,

II

Let us read the Sermon on the Mount. We observe that, to the *symmetry* of the traditional Law—"an eye for an eye, a tooth for a tooth"—characteristic of natural justice (which, be it commutative or distributive, is always a rule of *equality*) Christ opposes a *dissymmetry*. "If someone hits you on the right cheek, turn the left cheek," "love your enemy," which is therefore,

---

or posed, as someone who takes part in a certain confession (cf. the Introduction). I am *not* Christian, if by "Christian" one understands "non-Jew." I am Christian, on the other hand, in that I am seized by fear and by love before the Cross of Christ, something which I do not see why a Jew could not approach in the same way, as soon as he reads the Gospel with the Reason that Levinas demands and as soon as he challenges, at any cost, every prejudice foreign to the drama that unfolds there.

I am convinced that all the differences that prevent us from perceiving or confessing to the spiritual convergence of Judaism and Christianity are, in the final analysis, of sociopolitical origin. And also that the difficulty of clearly articulating convergences and divergences rests to a large extent in a mutual ignorance, still very great today.

Levinas himself has on many occasions underscored the absolute universality of ethics, which consists in being responsible for *everything* and for *everyone* before *everyone*. How would the discourse that clarifies this universal ethics not be common to all upon whom it is incumbent? That everyone does not reply "Here am I!" to the ethical demand does indeed trace the outlines of a "chosen people." But no one will maintain the thesis—which must be qualified as immoral—that the election would be a matter of ethnicity. The door is—alas—open to all. "The notion of Israel," writes Levinas, "designates an elite, of course, but an open elite. . . . This . . . helps us once and for all to get rid of the strictly nationalistic character that one would like to give to the particularism of Israel" (*Difficult Freedom*, p. 83).

To be sure, if there has to be confrontation between Judaism and Christianity, I understand an express confrontation between their fundamental options and presuppositions, and between their theoretical and practical consequences—at such a confrontation each party must arrive naked, threadbare, committed to the sole interests of truth. Philosophy is not a diplomacy. It is nevertheless that which makes wars and alliances that matter and that endure.

strictly speaking, an injustice.[5] Unlike natural justice, which obliges me only not to harm others, to carry out my own promises and to repair damages I myself have caused, Christ asks me to repair also the damages I have not caused, to honour even the promises I did not make, and to clear the path for others even of the evil which I did not cause. *Justice* consists in rendering to the other what is his due, *mercy* what is not his due. Mercy is one-sided; love is an unsymmetrical relationship.

By saying that, Christ anticipates and announces his Passion. He knows that this conduct is not compatible with natural life and natural society. Those who will follow him will be "insulted," "persecuted," others "will speak all kinds of calumny against [them]" (Matt. 5.11). Greater reason against their model: "The Son of the man is about to be handed over. . . . He will be ridiculed, scourged and crucified" (Matt. 20.18–19). To Peter who contests this logic, he says: "Your thoughts are not God's thoughts" (Matt. 16.23).

All this is strictly parallel to Levinas's analyses of the ethical demand and the responsibility for others. The responsibility

---

One will contemplate from the outset a text of Levinas which thus justifies the Jewish "No" to Christianity (*Difficult Freedom*, p. 104): "The misery that calls out for our pity, our justice, our freedom and our work, is [in Christianity] replaced by an ambiguous passion, in which grief is transformed into ritual and sacrament, and unfolds like a scenario. It is as if its human meaning were not sufficiently full, as if another mysterious night enveloped the night of human suffering, as if some celestial salvation could triumph without ridding it of visible misery. The efficacy of the work it replaced by the magic of faith; the austere God appealing to a humanity capable of Good is overlaid with infinitely indulgent divinity that consequently locks man within his wickedness and lets loose this wicked yet saved man on a disarmed humanity." This analysis, indeed, makes one think. The present exposition is, in a sense, its commentary.

[5] Levinas notes (*Difficult Freedom*, pp. 146–48) that, if the prescription "eye for an eye, tooth for a tooth" is indeed to be found in the Old Testament (Lev. 24.20), so is the commandment to "turn the other cheek" (Lam. 3.30; Isa. 50.6).

for others is a fundamentally unsymmetrical relationship; it consists in the recognition of an infinite debt, a "debt exceeding one's means,"[6] and one which has been due prior to every voluntary and explicit commitment on my part, simply because I am human. When we are born, we are already in debt.[7] We are already off-balance, we are not, and never will be, adequate to the order of nature; it is already impossible for us to live. The debt increases in measure to one acquitting oneself of it: "the more just I am, the more guilty I am."[8] Hence it is impossible to pay it off, hence it can only devour all Being and every claim to life.[9]

In *Transcendence and Intelligibility*, Levinas himself grants the similarity between this ethical situation of the human being, as he describes it, and the kenosis of the Christ. He approves of an interlocutor[10] who applies to Christ the following passage

---

[6] Levinas, *Otherwise than Being, or Beyond Essence*, p. 109.

[7] This is the meaning of the "original sin" as Levinas's analyses restore to it a rational sense based on a phenomenology of actual ethical experience rather than on adherence to a myth of origin.

[8] *Otherwise than Being, or Beyond Essence*, p. 112. See the whole of chap. 4, "Substitution."

[9] For Levinas, the dissymmetry and the depletion of the I as it pays off an infinite debt, however, only concerns the first ethical relationship, my relationship with the neighbor. In the presence of a third party, ordinary justice resumes its sense. For, as Levinas says, the third is also my neighbor, and how can I settle a difference between them? Whence the indirect ethical value of distributive and commutative justice, of human law and of the judicial order judicial whereby rights and obligations are distributed. Levinas affirms the absolute priority of the responsibility of the subject no less. Between others, there is equality. Between me and others, there is always dissymmetry. It is by this personal responsibility, nontransferable and primary, that Biblical Law breaks with all natural law, where the collective is prior to the individual, includes and drowns the individual.

[10] This text transcribes a dialogue that took place in Geneva in 1983 between Levinas and friends, rabbis and Christian theologians. Cf. *Transcendance et Intelligibilité*, p. 58.

from "God and philosophy": "as responsible, I am never finished with emptying myself of myself. There is infinite increase in this exhausting of oneself, in which the subject is not simply an awareness of this expenditure, but is its locus and event and, so to speak its goodness."[11]

The parallel between the Levinasian righteous person and Christ goes far therefore. But there is a point where the parallel lines diverge.

"Happy those who are persecuted in the cause of right," says Christ, *"for theirs is the Kingdom of Heaven"* (Matt. 5.10). Opposite the hell of the infinite debt that one pays off only by depleting oneself till death is placed a "Reign of God."[12]

That changes everything! The equation of natural justice, equality between two finite terms, had been destroyed by mercy, inequality between a finite term and an infinite term. With the "Kingdom of Heaven," which is an Infinity, an equivalent is camped opposite the Infinity of mercy. Thus a new equation is established. My works will never redeem my debt, my sin; I must, in the face of the other man's suffering, give everything, up till my life; love asks for an infinite gift. But that, says the Gospel, will be rendered back me "a hundredfold." Therefore I do not give "for nothing," I will obtain justice. Love is infinite like death, it bears up in the face of death victoriously.

It is true that no calculation is possible with infinite quantities; the Sermon on the Mount does not reestablish any "hypothetical imperative." Mercy gives without calculating; or rather, it is noncalculation, if we may put it that way, that is ascribed

---

[11] Levinas, "God and Philosophy," *Basic Philosophical Writings*, ed. Adriaan T. Peperzak, Simon Critchley & Robert Bernasconi (Bloomington: Indiana University Press, 1996), p. 144.

[12] Which other formulae of Beatitudes adumbrate: *they will possess the earth, they will be consoled, they will be sated, they will obtain mercy, they will see God, they will be called son of God, their reward will be great in Heaven. . . .*

to justice with the "poor in spirit" (as Abraham's immediate reply, free of ruses, hesitations or detours, his "Here am I!", was ascribed to justice). The new justice shatters the wisdom and the moderation of Aristotle, of Cicero and of jurisconsults, together with the morality of Job's three friends and all Jewish and Christian theodicy.

It reestablishes a *rationality* of ethics to no lesser degree. If the one commanded to mercy is sure to always suffer more, to descend into an always deeper hell, how will love be distinguished from hatred? How will the Law of God be distinguished from the Law of the world? On the contrary, for the one who puts his hope in a "Kingdom of Heaven"—a kingdom that "is not of this world," a kingdom "otherwise than being"—there may be a *sense* in gratuitously serving others whatever may happen. In other words, the perspective of salvation here, far from *exempting* one from the Law, may well serve to *ground* the Law.

A serious alternative to Levinas's conception of the Law. In the two cases, it is a matter of approaching the Good. The salvation provided by Christ does not consist in giving the sinner a right to abide in his sin (to be a "saved evildoer," as Levinas says), but in giving him a weapon for combating evil without which the fight would be lost from the beginning.

This has meaning only if one can believe in the promises of Christ, and if Christ changes something in our condition and in History, if the Gospel is momentous.

What extends credit to these promises is, I think, not the reputation of divinity of the one who makes them, a divinity that would be certified and stamped by the supernatural fact of the Resurrection (rather, this fact is what is to be proven). Rather, what imbues the words of Christ with power is his death. If it is necessary to believe in the Kingdom in order to love unto death, and if Christ accepts death, it is because these promises are, for him if for no one else, the word of truth. His death demonstrates the Kingdom. It is the Passion of Christ, his suffering, his wounds, his blood, that give a meaning to his words, according to which love exceeds death.

It is true that, for Levinas, all human beings who are truly human are, in this sense, Christs. Every individual who "discharges" and "empties" himself of himself in order to respond to the call of the face and the misery of others, no less than in Christ, radiates with the "glory of the Infinite."[13]

Nevertheless let us grant the Nazarene a unique power of testimony. For in his gesture, Love and the Word comingle in a manner the like of which I do not see elsewhere.

Which lover calculates his love less than he does? He dies in order to ease the miseries, not of his friends, but of all men to come after him, men whose faces he does not see, distant humanity with whom he would be neighbour. No element of reciprocity is mixed in with his act; the dissymmetry of the ethical relationship, which is for Levinas its essence, is total here, and consequently so is Love. On the other hand, Christ accomplishes this act of love even as he is in total dereliction, one equal to Job's. His soul is sad to die (Mark 14.34); he cries: "My God, my God, why have you forsaken me?" (Matt. 27.46). The Cross is manifestly "non-integrateable" into his thought. His confidence in the power of love does not have a hold on any external insurance, supernatural or ideological, therefore; as with Job, it only holds on to Love itself, which thereby becomes an irrefutable Word.

This Word is *momentous*—and so we come to the second aspect, one so problematical for Jewish thought about God. In and by the Passion, a change of situation is put into operation *for the whole of humankind*, a messianic "rearrangement in the objective order" (to speak again like Levinas, cf. *infra*).

---

[13] Cf. *Otherwise than Being, or Beyond Essence*, pp. 140–52. *Ubi caritas et amor, Deus ibi est.*

The Gospel, after all, does not say simply that the Christ takes on the world's sins—the Levinasian righteous person does that also: that is the very meaning of responsibility for others—it also says that, taking the world's sins upon his shoulders, he *accordingly alleviates our burden*. In other words, the Christ *atones* for us. His sufferings would be our recovery, as Isaiah says of his "Servant" (for which reason Levinas would gladly exclude chapter 53 of Isaiah from the Bible!).

This idea, to be sure, is not self-evident. If every responsible human being is "responsible for my responsibility"—it is *his* affair, says Levinas—how could I, for my part, accept assistance as this would cancel my *own* responsibility? In allowing the violence that has fallen upon me to fall upon him, instead of recognizing it and repairing my situation, do I not commit a crime? And he who offers me this expedient, does he not become an accomplice to this crime of which he is the victim? Indeed, it seems that here "another mysterious night envelopes the night of the suffering human,"[14] a night where mendacity and immorality are in danger of being concealed, together with magic and the sacred, together with an infinity of other crimes, now and in the future! A night that Conscience must refuse, if it is true that it is always a burning lamp.

I think that the force of this objection is great, but that it does not exhaust the meaning of Christ's gesture.

For I believe that the act of Christ—like other extraordinary acts at work in the Bible—actually change the human condition and the face of the Earth. One can maintain that Christ opens the way like a soldier out in the vanguard. By daring to suffer the first blows, by offering himself as hostage and as victim, as Lamb—by voluntarily placing his head on the block of immolation, to quote an admirable hymn by Paul Gerhardt

---

[14] Cf. *supra*, note 4, Levinas's text on Christianity.

paraphrasing Isaiah, he makes a gesture that produces real effects. For if it is true that he thus gives credit to his own commandment to love, as we have suggested, then it is true that he augments the Good and creates the conditions of a messianic approach of justice. He takes the lead of a whole people who are summoned to join with him in the fight against evil, to upset the equilibrium of the simple and hard justice of nations, and thus to change the face of the Earth (I have in mind the anthropological theories of René Girard).[15] The Passion is not in vain. It will not cease bearing spiritual and practical fruit in History. *Oleum effusum nomen tuum.*

---

[15] The Christ, for Girard (*Violence and the Sacred*, trans. Patrick Gregory [Baltimore: John Hopkins University Press, 1977]; *The Scapegoat*, trans. Yvonne Freccero [Baltimore: John Hopkins University Press, 1986]), is the last scapegoat, and after him this foundational mechanism of sacrificial societies has been dismantled. Indeed, the religion that Christ founds inscribes for posterity, not the version of the collective crime as given by the assassins, i.e. the myth, but the version given by the victim. Henceforth, a moral weapon exists against the mechanism of sacrifice: when proceedings of collective violence are initiated, the victim finds defenders, so that unanimity is not achieved and the myth and the rite cannot be reinstated. Whence the emergence of new societies in which individual liberties, critical thought and science, and human rights are able to flourish. In this sense, the Bible (because Girard clearly discerns that the ethics of Christ is the same as that of the Old Testament, and that Christ simply carries it to an unequalled degree of clarity and conscience) has truly transformed the world, has truly introduced something new into History.

As for the Crusades, the Inquisition and the pogroms that the historical memory of the Jews intimately associates with the Cross because assassins carried its symbol, these are, for Girard, remnants of sacrificial sacredness in a society where the Christian message has been proclaimed, where gods therefore have taken Christian names, but where the social bond has remained at heart that of prior sacrificial societies, a bond based on a *mimesis* of violence and on crowd-behaviour. The real comprehension of the message has been attained in Judeo-Christian societies only gradually and, initially, only by small minorities. A long incubation period lasting seventeen or eighteen centuries was required, says Girard,

Now this Christian *event* is in no way a natural or a historical necessity. It might not have occurred. It is a gift of God that objectively changes Being. Like every prophetic act, it is nothing less than a rearrangement of Creation, a change in its objective order (this is what Levinas says of the messianic event; cf. *infra*).

But I do not want to explore the mystery of Jesus any further here. I have quoted the Sermon on the Mount only because it offers, at closest range to Levinas's ethics, a notion of what Levinas would apparently absolutely exclude from ethics: a gratuitous gift from God, a salvation that we do not deserve.

This notion, as it happens, is Christian. But I do not believe that the conflict between the two conceptions of ethics and of the relationship to God adumbrated here is reduced to an opposition between Christianity and Judaism.

1. According to one conception, the "hardness of the philosophy" has the upper hand over all "consolation." What is necessary is the "ethical order," to act in this world, within the

---

for the just society to flower in modern Europe, a liberal and democratic society which he sees as a beginning of the incarnation of the Judeo-Christian ideal.

The Crusades, the Inquisition and the anti-Jewish pogroms would thus have *nothing* to do with the Christian message in its spiritual exactitude. The proof for this is that collective massacres have existed throughout archaic humanity and continue to exist in our days everywhere where this archaism resides or irrupts anew, independently of all Christian teaching and semiology. Nazism has been, doctrinally, an anti-Christianism, an explicit attempt at the resurrection of paganism. Is it in the name of Christ that millions of Gulag victims were assassinated? Is it an application of Gospel precepts that Turks assassinated Armenians, that today Iraqis massacre Kurds, and Houtou massacre Tutsis (or vice versa), etc.? Every crowd, as crowd, when the individual moral conscience does not bridle its outbursts, is criminal. Is it in the name of Christ that the Jewish crowd cried out for Christ's death? I turn to Girard's magnificent explanation of the words: "Forgive them *for they know not what they do.*" The crowd does not know what it does. Biblical ethics teaches this to every human being who belongs to it.

imbroglios of injustices in this world, without escaping to an ideal world, owing to a separation between the sacred and the profane. The enthusiasm for the sacred is not only a "utopianism," it is an injustice; it is injustice itself. "The man of the utopia wishes unjustly. Instead of the difficult task of living an equitable life, he prefers the joy of solitary salvation. . . . He is nothing but Desire."[16]

2. According to the other conception—that expressed in the Gospel, but also in the salvational verses of Job—we are not alone in the fight against evil. Our Desire is granted. Someone holds out a hand to help us cross the *nada* of existence. He takes a part of our load upon his shoulders. And he does this because He himself suffers, He himself atones. It is only in so far as we receive this help from Him that we may try to walk straight. For the salvational verses of Job as for the Gospel, there is salvation at the same time that there is ethics, and likewise there is ethics only because there is salvation.

What is the source of this duality of conceptions?

Levinas's philosophy has been reproached for its lack of "humility":[17] can the moral subject *truly* carry the world by himself alone? Is it not the Creator who supports Creation? If it is the moral subject, then, as we have seen, it is necessary to say, and Levinas says this, that the Jew is culpable for Auschwitz. I believe this is an unacceptable consequence, and I take this unacceptability for a sign. Like the unjustified suffering of Job, Auschwitz is an evil in excess—in excess of this very moral force that Levinas wants to be infinite. Job sees very well that, *culpable or not*, he suffers *more than* he deserves to suffer. Similarly, Auschwitz is an evil surpassing every human power of

---

[16] Levinas, *Difficult Freedom*, p. 101.
[17] Cf. Jean-Louis Chrétien, "La dette et l'élection," *Cahier de l'Herne. Emmanuel Lévinas*, (Réed, Livre de Poche, Biblio-Essais, 1991), pp. 257–77.

word and intellect; it is the "non-integrateability of the non-integrateable."

In this sense, Levinas, who has analyzed the *creatureliness* of human beings more radically than any theology that I am aware of—for he describes the subpoena, the accusation that constitutes me as responsible, and as unique, chosen, for this responsibility, as "a passivity more passive than any passivity correlative to action"—might misunderstand a fundamental aspect of creatureliness. He reproaches me for "never putting the suffering of the other in the foreground." By I return the objection to him. Levinas never puts my suffering in the foreground, understood as a burden that has become too heavy. *This, no less than the exposure to a Law which one did not freely contract, attests to the creatureliness of humans.* Is the creature who is created under the condition of a fundamental exposure—without protection, without shade, as if under a lead sun, says Levinas—to the Law less exposed to God's salvational project for his creation?

It is there, as we have seen, that we find the paradoxical source of Job's hope. This hope is not founded on his own moral force, the fragility of which Job is aware of; it takes on meaning in the fear and adoration of the creator God. It is because he does not see the specifics in the experience of Job (and in this section of Biblical Revelation) that Levinas rebels against the idea of a God who serves.

The divergence of views regarding the significance of creatureliness would be, in the last analysis, the ground of the difference between the two foregoing conceptions of ethics—and it is through this divergence that, anecdotally, the fraternal quarrel between Levinas and myself may be explicated.

III

Now, as it happens, the Talmud—commented upon at length in the magnificent chapter in *Difficult Freedom* dedicated to this problem of messianism and the "world to come"[18]—provides us with grounds for both views! Here we see yet again that the problem does not in any way throw us back upon an opposition between Judaism and Christianity.

Indeed, among the Rabbinical opinions related by Levinas that deal with the conditions of the advent of the "messianic era" and the "world to come," there are some that confirm one of the theses developed above, and others that confirm the other. Actually, there are three schools of thought.

1. *The advent of the messianic era depends on man alone.* This is the position of Rav: "We are past the deadline and [the advent of the messianic era] depends on nothing but repentance and good deeds." Levinas comments: "The messianic advent is at the level of an individual effort which can be produced in a full possession of the self. Everything is already thinkable and thought; humanity is ripe; what is missing is repentance and good deeds."

2. *The advent of the messianic era depends on God alone.* This is the position of Rabbi Shmuel: "The mourner has mourned enough." The messianic era will come because God is tired of waiting in vain for the repentance of humankind, and because God will make a unilateral decision to intervene. "The objective order of things cannot rest eternally upon a failure, it cannot rest eternally in a state of disorder, things will turn out all right and they will turn out all right objectively," that is to say, upon the initiative of God, through what we must call—however much Levinas dislike this word—his grace. Human merit counts for almost nothing here; the only thing God takes into account is human suffering, which therefore can be said to have redemptive potency in and of itself.

---

[18] Levinas, *Difficult Freedom*, pp. 59–96.

3. *The advent of the messianic era depends upon humankind and God both.* A commentator from the seventeenth century, the Maharsha, rejects the idea of a "redemption obtained solely through the effects of suffering and without any positive virtue." He thus suggests that it is Israel that is designated in Rabbi Shmuel's phrase and that the phrase means: Israel's suffering will incite it to repent, and this repentance will permit the advent of the messianic era. Through suffering, God awakens man; and man mends his ways; each one walks part of the way. "In the economy of being, therefore, suffering has a special place: it is not yet moral initiative, but it is through suffering that *a freedom may be aroused.* Man receives suffering, but in this suffering he emerges as a moral freedom. The idea of outside intervention in salvation becomes reconciled in suffering with the idea that the source of salvation must necessarily lie within man. *Man both receives salvation and is its agent.*"[19]

In the pages following that, Levinas cites other Talmudic passages which offer more or less the same options, these apparently being three permanent indices of Jewish thought, with no option ever ousting the others definitively.

What is the personal stance of Levinas? His concern before anything is not to let himself be drawn into the pure "grace" thesis. God would not extend his grace to a sick individual who does not want to fight, who has become complacent in his illness. As for the individual, he cannot put up a fight without the aid of medicine. "Return to me and I shall return to you" (Mal. 3.7). Between God and the human being, there is an equality of freedom.

Nevertheless, Levinas understands that the symmetry between them is not perfect. For, pushing it to the extreme, affirming the total freedom of the human being, one will arrive

---

[19] Ibid., p. 71, our italics.

at the very negation of messianism. Indeed, to say that we are entirely free is to recognize that we can choose not to observe the Law. Utter immorality, and thus the definitive adjournment of the messianic era, would then be conceivable! The injustices, the wars, the suffering could continue forever. No progress, no hope, the worst yet to come, evil definitively gaining the upper hand.

Before the evocation of such an hypothesis, the Rabbis of the Talmud recoil in horror, and Levinas with them. God would not let things come to that. It is impossible that evil should triumph. We have here the same reasoning as Job's: for You too, the adventure of Creation has a sense, You who instigated it, instigated it by love yourself, You cannot go back on your decision. Faith in God, in effect, is *rationally* equivalent to a certainty in the ultimate triumph of the Good. And Levinas posits what may well be called a "postulate of pure reason" (despite what he says on the matter in "Transcendence and Evil"): we cannot practice the Law if we do not think that, at the end of all ends, the Good will triumph. Our very idea of God implies the triumph of the Good, *therefore* the Good will triumph. "God is here the very principle of the triumph of good. If you do not believe this, if you do not believe that *in any case the Messiah will come*, you do not believe in God."[20]

The two doctors who are, at this point, the protagonists of the Talmudic discussion, Rabbi Eliezer and Rabbi Yehoshua, find unanimity again on this crucial, first and last affirmation. It is self-evident to the latter, who is a partisan of divine "grace," and who cites a number of lively Biblical verses supporting this grace. But Rabbi Eliezer, who himself sides with human responsibility, also concedes to it by the simple fact that he demurs from citing verses to the contrary. In fact, he throws in the towel. By his silence, he accepts Salvation.

---

[20] Ibid., p. 77, our italics.

As Levinas observes, nothing distinguishes him formally from the atheist. He holds fast to his rejection of miracles and of all sacrality, and this stance, insists Levinas, will always be exemplified at the heart of Judaism. But since he believes in at least *one* miracle, that of the Law and of the "glory of the Infinite" resplendent within the Law—this is how he differs from the atheist—he admits that the Infinite is greater than his conscience, he welcomes grace and love.

I think that this is the stance of Levinas, who, if he did not assume this stance, would not have devoted many pages to messianism and the world to come, notions of a saved world, *saved although it did not cease from being wicked.*

Levinas paints an extremely interesting picture of this world, from which I will only recall characteristics that strike me as directly corresponding to the notion of the "excess of good," which I have invoked in connection with Job's hope.

The messianic outcome is not, for Levinas, a life expelled from time, a "pure and gracious spiritual life"—a beatific state consisting of "absolute knowledge," of "artistic activity" and of "friendship." It is a life where the issue is still and always that of living in ethical relation to others, that is to say, of "giving," this being the "original movement of spiritual life." This life implies incarnation and even economic relations. But it is then that "giving" attains its "full blossoming," its "greatest purity," and procures "the highest joys."[21] "Deliverance by God coincides with the sovereignty of a living morality that is open to infinite progress."[22] In the world to come, time will not stop, it will not cease from begetting the New. For this reason, the messianic outcome is not an outcome that will have been "prepared" by "ethical order." "The ethical order does not prepare us for the

---

[21] Ibid., p. 62. Let us note the word "joy," which is infrequent with Levinas.

[22] Ibid., pp. 82–83.

Divinity; it is the very accession to the Divinity."[23] Living charity, at once suffering and joyous, is the very access to God.

In this Levinasian notion of the *epectasis*, the "eternal life" spoken of in myth is inverted in "diachrony." We are far from Dante's Paradise.

Levinas has a thought which is still more radical. Salvation must be thought even beyond ontology. Meaning does not arise from Being; it is the Good that gives meaning to Being. Whence the idea that death is inevitable ("Mortality renders senseless any concern that the ego would have for its existence and its destiny. It would be but an evasion in a world without issue, and always ridiculous")[24] and, at the same time, death is nevertheless impotent against a meaning that traverses it and annuls it. Death, which belies "pleasure," can no longer "introduce the absurd" into the ethical act, "despite all its adversity." "No one is so hypocritical as to claim that he has taken from death its sting, not even the promisers of religions. But we can have responsibilities and attachments through which death takes on a meaning."[25] If the truly human human being is "otherwise than being," he is also otherwise than nothingness. As little as that human being may have been made for life—is that same person made for death.

It is permissible to interpret these pages from Levinas as a picture of a kind of salvation, even a personal salvation,[26] even if this notion takes on an altogether new significance when it is passed through the fire of philosophical thought and Reason. This salvation is not a fleeing, nor a repose, nor an egoism. It is sociality, alterity, opening, life. It is an "excess" of the Good, that is, something other than a satis-faction, but also other than

---

[23] Ibid., p. 102.
[24] Levinas, *Otherwise than Being or Beyond Essence*, pp. 128–29.
[25] Ibid., p. 129.
[26] What would be the "world to come" as opposed to the "messianic era."

a dis-satis-faction, since through it every waiting, every prayer, and finally eschatology itself are outstripped—for this Good is not "to come," it is accessible to us at every moment, just as at a certain moment it became for Job the provisions for the journey that was his *via dolorosa*.

Translator's Postscript

Michael Kigel

> Reish Lakish said: "He is the Accuser [*ha-satan*],
> he is the Evil Inclination, he is the Angel of Death."
> —*Baba Batra* 16a

1. THE PRESCRIPT

The complaint brought forward by Levinas against Nemo states that: "the problem of the relationship between the suffering of the I and the suffering that an I can feel of the suffering of another human being never appears in the *foreground.*" (*supra*, pp. 179 ff.). It is a formal complaint, a complaint brought forward on behalf of a client, "another human being."

As part of the same general complaint, moreover, a specific complaint is brought forward on behalf of a certain "pietism" that Nemo's exegesis has methodologically abandoned, a certain unabashed *eisegetical* style and prejudice. On behalf of another human being, Levinas would gladly have us "read too much into" the Book of Job. After all, where *in the Book of Job* does the suffering of another human being—other than Job—appear in the foreground? We imagine a young law student articling in the firm of Levinas making the suggestion that the case be presented as a Talmudic lecture on the passage from the tractate *Baba Kama* (92a) where we read: "Raba said to Rabbah bar Mari: Whence do we get the saying spoken by the Rabbis, 'Whoever solicits mercy for his friend while he needs the same thing, he will be answered first'? He said to him: It is written [Job 42.10], 'And the LORD returned the fortune of Job when he prayed for his friends'." We imagine such an unabashedly eisegetical suggestion being welcomed by Levinas.

In court, of course, it would meet with grave objections. For one, exegetical standards for biblical interpretation would hardly be satisfied by this Talmudic approach to the Book of Job, which would solicit[1] the meaning of the whole book from a single verse in its epilogue, verse 42.10, with the conclusion that it is the sheer *drama* of the dialogues between Job and his friends that conveys the meaning of the book rather than the thought-provoking content of these dialogues. In Levinas's terms, the meaning is in the "saying" rather than the "said." But even apart from that, since there is more at stake here than biblical interpretation, since an eisegesis of the Book of Job is also an eisegesis of evil, as it were, such an unsatisfying solicitous hermeneutic must also produce, or rather, presuppose, an unsatisfying *phenomenology* of evil. For a phenomenology of evil, Nemo's basic plan is the only viable one: the suffering of the I must stand in the foreground. Phenomenologically and exigetically, one simply cannot speak of the suffering of others, of "Holocausts," before posing the question of personal suffering. As Nemo says, when I see death coming, it comes for me, personally. Would Levinas propose that when death approaches you and me, I am to worry about your death before my own, as if death itself, my own death, the last possession I might have hoped to still claim as my own, were public property first? In a court concerned with strict exegesis, strict phenomenology, and

---

[1] *Solicitter*: Levinas's technical term for this Talmudic hermeneutic.

strictly fair and impartial distribution of property—property such as my "own" death, *ma propre mort*—Levinas's complaint would fall on deaf ears.

A more thoroughly critical court, on the other hand, would be mindful of the fact that strictness of exegesis is itself just a special mode of eisegesis, and that strictness of phenomenology means admitting to the limits of phenomenology. A court concerned with more than distributive justice, moreover, would take into consideration more than issues of property. In such a court, Levinas's complaint might indeed be heard and justified, the Talmudic eisegesis might be validated as an exposition of the essential theme of the Book of Job, and it might be legislated that, at the limit of any phenomenology of the suffering I, my efforts to shed light on my suffering as a phenomenon must be redirected toward making suffering, my personal suffering itself, into a scene in which the Other's suffering is apparent, and talking. And in fact, Nemo himself enthusiastically justifies this complaint.

Indeed, there isn't so much as an out of court settlement between Levinas and Nemo. Quite the contrary, we see them shaking hands like two attorneys working for the *same client*. Levinas's complaint is his only complaint. Enthusiastic about Nemo's book, Levinas doesn't deny the need for a phenomenology of evil and an exegesis of the Book of Job. At worst, his accusation is aimed at a sin of omission. Nemo's book is coherent in the discourse which it puts *au premier plan*. What's missing is another plane of discourse. Far from denying the need for a phenomenology of evil, moreover, this other plane of discourse Levinas has in mind can be placed in the foreground only when such a phenomenology is upstaged, which is just what Nemo produces in his "other other scene." Nemo, says Levinas, speaks of what is "familiar and dear to us": "a 'beyond' transcending the closed dimensions which are delineated by the judicatory operations of the intellect and which the forms of logic reflect. It is in the same way, in fact, that transcendence seemed to us

to shine in the face of the other man. . . . That the evil suffered
by another man afflicts me in the evil that pursues me, that it
touches me, as if the other man were calling out to me right
there and then, putting into question my *relying upon myself*
and my *connatus essendi*, as if before my lamenting over my
woes here below, I have to answer for the other—*is it not this
that is a breach of the Good into evil, into the 'intention' that
targets me so exclusively in my woe?"* (*supra*, pp. 180 f.)

We must be careful how we read this. Levinas claims that
transcendence shines in the face of the suffering Other *de la
même façon* that it is illuminated in Nemo's phenomenology of
the suffering I. This is an interpretation of Nemo. Levinas's
rhetorical question gives an eisegesis of the Intention. In Nemo's
complex analysis of the courtroom scene where the inner logic
of the Intention is poetically reflected and refracted into litigational personae, the only identifiable plaintiff is Job. Levinas
would add another plaintiff. And therefore another Intention
curtained within the innermost room of the inner logic of the
Intention. If my suffering is somehow intended by some judge
or jury or prosecutor, it is intended on behalf of someone other
than this judge or jury or prosecutor. The Intention *represents*
someone. Who? we might ask. After all, one must keep in mind
the sin of Job's friends, how they accused Job, without proof,
merely on the basis of a neat dogmatic deduction drawn out of
a book that was never opened, of crimes against humanity which
he never committed. Would Levinas not be joining in with the
company of these well-wishing cannibals (as Job refers to them)
in further compounding the case against Job? It's certainly not
an impossible Levinasian reading of the Book of Job. It has the
peculiar logic of Levinas's own suggestion that God's "Where
were you when I laid the foundations of the earth?" is a charge
of truancy: Job should have been there when God laid the foundations of the earth![2]

---

[2] "We have been accustomed to reason in the name of the freedom of

But we have already noted an alternative that is more easily developed from the textual resources of the drama itself even though it is also harder in its moral implications, namely Rabba bar Mari's eisegesis: God accuses Job for not letting himself be falsely accused by his friends, even as God accuses the friends for falsely accusing Job. This would be quite consonant with Levinas's reading of Lamentations 3.30, "To offer the cheek to the smiter and to be filled with shame": "In the trauma of persecution it is to pass from the outrage undergone to the responsibility for the persecutor, and, in this sense from suffering to expiation for the other."[3]

In short, what is at stake for Levinas is a properly ethical question. It is the question that Levinas develops, for example, in the context of a Talmudic discussion in *Yoma* 85, which is directly related to the discussion in *Baba Kama* 92a.[4] The general form of the question is: *Who* is the one who accuses me when I stand accused of a crime against a fellow human being, God or the fellow human being? But what makes it properly

---

the ego—as though I had witnessed the creation of the world, and as though I could only have been in charge of a world have issued out of my free will. . . . That is what Scripture reproaches Job for. He would have known how to explain his miseries if they could have devolved from his [sins]! But he had never wished evil! His false friends think like he does: in a meaningful world one cannot be held to answer when one has not done anything. Job then must have forgotten his [sins]! But the subjectivity of a subject come late into a world which has not issued from its projects does not consist in projecting, or in treating this world as one's project. The 'lateness' is not insignificant. The limits it imposes on the freedom of the subject is not reducible to pure privation. To be responsible over and beyond one's freedom is certainly not to remain a pure result of the world. *To support the universe is a crushing charge, but a divine discomfort*" (Levinas, *Otherwise than Being or Beyond Essence*, p. 122. Italics in French text). Cf. *Nine Talmudic Readings*, p. 85. Texts written before 1978.

[3] *Otherwise than Being*, p. 111. But Levinas will not have this confused with "offering the other cheek" of Matt. 5.39.

[4] See "Toward the Other," *Nine Talmudic Readings*, pp. 12–29.

ethical in Levinas's sense of ethics is the specific form: *From whom* do I beg forgiveness? *To whom* must I make reparations? This question is posed, as we say, within ethics proper, it is already an ethical question, where by ethics, moreover, we already understand Levinas's *ethics of alterity*.

But Levinas doesn't enter into this question with its proper plane of discourse, insisting that his book review is no place to propose "improvements" to Nemo's book.[5] That is the rule of his book review—and it is the rule of the present postscript.

The priority peculiar to Levinas's question is not in question here. That is taken for granted. It is as an aside to this question that we wish to posit yet a *third discourse*, accompanying Nemo's and Levinas's,[6] while maintaining the general form the question, "Who accuses?" in this discourse. For Nemo, God accuses. For Levinas, the Other accuses. These, in any case, are useful oversimplifications; after all, Nemo is no theologian, and Levinas, in his analysis of *illeity*, would have the Divine Other and the mortal Other taking turns popping their faces out each from behind the other's face. We oversimplify only in order to sidestep an analysis of the complex turns of these faces within faces, taking instead the complaint of Levinas to mean that you can never have too many angles from which to be accused. We add a third type of accusation, then, in a third discourse, one which may be useful in translating Nemo's phenomenology into Levinas's ethics and vice versa, a discourse minimally phenomenological and minimally ethical.

For the sake of simplicity, we refer to it as *prescription*. The term is meant to convey relatively little, particularly about ethics.

---

[5] Levinas goes on to sketch an analysis of an *alterity of evil* in "Useless Suffering," trans. R. Cohen, *The Provocation of Levinas*, ed. R. Bernasconi & D. Wood (London: Routledge & Kegan Paul, 1988), pp. 156–67; an essay motivated by Nemo's book in a number of ways.

[6] What! Like a third comforter to Job, perhaps? No doubt, no doubt.

2. WHO PRESCRIBES?

In the section of the Talmud where the Book of Job is dealt with at greatest length, the identity of the Accuser, *ha-satan*, is touched upon. "'And the LORD said to the Accuser: Have you noticed my servant Job, that there is no one like him in the land, etc. But he still holds on to his integrity, and you provoked me against him, to devour him, for nothing' [Job 2.3]. Rabbi Yohanan said: Were this verse not written, it would be impossible to say it. As if it were a human being here whom others provoke, and he is provoked." (*Baba Batra* 16a) No sooner is the Accuser identified than the unthinkable question arises: *Who hears the accusation?* What jury or what judge? It isn't enough that the accused alone should hear it, for then it would not be an accusation at all. For the accused to hear his own accusation, he must already be standing before a judge. To hear the accusation, merely to hear it, is to hear it as a judge hears it. A judge must be provoked. But can God be provoked? It is impossible to say this. Or rather, it would be impossible to say it were it not written. A little further in this same Talmudic discussion we read: "A Tanna taught in a *baraita*: he [the Accuser] descends and tempts to sin, and ascends and provokes, takes permission and takes the life." (Still further elucidated by the saying of Reish Lakish.) But if, strictly speaking, God cannot be provoked, then perhaps, strictly speaking, he also never gives permission to anyone to take a life, and perhaps, strictly speaking, *no one is ever tempted to sin.*

Who accuses? The Satan. But this means nothing. For the Satan is precisely the one who is not a "who" at all. A provoker who provokes no one. The Satan is very much the *question* "*Who?*" His body is this question. And so our question remains a question, a question without a discourse. And yet, if we take away the Satan, for the sake of a stricter speaking, what—in heaven's name!—will be said of *God?* After all, is it not God who asks the Satan, "Have you noticed my servant Job, that

there is no one like him in the land"? Is it not God who provokes the Satan—to provoke God? Is it not God who provokes
God? Provocation isn't all that different from temptation moreover. So is it not God who tempts God? And temptation itself
includes an accusation and is a kind of accusation, for Satan in
a sense prosecutes God, the Judge himself, for failing to pros-
ecute Job. So is it not God who accuses God? Is it not God who
deals, so to speak, *satanically* with himself?

This same question swirls down into a vertiginous pit in the
stomach, where not just theology but discursivity itself becomes
a little nauseating, in Nemo's pronouncement: *Dieu est le Diable
et Satan est Dieu, et Job n'est Job que par le Jeu de Dieu-Satan.*
"The Divine *is* the Devil and Satan *is* God, and Job is Job only
by way of the God-Satan Game."

It sounds a little bit like Nietzsche's epic pronouncement,
"God is dead." And yet, Nietzsche, with his epoch-closing *Wort*,
locates the abyss within language, at the edge of the world,
and, with a martyr-like resignation to the fact that the price
he must pay for his pronouncement is an abyss that returns
his gaze and looks back into him, an awareness that he must
become a monster, *monstrum in fronte, monstrum in animo*, in
order to make his pronouncement, Nietzsche sails off the edge
of the earth, into his abyss, all in order to drag the word "God"
down with him. Indeed, he is Captain Ahab coiled in harpoon
wire against the body of a great white whale as it sinks into
the depths. It is a consummately tragic gesture, enacted, as
Gide remarked, in a singularly passionate envy of Christ. The
word is both too much and not enough in comparison to Nemo's
word. For Nemo's word isn't a word on God. It isn't theology.
Nietzsche's word is still a theology. It is atheology. For Nietzsche
understands that the word "God" doesn't really belong to language, that, strictly speaking, it is impossible to say this word.
Nietzsche experiences language like a bare-chested man standing on a snow-heavy cliff, as something natural, something "fatal." And the word "God" is hardly a word that can be considered

natural. From the standpoint of Nature as that which cradles the Normal in its bosom, the word "God" must in fact look like a freak of nature. It must be an embarrassment to language. But in the way that a parent whose continual supervision of the child's game becomes loathsome for the child, who wants to take his destiny into his own hands and to play with the other children away from the demanding gaze of the parent. By a kind of oedipal decision, Nietzsche must sacrifice this word in order to set language free.

And Nemo's word? It is the other possible course: *language is sacrificed in order to set God free*, free to continue his demanding supervision, until *God* decides we may be left on our own. Is Nemo's refusal to sacrifice God the basis for his "Why I am not a Christian"? Or is it his profoundest commitment to the essence of Christian wisdom which itself refuses to confuse the Passion with its parodies, in Nietzsche, in Melville, in all that is still Greek tragedy? Questions to keep in mind, albeit not to be addressed here.

Nietzsche's sacrifice of the word "God," let us note, is itself not simply "beyond," or simply inimical to, the sacrifice of language. It is necessitated by his attachment to a single type of discourse which for him exhausts the possibilities of language. For Nietzsche, language is a tragic event, it is a gift of nature, language happens. And yet, because at the same time Nietzsche also hears an imperative that invites him to overcome tragedy, to overcome tragedy from within tragedy itself, from within the discourse in which tragedy is inscribed, Nietzsche too must strain language, and hence suffer at the hands of language. What doesn't occur to Nietzsche, because, again, he is tragic by nature, is that there is another discourse at hand all along.

Nietzsche remains and suffers by *description*. This is the type of discourse that Nemo makes use of, and indicates, in his own pronouncement in italics, although for the sake of a different sacrifice. Nietzsche's word, the adjective "dead," which Nietzsche pronounces, pronounces of God, is only possible on account of the "*is*" that holds the pronouncement together. The "is" isn't a word, not even a word like "God" which should not have made it into language. On the contrary, *the "is" is the discourse itself*, descriptive discourse. This is something that we know from Heidegger. But Nemo doesn't delve into this discourse and the possibilities it contains within its depths in the way that Heidegger does. For Heidegger too is a tragic thinker, even more so than Nietzsche, perhaps a thinker who would think the essence of tragedy itself as something from which discursivity itself bubbles forth, as the "earth hath bubbles," even before tragedy is able to come to language in a discourse. Nemo, like Levinas, settles for less than Heidegger does: not what lies before, or deep within, discursivity, but merely another discourse. It is enough. The way to bring the "is" into question, Nemo tells us, is to place it beside the word "good."

To present an alternative in this way, very simply, is of course very naïve at heart. Such naïveté could not hope to survive a Nietzschean "re-evaluation of values," where the good is rendered just that, a value, a value among other values—*less valuable* than the "is," which is also a value, but a value that is less naïve. To safeguard against naïveté, which means in positive terms to love truth before any other value, it is necessary to cultivate deep misgivings and suspicions about the word "good." One would have to value truth *less* and be, as it were, skeptical about truth, or critical about it—evidently by a skepticism and a critical faculty that is no longer invested with the ability to discern between the true and the false, or between the illuminated and the withdrawn—in order to free up one's soul to the naïveté required to love the Good. A very different kind of childishness is needed than the kind Nietzsche expresses longings for.

The word "is" is the horizon of a discourse. The whole of descriptivity is inscribed within the "is." And for this reason, the word "is" never really makes it *into* language as a word, a word like other words, not cleanly. Its appearance in language is always something of a residue that bespeaks what is beyond all that can be clearly spoken. And as this beyond, as the horizon of discursivity and the transparent light, bright and also weightless, as *Lichtung*, within which words can show all that can be seen, the "is" is invisible. The "is" illuminates all phenomena and all ideas. It is something of an irony, therefore, that the word "good," like the word "God," can succeed in making it all the way into language, precisely because it is not illuminating. The word "good" makes a clean jump and a square landing precisely into the discourse of the "is." Words like "good" and "God" can be coupled with other words. They are precisely opaque.

But it is also here, at the point of landing, that these words fall through language, as if through the paper of the written page. The opacity they attain as soon as they touch language exposes them to tragic fates at the hands of the descriptive "is." For these words are not opaque like other words: they are more opaque than any other words. Hence they in turn are quickly destined to be invisible, albeit not in the way that descriptive language is invisible by way of transparency, but by way of opacity, like black holes. One falls into the words "good" and "God," as into the dot cradled in the arms of the first letter of the Torah, in order to emerge into another universe. They are passageways to another discourse, here called prescription.

"God is Satan" means description is dead. The "is" is dead, and hence every "who" named in such an utterance is no one at all. He is not dead, but never was, and only seemed to be a "who" in a language that was commanded (by who knows who) to give this semblance, right up until, but not including, the point that the utterance is made. Before one writes, "God is Satan," the commandment is revoked, so that this sentence drifts meaninglessly into the void.

The only one "who" still remains alive within such an utterance, if only barely alive, is Job. Job *is* by way of the Game between God and Satan, the Game where the one switches places with the other and then switches back again. "God is

Satan" is just another way of saying "God is provoked." Is it even worth writing? If it is worth writing, it's only because it's worthwhile to give a description of the temptation of Job. Job is the real "who" in question, *but a "who" whose identity must be posed as a question in a purely prescriptive discourse*, a "who" who isn't a "who is. . . ." Job "is" Job only because God is provoked. But God provokes Himself. Therefore Job is provoked by God. But this too only means, in strict description, *Job provokes and is provoked*. For, to be sure, to be precise and to speak clearly and logically and without poetry, God was never in all eternity provoked.

3. PRESCRIPTIVE THEODICY

What this amounts to saying is that theodicy, the litigational process that attempts to justify the ways of God to humankind, is a very poor species of discourse. For in the dizzying dialectics of the "is," what theodicy really ends up doing is spending most, if not all, of its time and efforts justifying the ways of the Satan. Theodicy is the discourse that attempts to describe the Satan. This is what happens to any defense that goes on the offence. One should have learned from Nietzsche how fighting monsters can make one into a monster. Theodicy, as the prosecution of the prosecutor, remains essentially monstrous and satanic, against its own wishes. But, of course, this only results from the fact that the discourse which theodicy has chosen for itself is description.

We can pose the problem in another way. Theodicy is a discourse of faith, for faith is something that is edified by a description of God vis-à-vis evil. Faith needs a description of the *necessity* of evil, necessity, like nature, like tragedy, being the domain of description. Only such a description can reconcile the soul to God's world as God's. But this is precisely what undermines the *freedom* that is needed for the soul to fight evil. Prescription is enervated by faith, as faith has always already rendered the soul passive in the face of evil. Indeed, evil provides faith with its very passion. And hence also with its compassion. But neither passion nor compassion is adequate to prescription, at least not in so far as the pathos, the suffering, is embraced. What is essential to prescription is that all suffering be fought off pitilessly to the extent that it can be fought off. To embrace suffering, even as a secret joy, is to give Satan an identity. And this may be a valid and useful enterprise from the standpoint of religious aesthetics, and even indispensable for morals; it is better to bring the Satan into one's service of heaven,[7] rather than to serve heaven by bolting the door on the Satan's face. Indeed it may be very useful to find a truly decorative purpose for that part of suffering which simply cannot be fought off. In beauty, and above all in the beautiful works that have been carried out for the sake of heaven, the very uselessness of suffering can find a kind of use for the soul. But for this reason, because passion is the helper of morality, it isn't the moral agent.

The ironic fate of faith is that it is supposed to accomplish by itself that which can only be accomplished by activity. It has blocked its own path with a descriptive discourse. Description—and hence, some would say, philosophy itself, "Greek thinking"—is possible only within passivity, the passivity of belief, of believing something to be true, of knowledge; that is its proper strength, to poetize, and to that extent all descriptions of evil can be beautiful poems. But again, to expect poetry by itself to generate activity is to end up writing tragedy. Faith is to grow from the soil of Greek tragedy, which in its essence is prescriptively arid.

---

[7] "Rabbi Levi said: The intentions of the Satan . . . were for the sake of heaven. When the Satan saw that the Holy One, blessed be He, was partial to Job, he said, 'God forbid that He will forget Abraham' . . . Rav Akha bar Jacob taught this in Papunia, and the Satan came and kissed his foot" (*Baba Batra* 16a).

But we must still grant theodicy the benefit of one more doubt, the most important one. We must acknowledge its good intentions: it is the intention of theodicy, and of faith, to accomplish what activity accomplishes, despite the essential tragedy to which it capitulates. If theodicies are all descriptive by nature, their intention is no doubt prescriptive as well as descriptive. Hence Plato, forefather of all theodicies, includes "matter" (which already for Plotinus is tantamount to the substance of Evil) in his description of reality, not just as a necessity (*Ananké*), but also by way of a rhetorical and pedagogical encouragement to the soul to break the shackles of necessity and to ascend to the Good. And, in due course, when Augustine rewrites matter or evil negatively as a *privatio boni*, he is pushing description to its limits in a way that must have a prescriptive effect. The possible prescriptive intentions of such theodicies are evident in their efficacy as poetry. Unfortunately, they also are read as mere descriptions and nothing more, and this is when they must end up, in the final analysis, repeating the very Manichean sin that they intend to overcome. This is the effect of Nietzsche's Zoroastrianism, which is also intended as poetry and prescription: it discourages, because it says too much, it describes the enemy as a giant and itself as a grasshopper. The essence of the Manichean heresy isn't a matter of theology, as if the dualist description of the divine, the equality between God and Satan, were an offence to God and His own estimation of His place in reality. The superficial heresy is that a God-sized Satan would rob God of his divine power; the deep heresy is that the necessity of Satan robs man of his human freedom. Otherwise, Manicheanism itself is in principle redeemable, if it only rewrite itself into a *prescriptive Manicheanism*.

And, for that matter, Manicheanism is not something that prescription can ever escape. From the standpoint of description, the purest prescriptive discourse—Levinas's, Nemo's, anyone's—is recognizable as a theodicy, and not by attempting a theodicy but merely by prescribing. Prescription as such is a defense of God and a justification of God's ways, one that works, not by bringing God into court, a move certain to blow up in the faces of those who would attempt it, but by a far more clever ruse, namely, convincing the jury that the very justice of God and God's ways is besides the point. But to avoid the God-issue as "irrelevant material" is just another way of dropping the charges against God on account of God's inscrutability. "Canst thou by searching find out God?" (11.7). God thus would be justified under the noses of the jury without anyone even suspecting that a theodicy had taken place. It is just such a conspiracy carried out by religious exegeses of the Book of Job that Jung tried to expose in an attempt to rekindle the holy indignation of Job and to taste his bitterness once more. However, what is besides the point is the very *standpoint of description* from which this objection is raised. If prescriptive theodicy justifies the ways of God, it is only by *being just* ourselves as God would be just, by seeking out "justice, justice." God's innocence, defended as irrelevant, means nothing in itself; it merely signifies that *we* are guilty and defenseless, without defense.

Hence to sidestep theodicy, as Nemo does, is also to take hold of the essence of theodicy. For there is nothing wrong with theodicy as such. The passivity of faith is not the result of description and of "speaking Greek." Greek merely presents the soul with the general opportunity for passivity, which opportunity often must be seized. Greek is not a sufficient reason for passivity. There is no sufficient reason why one doesn't listen to a commandment, after all, for if there could be such a reason, the commandment would be rendered effectively mute from the start by a necessary deafness in its addressee. If anything is to *blame* for the passivity of faith, it lies within the domain of prescription, in a temptation within "Hebrew" itself, a temptation to turn a deaf ear to Hebrew, and to then hide beneath the foliage of another discourse offered as an alibi. The ability to speak Greek merely equips us with the ability and the opportunity to *pretend* that we do not understand Hebrew.

In other words, there must be other ways to define faith. What would be required is a definition of faith as something other than a species of belief, this genus which also contains the species of fruit called knowledge. Faith should be nothing like knowledge of the truth.

4. PRESCRIPTION AS CENSUS

As an afterword corresponding to our postscript, we pick the word *pikud* to make our point, in particular its instance in Job 7.17–18. In the King James translation we read:

> What is man, that thou shouldest magnify him?
>   And that thou shouldest set thine heart upon him?
> And that thou shouldest visit him every morning,
>   and try him every moment?

This is a parody, which is a kind of an exegesis,[8] of Psalm 8.5–6.

> What is man, that thou art mindful of him?
>   And the son of man, that thou visitest him?
> For thou hast made him a little lower than the angels,
>   and hast crowned him with glory and honour.

The Hebrew word *pikud* is what the King James renders as "visit." In each of the two situations described in the above passages, God pays man a visit. He knocks on man's door, and looks. *Pikud* means inspection, a looking-into something; circumspection, a looking-around once one has stepped into something;

---

[8] Michael Fishbane, *Biblical Interpretation in Ancient Israel* (Oxford: Clarendon Press, 1985), pp. 285–86.

search, a looking-for something that is presently invisible; and finally, a looking-out-for, a providence. Hence the King James *uisitare*.

What, then, constitutes the difference between the two situations? Why is the Psalmist joyful to be paid a visit by God while Job is very much inconvenienced? Why does Job only desire to *hide* from his visitor? In the same chapter, Job describes himself as a servant longing for shade (7.2), a sea-monster that God sets a watch over (7.12), God's target (7.20). But Job's desire to hide from God is to be found everywhere in the Book of Job; the whole of chapter 3, Job's opening lament, for example, voices his desire to hide in death's womb.

Would it be sufficient to say that Job wants to hide from God because God is hiding from Job?[9] The visitor in Job 7 is God invisible. God isn't a visitor at all, but only a spectator, a detached inspector; indeed, he seems little more sympathetic to his human host than does Ananké herself, Blind Necessity, that all-but-maternal figure of Justice in a blindfold. But is this reason *enough* to forsake joy? Psalm 8 rejoices in God's intentions with humankind, in the fact that God looks for human beings, while Job laments the very lack of divine intentions behind the hard divine stare. But does this necessarily mean that the Psalmist rejoices in the LORD, the God of mercy, while Job laments over the visit paid him by God the stern Judge? What is being suggested here is the possibility of *rejoicing in the hard stare of the Judge*.

My own suspicion is that the deepest meaning of *pikud* is revealed in the Pentateuch on the different occasions that a

---

[9] The biblical theme of the "hiding of the face" (*hester panim*) arguably finds its most intensely and consistently "Greek" *thematization* in Job. In the *Prophetic Faith* (*op. cit.*, in ch. 4), Buber takes it to be the basic theme of Job. Some have even taken it to be the biblical theme *par excellance*; e.g. Samuel Terrien, *The Elusive Presence* (San Francisco: Harper & Row, 1978).

census is taken. *Pikud* in these contexts means census. Here I can only cite a comment by Rashi[10] on the census decreed at Exodus 30.12, "When you count the heads of the children of Israel in a census, each man shall give an atonement for his own soul to the LORD in their census, so there will be no plague in their census." Rashi explains: "For the evil eye can gain mastery over the numbered, as we found in the days of David." When David ordered a national census, 70,000 died in a plague. A census gives the evil eye permission to roam the land, in the same way that God deputizes Satan in the prologue. A census is a day of judgment.[11] But again, whose eye is this evil eye? Satan's? Satan's lord?

The difference between the joyful Psalmist and the bitter Job depends on the identity of the one with the evil eye. And the rule of prescriptive discursivity dictates that this difference is not to be sought in a theology of these two passages which would uncover a difference between God here and God there. Again, we are assuming God is Judge for the Psalmist as well as for Job. The difference, therefore, must lie in *you*. Somehow the evil eye is your eye—or ought to be yours. Are you a Job or are you a singer of psalms?

Penitence, the penitence awaiting you on a day of judgment, is possible only in the face of the blank stare of Blind Necessity.

---

[10] Rabbi Solomon Yitzhaqi of Troyes (1040–1105), *first* commentator in any Jewish edition of the Bible.

[11] According to *Midrash Job* and the Targum, the day that the "sons of God" (or "the Judges"?) assemble themselves before the LORD, "and the Satan was among them" (1.6), is Rosh Hashana, the head of the year. Rashi (at 1.6) explains: "For that is the day of the blasting of the ram's horn and the Holy One, blessed be He, commanded the Satan to bring forth the merit and the guilt of all creatures; this is the meaning of 'From going to and fro in the earth'." It is ten days later, according to the Targum this time, that the same company is assembled again: the Day of Atonement. That is the day Job loses his health. These are the ten days known as the Days of Awe.

As the hangman must be hooded, the judge indeed must be blindfolded. The work of penitence is the appropriation of this blank stare of God's scrutiny.

But this means that we must not place too much weight on the question of whom the blank stare belongs to. The very appropriation of this stare, which makes the evil eye your eye, can't become prescriptive to the point of personalizing everything and making the stern Judge into a merciful Lord. This would ruin penitence itself. The blank stare must remain *blank*, impersonal, "yours" but not possessed by you, "yours" only in the sense of your nemesis, your accuser and critic. For this reason the blank stare must not be *aufgehoben* into a moment of prescription, but should be preserved *descriptively*. Prescription itself rests in a prior descriptivity, in the way that the revelation of the commandments rests on an account of Creation.

For Job, this blank stare is too much to bare. For him, it means that there is no judge—"There is no arbiter betwixt us" (9.33)—or that the judge and the prosecutor are one and the same person, "God is Satan," and consequently that any attempt at defense would be useless—"My transgression is sealed up in a bag" (14.17). But what if Job's only transgression is, indeed, not something belonging to the past, but is his present bitterness in the face of prosecution and judgment? Job is embarrassed by the suggestion that he is guilty. "If I am guilty, then let me be guilty! Why this interrogation?" The basic assumption of theodicy, and it seems *natural* enough, is that innocence and righteousness should no longer desire to be prosecuted and judged. But what if the commandment to rejoice in the commandments is a commandment to seek out joy precisely in the identity of prosecutor and judge and precisely in the prosecution of the innocent? Worse, what if this *is* joy? A hard doctrine, no doubt.

Pikud then would mean inquisition. Its intention is to bring a lie into the light—and into fire. And for this, indeed, the judge and the prosecutor must be one and the same person. The hybridization of judge and prosecutor is precisely what makes it impossible for the defendant to argue his case, as Lyotard shows in *Le Differand*, as there is no common language between the defendant and the prosecuting judge. Is a Nazi judge a *judge* at all? (And yet a Nuremberg judge *is* a judge!) But if such a hybrid can produce the most deplorable situation in the domain of interhuman law, the domain of law between the human and the divine is a different matter. For God is one before he is two. Who is beyond *divine* inquisition? Who sees oneself better than God sees one? "If I justify myself," says Job, "mine own mouth shall condemn me; if I say, I am perfect, it shall also prove me perverse" (9.20). After all, the Judge whom my mouth would address also happens to be the One who brought my mouth into existence. So if this mouth betrays me, what should I trust, myself or my mouth? Which betrayal would be the deeper self-betrayal? We must not assume that the word "myself" is closer to the self than the word "mouth."

From the example of the Spanish Marranos, we know that it is possible for some to believe that they can feign an identity, in the certainty that they will be able to conceal their true identities from others and thus shield that from harm. But we also know that this certainty can prove to be a shortsighted and all too flimsy grasp of human psychology. For when one's true identity is hidden, hidden within a lie, this very hiddenness can take on an identity and a life of its own, so that the true order of what is inner and what is outer—which order itself is supposedly taken into hiding with what is inner—can come to be forgotten. One may begin with a jealousy for the true identity behind the mask; but precisely for this reason, precisely because one isn't jealous for the mask itself, the mask can readily acquire more power than is originally lent to it. And one finds oneself, many years after having donned it, unable to take it off, even in the strictest privacy. For one has become the mask, one has become that which one would have feigned: one has become someone else. Masks are also alter egos. And consequently, the Inquisition that would tear down the mask may also be—its own over zealous intents, and its own satanic immorality notwithstanding—an act of God.

One may have reason to rejoice in inquisition, therefore, to rejoice in it as an act of divine grace that gives one the gift of penitence. To defend oneself joyfully is to want to discover one's errors and sins, and precisely on the assumption that one is innocent, an assumption that would be part and parcel of one's guilt. The consciousness of innocence, the certainty that "the spirit of God is in my nostrils" and therefore that my tongue is incapable of deceit, that "my heart shall not reproach me as long as I live" (27.3–6), the certainty that I am not a hypocrite[12]— this certainty is as susceptible to the forces of self-delusion, and indeed of hypocrisy, as is the consciousness of happiness. "Happiness is the most cherished hiding place of despair" for the same reasons that a consciousness of innocence is the favorite hiding place of hypocrisy.

The inquisitor is there to *tell* sinners of their sins—to tell, and not "to remind," for the sins in question, in a prescriptive discourse, are not sins that they will be able to recognize as their own, even if in another discourse it would be possible to induce such a memory or simply to overrule any alibi for its absence. As far as prescription is concerned, these sins are buried in an oblivion that cannot be excavated. The story of Eden

---

[12] Kant was sufficiently impressed by Job's certainty on this score to make it the exegetical basis for his own prescriptive theodicy. See Immanuel Kant, "On the Failure of All Attempted Philosophical Theodicies," trans. Michel Despland as the appendix to his *Kant on History and Religion* (Montreal: McGill-Queen's University Press, 1973). But it is also this confidence in the possibility of *Redlichkeit*, which Kant sees embodied in Job 27, that limits the prescriptive force of Kant's prescriptive theodicy and keeps it from taking up repentance as a task that is never completed.

too is a *revelation* of an inherited debt, and not a Platonic recollection and recognition of it. Sin is a patrimony—but *you own* it now.[13] Your father sinned. But you are your father now. Therefore you are a sinner. Again, *who* sins isn't the real issue. Forget Freud. The issue for prescription is, who will redeem you?

—If not *you*? Inquisition is the only possibility of self-redemption. To this extent the Christian teaching of the indwelling Redeemer may provide a new prescriptive twist on the old Christian interpretation of Job 19.25: "My Redeemer liveth." When a human court appoints an impartial judge to oversee the process of law, this is done partly in order to shield defendants from the prosecutor who, in a sense, is more a judge than is the judge. Like a Fury, the prosecutor is perfectly *judgmental*, critical, partial to justice, whereas an impartial judge, in this very impartiality, is partial to a kind of mercy. The judge assumes defendants are innocent until proven guilty; only the prosecutor is permitted the wisdom that all people are in need of penitence.[14] Only the prosecutor *cares* about the guilt of a defendant. The judge doesn't care. To be sure, the care that the prosecutor demonstrates is not intended to make defendant innocent or the defendant's life more pleasant. The prosecutor cares, as it were, categorically. But it is just this, the fact that defendants are placed under the *katégoria* of care, that makes it possible for defendants to work, with even greater care, toward their innocence, and if not merely in words then in works, if not merely to prove it then by proving themselves.

---

[13] Kierkegaard described this hereditary sin before Levinas. And for him, too, what was at stake was not so much the description as such as its rhetorical use for a prescriptive theodicy. To *be* a sinner is to be *commanded* to repent.

[14] This is a policy of Roman justice, in any case, which inverts the ideal presented in *Pirke Avot* 1.8 that says a judge should assume all parties guilty until they are proven innocent. A prescript to judges themselves to be *inquisitive*.

In a human court of law set up to shield defendants from the fury of the prosecution, the defense must come from an advocate other than defendants themselves. You are too biased to defend yourself. A more impartial defense attorney is needed, one more like a judge. But then, if your own attorney is like a judge, who will truly *defend* you—not just for your sake but for the attorney's own sake, as if *the attorney's* life depended on it? Who will defend you hotly, with bias, with a care and fury to match the care and fury of your accuser? Who will show you where you are wrong, and bring you to an actual innocence and not just a convincing one, an innocence that may well require you to commence the hard work of penitence? Who will defend your soul—if not you?

When you have no advocate, when like Job you are your only defender before a judge who is also a prosecutor, then and only then can you take your innocence into your own hands. Then you can begin to feel the full power of the ethical and begin to rejoice as the blind spots on your soul are pointed out to you and you can perceive the possibility of becoming a *better* person, the possibility of genuinely eradicating feelings of guilt and bad conscience, not through some hocus-pocus or psychoanalysis that makes the guilt *feelings* disappear, but by paying your debts and working off the guilt itself. "What is man, that thou hast made him a little lower than the angels, and hast crowned him with glory and honour"? Our self-respect, our well-nigh-angelic nature, depends on divine inquisition. To appoint oneself one's Redeemer is to stand face to face with the Inquisitor: He is the judge who prosecutes, and you are the defendant who becomes judge.

Job, then, would be guilty of a sin of litigation. Instead of defending himself, he accuses his accuser, he appeals. Instead of living *sans appel*, the existential condition of moral responsibility and of dignity, he is embittered by the very call to dignity. It is the sin of Joseph K., which only begins after the Trial has begun. With Job too, the crime is committed during the trial

itself, there being no crime to speak of before the trial to which
the trial refers.

If descriptive theodicy is a defense of the Judge, then a formula
for prescriptive theodicy would be: defense of the Inquisitor.

And then indeed the Messiah may come. If one will defend
one's Inquisitor, the Inquisitor may then become a trinity. Besides Prosecutor and Judge, He may show up, "at the last upon
the dust," as one's Witness in heaven (16.19) and one's *other*
redeemer. (19.25; cf. 23.4–7).

5. CENSURE AS PRESCRIPTION

We should mention that, to the parodic exegesis of Psalm 8
that Job gives in Job 7, there is added a parody of the parody in
Job 15 given by Eliphaz, bringing the whole discourse around
full circle.

> What is man, that he should be clean?
>   And he that is born of woman, that he should be
>   righteous?
> Behold, He putteth no trust in His holy ones;
>   Yea, the heavens are not clean in his sight.
>
> (15.14–15)

Eliphaz, like a good wrestler, makes use of Job's antagonis-
tic momentum against Psalm 8 to make him tumble right back
into the psalm. Where Job resented the divine inquisition as
something that targeted him, like a bull's-eye, Eliphaz brings
Job some comfort by assuring him that in fact nothing lies outside this inquisition, and that God isn't shooting arrows but
rather throwing grenades. To some extent, Eliphaz's parody
enters into collusion with Job's parody against the psalm. For
the angels in the psalm who are just above humans in dignity
are considered to be as dirty as humans. Then again, this is

consonant with the idea that the dignity of humankind sprouts from dirt. There is no such thing as a "passive dignity"; such an oxymoron isn't even possible in heaven. Human beings can only attain dignity through toil with what is soiled, the eternal assumption of their unending debt, and if angels do not get their own hands dirty in some comparable manner, then dignity is not a possibility for them. Eliphaz thus opens the gates of repentance, precisely by denying an a priori innocence to everyone and everything, "even the heavens."

Again, we find ourselves with the dogmatic problem of hereditary sin. Let us not say too much about it—let us not describe it.

Hereditary sin means that we are *born deserving punishment*. This strikes us as a curious thing to say because it both invokes an idea of innocence and revokes it. At birth, we are innocent. To deny this, would that not be to deny—birth? Our basic assumption is that the innocent do not deserve punishment. This for us is a matter of definition. It's not an empirical claim. To deny this is to contradict ourselves. In fact, even before it is a question of just deserts, to say that someone innocent is being punished is, strictly speaking, contradictory. The most we can say is that the innocent suffer. "It is all one—therefore, I say: He destroyeth the innocent and the wicked." (9.22) The innocent suffer unjustly; they are not punished.

But in what *discourse* does the contradiction in question take place? Evidently in the discourse that worries about contradictions. May we then try to re-inscribe the statement, "The innocent are punished," into a paradoxical discourse, and leave it at that, as a paradoxical dogma? To be sure, there is a place for dogma, perhaps as a propaedeutic to poetry and even to faith. But we can also simply over-leap the leap of faith for the sake of another discourse, one that isn't a dialectical response to the logical discourse of innocence, a discourse that is neither illogical nor supra-logical, but merely *besides logic* and beside logic.

Instead of renouncing the word "punishment," we can bypass

the discourse in which the word has been inscribed. In descriptive discourse, punishment is justified—for description itself is a mode of theodicy, it justifies—by reference to an action done in the past. In a prescriptive discourse, which is essentially *future-looking* or providential, such reference is beside the point. Guilt itself cannot have any meaning with reference to the past. Prescriptively, *guilty is what we are about to be.* This may be a continuation of past guilt, but that is beside the point. The point is to see the guilt as something that is approaching, something that threatens like a danger, and not as something that haunts like a painful memory. Look out! You're about to be guilty! Your suffering is about to be punishment! That is the significance of punishment in prescriptive discourse: it is the upcoming revelation of the meaning of suffering. But this revelation of meaning is no mere semantic event, as if a psychological dimension had to be added to physical suffering, to complete the picture, in the way that unthinkable nightmares complete Job's unspeakable days. One should not expect this revelation to be pleasant, just because it is a revelation from God. God did not promise to be nice. The revelation *is* punishment. If it has the positive meaning of a messianic promise, the positive meaning itself is to be dreaded, as the Rabbis in Tractate *Sanhedrin* (97b–98a) dread the coming of the Messiah: "Let him come, but let me not see him!" Prescriptively speaking, all *punishment is apocalyptic.*

This is the desired effect of the apocalypse, to put one on the spot, face to face with the *d'emblée éthique*, the "right here and right now ethical" of the face of the Messiah. The nearer the apocalypse, the more effective for ethics. This means we are not talking about the kind of apocalyptic feelings that merely nudge a compass needle magnetized to describe a fact accomplished in the past to now point in the other direction, to a future necessity, a pastlike future. The kind of apocalyptic paranoia that such an obsession with *dates* promotes, apocalypse as doom or as destiny (*Schicksal*), has little to do with the true nearness of the apocalypse. It belongs to a German way of thinking about epochs and their faceless closures.

There is no way to *know* whether suffering is punishment. The revelation can never be like those in the historical passages of Scripture. The revelation of suffering as punishment is like the revelation, better yet, the speaking, of the *prescriptive scriptural*, the commandments. We cannot so much as say that one feels or experiences divine punishment. To be sure, it is painful. But the essence of the pain is its commanding voice, the call to atone for one's sins regardless of one's sense of innocence and one's knowledge of oneself.

Punishment is, in a sense, the place where the sin occurs. In order to be recognized by the eye of judgment, the sin must be occurring on the day of judgment. In a sense, a prescriptive sense, *punishment precedes the sin. And therefore repentance precedes the sin.* Repentance is something that must takes place in innocence, if we are to think it prescriptively. It is precisely the innocent who must repent. It is the angelic, the heavenly, those who would live on earth as if it were heaven, the utopic, those nostalgic for Eden, the beautiful souls, the childlike, the victims—who must repent. Sartre was only wrong descriptively when he said that there are no victims. The perception of oneself as a victim, the certainty that there is a child within, the certainty of one's radical innocence—is the root of sin. Truly, the worst criminals are the purest victims; a well-documented psychological fact. If one is to begin the dirty business of repentance, therefore, it is only from the purity of such victimized innocence. And indeed in order to repent, one must seek out this innocence in every corner of one's soul with a candle.

If the righteous may not stand in the place of the penitent, it is because they are not truly righteous, for the truly righteous are never finished repenting. And here as everywhere we must be careful not to allow this idealization of repentance to slip into a descriptive theodicy of the *felix culpa* type, such as we find in the monologue of Elihu. Rather we must conscript such theodicies into the services of prescription.

The Apocalypse has the face of the Messiah, and the Messiah comes, not so much to save, as to command.

The natural descriptive order of crime and punishment which says that first comes the commandment, then the transgression, then repentance, is, from the standpoint of the commandment, a miscommunication of its prescriptive order. The descriptive order assumes that the commandment can be heard in a place that is ruddy-cheeked with the innocent flush of pleasure, a place free of pain, penalty and penitence. But there is no chance of this. Pain, penalty and penitence describe the only possible place where the commandment can be heard. One would like to describe the fall of Adam. One would like to find the body of Adam and to dissect it until the pineal gland of sin, as it were— the mysterious point of transition between innocence and sin— is found, so that it can be surgically removed. One would like to see, to finally see, the *mis-take* in Eden, so that we might go back and take it back. But there is no chance of this. What Eden looks like, even today, is a flaming sword which turns every which way.

"Is pain necessary then?" The mind never ceases from desiring a descriptive theodicy, a proof that God is limited, limited by logic, by rocks God can lift but can't create or can create but can't lift, or here, by the sheer necessity to command. One would like to say that we are necessarily free, that the commandment is ultimately a paradox or a reconciliation of autonomy and heteronomy, something that binds us to freedom, a freedom whereby we bind ourselves to a higher order of slavery, a slavery that has been redeemed into a service. There is no harm in saying such things about commandments. But what do they have to do with hearing and keeping commandments?

6. TWO TYPES OF PRESCRIPTIVE RHETORIC

> That which is Jewish is first visible in countenance and trait in the
> old Jew. His type is so very characteristic for us as is for Christian
> peoples their youthful type.
>> —Rosenzweig, *The Star of Redemption*

> The descendants of Abraham, Isaac, and Jacob are human beings
> who are no longer childlike.
>> —Levinas, "From the Sacred to the Holy"[15]

> When I was a child, I spake as a child, I understood as a child, I
> thought as a child: but when I became a man, I put away childish
> things.
>> —1 Cor. 13.11

Finally, we come to the question of rhetoric, from which question no discourse can be free, least of all prescriptive discourse. For it is either the one discourse that is in greatest need of a suitable rhetoric, and is itself rhetorical discourse *par excellence*, or it is the one discourse that begs of us to remove the useless bronze armour of rhetoric that we have heaped upon it and prefers five smooth stones from the ground. Does prescriptive discourse need to *convince* or simply to *convict*? Here we can only touch upon this question.

The question arises in Nemo's reply to Levinas, where Nemo suggests that the discourse fashioned by Levinas on a grammatical case, namely the accusative case, could use the help of another discourse in achieving its purposes. This other discourse is one in which, in more than one manner of speaking, it isn't possible for me to be accused. In the simplest manner of speaking, it isn't possible for me to be called "you" by someone and hence for me to call myself "me." Nemo further argues that

---

[15] Levinas, *Nine Talmudic Lectures*, p. 98. But of course he adds with usual generosity: "any man truly man is no doubt of the line of Abraham" (p. 99).

Levinas's *accusative discourse* presupposes this other discourse, in a similar manner that in grammar the accusative case presupposes the existence and the common usage of a nominative case. This would make it a *nominative discourse*, one perhaps characteristic of a child's consciousness that is always saying "I" to itself. The nominative is the case of innocence. What Nemo finally suggests is that something like a translation, to use yet another linguistic metaphor, can take place between accusation and nomination. (By the latter term, we are indeed alluding to Nemo's very fine analysis of Jacob and the angel.) Such a translation would be an essential part of the usefulness of the nominative discourse in that it would pull this discourse up from its status as a presupposition and bring it into the light. For, as hidden, it might be worse than useless, it might be counterproductive. This translation, from an accused "me" to a named and hence innocent "I," is called *grace*. Grace gives me an ear, so I who have been silenced by the Other's accusative discourse am once again able to speak freely, "without restraining my mouth."

What is incumbent upon us, then, is to ask, in the name of Levinas, how the accusative could in fact use the help of the nominative. The stronger claim, that the latter *presupposes* the former, we wish to bypass; Levinas denies that there is a logical necessity for the desire for happiness.[16] As Nemo remarks, Levinas denies this explicitly in his critique of the way Kant, by a logical necessity within pure reason, postulates happiness in the Hereafter as divine reward for a reverence for the Law in the Here. And as far as we can see, this rejection doesn't come back to haunt Levinas in a statement like, "if you do not believe that the Messiah will come anyway, then you do not believe in God," for while this too may be a postulate, it is

---

[16] Right from the beginning of *Totality and Infinity*, he does this by rejecting a univocal interpretation of desire itself. If anything, the "metaphysical desire" beneath all desires is a desire for *unhappiness*.

not happiness that is postulated or is even hoped for. But if there is no logical necessity for the desire for happiness, and the nominative discourse is not logically presupposed, the question of the need for such a desire, its usefulness for something other than happiness, remains. It is on the question of the *uses of happiness*, a question proper to ethics,[17] that Nemo really contends with Levinas.

We see this in their common pursuit of a Talmudic dispute on the question of messianism. In *Sanhedrin* (97b–98a), Rabbi Eliezer argues that the messiah will come on the condition that Israel repent, while Rabbi Joshua argues that the messiah will come even if Israel does not repent. The arguments go back and forth until Rabbi Eliezer falls silent, proffering no further proof for his case. This, apparently, is Rabbi Eliezer's way of recognizing that at a *certain point* a nominative discourse on eschatology becomes useful and even indispensable for morality,[18] and Levinas brings this concession into language, out of Rabbi Eliezer's self-imposed silence, only to bury it beneath language once more as if that were its proper resting place. This, for Levinas, is an act of rhetoric true to the rhetoric of Rabbi Eliezer.

---

[17] Kant already insisted on the usefulness of happiness for the sake of duty to the point that it is a duty itself: "for discontent with one's state, in a press of cares and amidst unsatisfied wants, might easily become a *great temptation to the transgression of duty.*" *Groundwork of the Metaphysic of Morals*, trans. H. J. Paton (New York: Harper & Row, 1964), p. 67. Cf. Aristotle's *Ethics*, 1099a7 ff. There is no getting around the innocence of *ton khrésimon* that Socrates pursues in his ethical inquiries.

[18] "And this is why R. Eliezer *on this occasion* remains silent. He does so because this time the requirements for morality *reach a point* where, in the name of man's absolute freedom, they deny God—that is to say, the absolute certainty of the defeat of Evil. . . . God is here the very principle of the triumph of good. If you do not believe this, if you do not believe that in any case the Messiah will come, you do not believe in God. This helps us to a better understanding of the famous paradox that the Messiah will come when the whole world is wholly guilty" (*Difficult Freedom*, p. 77, italics added).

So it is the rhetorical *canon* of Levinas that Nemo is suspicious of; and for good reason: it is good rhetoric. Is it not more useful to keep Rabbi Eliezer's concession out in the light of day? Nemo has Kant's subtlety on this point. His suggestion isn't made simply for the sake of supplementing and rounding out the ethical imperative with something less categorical and more sensitive to the needs of the accused soul, as if the accusative discourse were mere skin and bones and needed to be fleshed out and beefed up. The incarnation that concerns Nemo, rather, is that of the imperative itself, as categorical. He would undermine Levinas's harsh rhetoric precisely for the sake of sharpening his accusative discourse and making the accusation *more* acute, and in order to enable the imperative as categorical. Nemo would play good cop to Levinas's bad cop, by a "fraternal" loyalty and singularity of purpose between those who enforce the law.

This is why he says nothing about "divine reward" as such in his reply, but prefers to speak of grace. Grace *enables* the soul—enables it with the ability to respond, hence, with responsibility. It does so by promising divine reward to those who will obey the law. By the same token, divine reward, and therefore messianism and any other question of eschatology, isn't something that should be discoursed upon apart from ethical considerations. For the description of grace is quickly lured into a discourse on the forgiveness for sins, mercy after the fact, and this can be ethically useless and even counter-productive in that it opens a door for "saved evildoers"—the ultimate and decisive evil issuing from *Schwärmerei*. What keeps the notion of divine reward firmly bound within prescriptive discourse is the fact that it is considered as a promise. Grace is mercy before the fact. As promise, as future-looking and providential, the question of grace is still something that enables the soul for prescription.

Nemo's argument, then, is that Levinas's accusative discourse falls short of its own potential and its own intentions. It isn't too harsh, it is too blunt; and so its action really causes needless pain. Its cutting edge needs to be *sharpened.*

And Professor Nemo, I suggest, is right on one condition: that which is to be enabled must be submitted to an assessment, in the way that the body is assessed for physical fitness in a medical examination. Nemo is right on the condition that we can say that it is the soul addressed by prescription that is disabled for some reason, that the ears of this soul are what fail to listen and that the eyes of this soul are what fail to observe, and that the will of this soul is what fails to obey, and that this is why we can then say of prescription itself that it is disabled, or less able than it can be. It is disabled as a discourse of the soul.

In other words: What if there are souls that *do not need such enabling*? Perhaps this is a fringe question, raised as if to give one counterexample in order to destroy an otherwise useful universal statement. After all, whom do we have in mind that would not need some help in being ethical? How useful would it be to introduce examples of unique individuals, individuals of ethical genius, in a discourse that is supposed to be heard, observed and obeyed by everyone? To be sure, the type of soul that I have in mind is rare. I am thinking of Abraham and Moses. But it is to such individuals that everyone turns when looking for ethics. It is precisely *as counterexamples* to the greater part of humankind that such men serve as human exemplars. It is why Nemo enjoins "the Nazarene." I am trying to further sharpen Nemo's point.

Let us consider Moses first. At the ford of the Jordan, as the Israelites are about to the enter the land to which he has guided them, he beseeches God for divine mercy: "My Lord . . . let me cross and see the good land which is across this Jordan . . ." (Deut. 3.24–25). Rashi comments: "Everywhere in the Bible the language of 'mercy' [*hinun*] signifies only a gratuitous gift [*matnat hinam*]: even though the righteous have good deeds on which to hang requests, they do not ask for anything from [God] except as a gratuitous gift." This same scruple Jewish liturgy puts into the mouth of the common person: "Master of all worlds!

Not upon our righteousness do we cast our requests for mercy before you, but on your abundant pity." The fact that Moses' request is refused by God only sharpens our point, and in a way that seems fitting in high tragedy. This is our first example, and it bears upon the mercy that forgives. Our second example pertains to grace proper.

Nemo makes use of a phrase, *Quelqu'un nous tend la main*, "Someone holds out a hand to help us cross the *nada* of existence. . . . We receive this help from Him only that we may try to walk straight [*marcher droit*]." The metaphor is an old one, and for good reason. Rashi recalls how it is employed to interpret the clause in Genesis 6.9, "Noah walked with God": "But regarding Abraham it says, 'Walk before me.' Noah was in need of support to hold him up, whereas Abraham would strengthen himself and would walk by virtue of his righteousness by himself [or: itself]." Noah was like a child holding on to his father's hand for support, but stronger than anyone else in his generation for at least wanting to walk by his father's side and wanting to learn from him. But Abraham was like an adolescent, a *bar mitzvah*, able to walk by himself.[19]

The command to Abraham, "Walk before me!" (*hithalekh*; Gen. 17.1), moreover, traditionally belongs to the stretch of Torah that begins with the commandment, "Walk forth" (*lekh lekha*; Gen. 12.1). In chapter 12, this commandment is followed by a promise, "I will make you into a great nation" (Gen. 12.2); and in chapter 17 this promise is sealed as a covenant, "You will be a father of many nations" (Gen. 17.4). And as promise becomes covenant, Abraham first comes into his name, having been Abram until then. This is Abraham's moment of nomination. How is it that he finds his most complete name, his most complete innocence, through an accusation—assuming that that is

---

[19] This is the parable of Rabbi Judah in *Genesis Rabba* 30.10 which Rashi is recalling.

what every imperative is? For Abraham is not disabled by God's letting go of his hand, but on the contrary, at that stage in his life, God's letting go of his hand *enables* him. But how is it that an accusation can enable—and nominate?

We would have to assume that *Abram* is not quite himself. Abram *is*, but he is not himself. To *become* himself, he must walk to himself—to Abraham. This is one way, as the Rabbis noted, to read the phrase *lekh lekha*: "Go to yourself!" It is only in so far as Abram *is*, is Abram, that he is accused. *Abraham* is not accused, he becomes Abraham by being accused as Abram. Only by leaving his homeland does he find his homeland; it is as if one were to return home without ever having been there, by way of something other than a *nostos* of nostalgia.[20] Only by forsaking his father does he become a father. But to do that, to become Abraham, he must suffer the most unrelenting, purifying accusation as Abram.[21] As Abraham, he no longer needs God's help. He would need this as Abram. And, as Abram, he would need it most in the moment when the accusation is so

---

[20] "To the myth of Ulysses returning to Ithaca, we wish to oppose the story of Abraham who leaves his fatherland forever for a yet unknown land, and forbids his servant to even bring back his son to the point of departure." Levinas, "The Trace of the Other," *Deconstruction in Context,* ed. Mark Taylor (Chicago: University of Chicago Press, 1986), p. 348. Cf. *Totality and Infinity*, pp. 33–34, 271. But perhaps, in one special type of discourse not to be confused with other types, probably the discourse of myth, there is something like a distant cousin of return in the way that a trace is a distant cousin of memory; for example, Canaan's relationship to Eden.

[21] I might read the comment of Rashi that immediately follows the comment presently occupying our attention, therefore, as a further elucidation. It is on a point of grammar: the third-person singular perfect (past), "He walked," which describes what Noah does or did is grammatically identical in form with the second-person singular imperative, "Walk!" which is a prescription to Abraham. This, Rashi seems to say, is merely a feature of *hithalekh* as an *hitpael* verb. But much can be made of this obviously.

sharp that he feels it as a knife at his throat, the moment of the *sacrifice of Abram*. But it is precisely as Abram that, in such a critical moment, a moment of crisis, of *krisis*, of turning, of *teshuvah*, that he does not receive a helping hand from God. Abram, as it were, must die. It is through the utter helplessness, the utter *nada*, the utter darkness of the night of the soul, where the commandment destroys the inner child *in its neediness*, that Abraham finds himself, as father, finds the child external to himself, the son whom he loves, Isaac. The two of them, father and son, will repeat the same weird logic in Gen. 22. It is the logic of Job's restitution. And it is the logic of the Passion, the "last sacrifice" which Nemo, upholding an old tradition, identifies with love itself, *agapé*.

Abraham, after all, is the first human being on record, in the Bible, who loves. (The word "love" first appears in Gen. 22.2.) He loves just because he gets no help. He loves not with a borrowed love, by means of some spiritual transitivity, but with a love that is utterly his own. He loves just because, at a critical moment, he himself is *unloved*.

If we introduce a simple consideration of time, of the "stages of life's way," into Nemo's "critique" of Levinas, then we have a useful model for seeing how their positions complement one another. The need for help that is insisted upon by Nemo may be seen, according to this model, as something that develops into a need to be released from the need for help. Salvation saves, but in the end it may save with the purpose of saving us from salvation itself. Nemo therefore may be seen as offering a *pedagogy* where Levinas gives us the school policy. And perhaps here lies one of the great secrets and lessons of the Sermon on the Mount, namely, that we may be more in need of pedagogy than we think, the inner child may need its hand held a little longer yet. We have yet to be as able-bodied as Abraham our father.

And this may help us to sharpen Levinas's problematical association of the imperative with the accusative. The imperative is indeed an accusation. But of whom? And at what stage in life? And what is the imperative besides accusation? Abraham, we have just said, is not accused. Only that which *is* can be accused; accusation is a modality of descriptive discourse, it borrows the essential indifference of descriptive discourse and intensifies it to the point that the indifference becomes pain. Abram, we must assume, suffers. But as Abraham breaks through Abram, as through the crust of a cocoon, he—this one, Abraham—immediately eludes descriptive discourse. "Abraham" would be a *prescriptive name*, so to speak. Indeed not so much a name as a nomination. And as named, as beyond description, he is no longer accused. Abram is accused, but *Abraham is commanded.* It is here that the greatness of his name would be found, in the fact that he has both hands free to receive something, to be com-manded. How exactly does he elude accusation? There is no simpler answer: by being a *tzaddik*, by being righteous.

"I will bless you," promises God to Abram, "I will make your name great, and you will be a blessing" (Gen. 12.2). This is a hint to whole problem: Abraham will not only be blessed, he, the one capable of walking the earth alone and unloved, will *be a blessing*. A walking blessing! "I will bless those who bless you and those who curse you I will curse, and through you all the families of the earth will be blessed."

In short, it all comes down to the question: *Who are you*? It is a question of "types" calling for better description. Are you Abraham? Not yet?

Now the question posed by the logic of grace is interior to this question. Grace asks: *How do you know who you are?* This isn't a rhetorical question. You know, yes; but *how*? There is only one way to be Abraham, if one is Abraham. But presumably there is more than one way to know it, as there is more than one possibility of interiority. To be sure, it may not be necessary to know who one is in order to be who one is. Interiority isn't necessary. Presumably Abraham did not become who he was with the help of the Delphic oracle. The interiority that Kierkegaard imagines Abraham to have wielded is, as far as we know, a pure anachronism—howbeit necessary eisegetically for the *Christian interiorization* of Abraham.

On the other hand, Socrates needed the oracle. And perhaps since Socrates, everything that has felt the touch of Greek thought, to some degree, necessarily, comes to be itself partly by way of interiority, if only to the extent that, since Socrates and since his oracle at Delphi, everything is partly, necessarily, interior. And what is Christianity if not the Greek interiorization of what is necessarily exterior in Hebrew? We are considering a historical necessity of "thrownness" here. Are we not all thrown into a need for interiority that is typically Christian? Do we not, still today, live in Christendom—all of us, if only because we are capable of *hearing* this question, and in fact incapable of honestly misunderstanding it? And hence is there not a certain necessity, or at least something useful, in knowing how we know who we are?

It is precisely in response to these questions that we are attempting a brief bricolage of typically Christian concepts such as grace and innocence—and not in order to return, nostalgically, to a pure type, a pure "Hebraism." (And note, we do not have to know very much about Christianity to attempt this bricolage; the very problem is that we already know too much.) If anything, the purpose is to purify the concepts of innocence and grace *as Christian*. We wish to attempt a bricolage of a tool to make the tool even more useful if possible, not a deconstruction that renders the tool useless.

Innocence is essential if we are going to be commanded. But the truly innocent soul, the kind we imagine infants possess, souls so innocent that they lack the least notion of innocence, which after all is dialectically related to guilt, cannot be commanded. One earns the capacity to be commanded by immersion in the fires of accusation and guilt, that is to say, by growing up. Christian thought seems to rely on a myth of innocence that precedes one's birth, taking place in Eden-time, a myth of the soul: so that the face of the child radiates innocence, but is known to be fallen. This is paradoxical, of course, as myth must be, but it is a specific kind of paradox: a paradoxical nostalgia. As it is too late to simply undo the paradox and get rid of the mythical reading of the "story" of Eden, we are better off trying to streamline its prescriptive usefulness. And we can do this by undoing the nostalgia of the paradox. Here is our bricolage; and it goes without saying that it is *pure Levinas*. Keeping in mind the implication of the quotation above, at the head of this section, from Rosenzweig: innocence belongs to the oldest face (*Typ*), not to the youngest. One walks toward one's innocence, one ages toward it; in Christian terms, one ages toward one's youth, or as Kierkegaard says, one begets one's father; in psychological terms, one looks for the inner child. It is a matter of rereading Eden.[22]

Innocence is essential if we are going to be commanded. But this means different things to the different "ages" of one's self. To the inner child, the child behind the old face, it means that, no matter how old we are, we must feel that that child can get away with *something*. Some lovely moment in the woods on some snowy evening. From this standpoint, the commandment is the work for which we are rewarded. Innocence is the reward. But from the standpoint of the old face itself, *the reward can only be the commandment itself*. Besides sheer pleasures of the soul, sacred pleasures which have been safely hallowed by ethical work, it is given to the old "type" to see how the holy itself,

---

[22] Such a rereading, formulated in terms taken from the fourth chapter of Hegel's *Phenomenology*, has been attempted by Howard Adelman, "Of Human Bondage: Labor and Freedom in the *Phenomenology*," in *Hegel's Dialectic of Desire and Recognition*, ed. John O'Neill (Albany: State University of New York Press, 1966), pp. 171–86.

even apart from every pleasure and *every conceivable heteronomy*, is good. It is the Kantian type of Good that Levinas calls *dignity*. With its face: reverence. And to be sure, this face does lack humility.[23] But from this standpoint, if the *Aufhebung* in question is truly to be a reflection of the holy, the reverence and dignity of the soul in the face of the divine commandment may well pass for an absolutely innocent stolen pleasure. Reward must remain an incentive for ethical behaviour, and the soul in its childlike innocence must continue to cultivate a real *joy* in the rhetoric that convinces it to be ethical. But within this child that is within the soul of the old person there is an even older soul that prefers to be convicted like a criminal rather than convinced like someone who is lazy. That soul's reward is *heavier responsibility*. The reward is sheer autonomy itself, a deepening participation in what Levinas calls the "religion for adults."

An old man's eyes, darkened and made heavy by time, see how a young man isn't able to grasp the seriousness of his own life. The old man sees the seriousness of the young man's life, even though the young man lives it. Hence the young man ages, ages well, to the extent that he darkens his eyes before time does, prescriptively, before the script of his life is written, squeezing himself out from his youth like a snake from its skin.

We have two types of rhetoric then. First, there is the nominative rhetoric that speaks to the soul in its interiority. What this type of rhetoric understands—something that the other rhetoric must dismiss and must fail to understand, if it is to work—is the way in which *taking*, the totalitarian gesture of the newborn and the selfish, can turn itself inside-out and spontaneously burst into a *giving* that is in no way diminished as giving by this spontaneity. This isn't metaphysical desire, but

---

[23] Contra Jean-Louis Chretien's charge of "arrogance," one might recall Kant's distaste, in the third Critique, for the *fear of God* as being a pale and merely "pathological" version of reverence.

the education of such a desire; an altogether unique phenomenon. The nominative rhetoric is able to lead the avaricious soul into a confrontation with the pain of its avarice, its masochism. For there is a point at which—if it isn't too late—avarice finds itself to be the consummation and perfection of utter solitude and loneliness. At that point one needs to give. Again, by a need that isn't reducible to any egoism, and isn't motivated by a commandment. One is convinced of love, and not convicted to love. The totality is exceeded not from beyond, by an exterior infinity. The excess burgeons from within totality's tight heart. In a sense, what is operative here is an accusative working from within the heart of the nominative. This is joy. It is the passion that is inseparable from compassion. And because it is something that happens in the severest interiority, which in principle could offer an infinite retreat into deeper and deeper pain, the moment in which the soul makes an about-face must be nothing short of a miracle of grace. The word that bursts from within the solitude of desire, not the commandment, perhaps, but nonetheless the word of the commandment, is given. Scripturally, Nemo has located this rhetoric in the New Testament.

The second type of rhetoric belongs to the prophets of the Old Testament. It is a rhetoric that calls sinners to repent, and hence recalls the commandments which have *already* been given in the Torah only indirectly. The kind of prescription that belongs to the Torah may well be, in itself, utterly free of rhetoric. But to hear it as such, as unrhetorical, to *return* to the unrhetorical, the prophet must speak rhetorically, in a kind of postscriptive prescription. A good example of such as rhetoric is Isaiah 6.9–10. Isaiah is being given his mission by God:

And He said: Go, and tell this people:
  'Hear ye indeed, but understand not;
  And see ye indeed, but perceive not.'

> Make the heart of this people fat,
>   And make their ears heavy,
>   And shut their eyes;
>   Lest they, seeing with their eyes,
>   And hearing with their ears,
>   And understanding with their heart,
>   Return, and be healed.

The intention, as God goes on to describes it to Isaiah, is to prune the people, so that only a ravaged stump remains of the old Israel, and this stump is to be a "holy seed" out of which Israel will continue to grow into the future. But in what manner is the failure to hear and see and understand and consequently to repent *predestined* by God? After all, were it merely a matter of destiny, the need for Isaiah to speak would be superfluous. Isaiah is sent, he is given a message to carry: the destiny of the people is only effected through a prescription, but one cloaked in rhetoric. It is this rhetoric itself, in a sense, that will punish the people, that will be its apocalypse, this covered-up and unenthusiastic way of prescribing repentance. God no longer cares to save; God's care has become strictly categorical. God's prescriptions are nothing more than accusations. The interiority of the people, their souls, are no longer God's concern. There is no commandment to repent. There is only a *dare* to repent. "Redeem yourself if you will," says God, "for I will no longer redeem you." God will no longer do the people's hearing and seeing and understanding for them, will no longer do their repenting for them, for that is what grace is essentially, *God doing our own repenting for us* in the way that mothers traditionally chewed solid food for their infants before putting it into their mouths. God will no longer be the Teacher, the Teaching has already been taught. God dares the people to be adults. This dare is the punishment from which prescription is heard.

And—that's it? Such an ungracious end! Will a conclusion be so easily purchased and the end of history so cheaply sold? We are talking about the apocalypse of the Teaching after all! How shall we endure such an apocalypse? The secret of the rhetoric of the prophets, which also explains why prophecy itself must suffer an apocalypse like the Teaching, that is to say, why these must suffer a canon, sprouts into the sunshine, from a seed, in the first verse of the first chapter of *Pirke Avot*: "Make a fence for the Torah." A fence of time perhaps, the very first step of time's door into history, and not in the least a shutting of the door. For perhaps the Teaching did not take place merely at some time, in mere history. Perhaps the Teaching has already been taught because now it remains for us to recite it, out loud to ourselves. A strange *because*, no doubt, but one dictated by the logic of the recitation in question. ("Recitation" here being a translation for "Mishna.") *Perhaps the Teaching is done so that we may now do the Learning.* ("Teaching and Learning" being translations for "Torah and Talmud.")

7. SUMMARY CONVICTION

Perhaps it is a little clearer how Reish Lakish answers our question, "Who accuses?" when he says: "He is the Accuser, he is the Evil Inclination, he is the Angel of Death".[24]

In terms of alterity, of ethics proper, accusation comes from

---

[24] Of this one saying by Reish Lakish, Maimonides goes so far as to say, indeed, so far as to command: "Hear the useful dictum of the *Sages* to whom the term *Sages* may truthfully be applied; it clarifies all that is obscure, reveals all that is concealed, and renders manifest most of the *mysteries of the Torah*" (*The Guide of the Perplexed*, trans. Shlomo Pines [Chicago: The University of Chicago Press, 1963], pp. 488–89). In a sense, this postscript has been nothing but, and nothing more than, a neo-Maimonidean effort to comment on this one dictum by Rabbi Simon ben Lakish.

the Other. But the prescriptive voice of accusation comes from the crime perpetrated against the Other. The crime speaks. The spilt blood of the Other calls out. Who, then, is the Evil Inclination, prescriptively speaking—*if not you?* Who is Satan, prescriptively speaking—*if not you?* You have yet to be yourself otherwise. Prescriptively speaking: *you are your Accuser.* You are the Satan. You are the sin that seeks itself out,[25] to accuse itself of itself.

And therefore, you are your own Angel of Death. The lives of the Evil Inclination and the Satan are in your hands, and to kill them, you must die *as them*, you who are them. If you do not kill them, but continue to live as the Evil Inclination and as the Satan, then you must also continue to live as the Angel of Death. If this Angel names you and kills you *by name*, the name whereby you will, God willing, elude your prescriptive identity as Evil Inclination, as Satan, and as Angel of Death; if you die thus, God forbid, *by name*, it will be because you have killed yourself by name. To kill Death, you must kill yourself as Death's Angel.

These strange-sounding propositions, of course, indicate the task of distinguishing who you are from who you are; or, to put it more traditionally, who you are from who you ought to be. But this further task doesn't invalidate or compensate for the fact that, within one discourse, namely prescription, this distinction is impossible, worse, forbidden. To try to undermine these propositions, for example by posing anew the "question of subjectivity," would be to deepen yet again the identity between yourself and the Evil Inclination, the Satan, and the Angel of Death. And furthermore, the "you," with its proper grammatical case, must be maintained and not substituted by "I" or "one." For every nominative pronoun is an evasion and a seeking refuge, a hiding, like Adam's, that lays the groundwork for

---

[25] Num. 32.23.

all sin. Only through the accusative can we reach the nominative in the sense of your *name*, the being at one with oneself which is atonement.[26] To be sure, when not speaking prescriptively, we must continue to distinguish players in the drama of crime and punishment: God prescribes, Satan provokes, you sin, and Death punishes. But in the terser session of prescriptive language, which Rabbi Yohanan urges us to keep in mind, in the session of learning out loud in spoken terms that which the written page says, pro-vocation is just a synonym for pre-scription. You prescribe, you provoke, you sin, you punish. And only after we have thus bound ourselves to the logic peculiar to prescription can we go on, then, to distinguish the prescript from the true *commandment*.

---

[26] *Nota bene*: Thus perfect sinfulness can result in perfect atonement, to wit, through the perfection of accusation. But, having sinned, one must take heed not to be tempted the last mile to *perfect oneself in accusation*. Temptation to sin itself may be the lure of *culpability*, the lure of being guilty, as if this promised the permanence of being addressed as You and hence the end of all loneliness, the final and eternal Sabbath at the table of the Lord.

INDEX